Moving Beyond the Presentation Layer: Content and Context in the Dewey Decimal Classification (DDC) System

Moving Beyond the Presentation Layer: Content and Context in the Dewey Decimal Classification (DDC) System has been co-published simultaneously as *Cataloging & Classification Quarterly*, Volume 42, Numbers 3/4 2006.

Moving Beyond the Presentation Layer: Content and Context in the Dewey Decimal Classification (DDC) System

Joan S. Mitchell, MLS, BA
Diane Vizine-Goetz, PhD, MLS, BA
Editors

Moving Beyond the Presentation Layer: Content and Context in the Dewey Decimal Classification (DDC) System has been co-published simultaneously as *Cataloging & Classification Quarterly*, Volume 42, Numbers 3/4 2006.

Routledge
Taylor & Francis Group
New York   London

First pubished by

The Haworth Information Press®, 10 Alice Street, Binghamton, NY 13904-1580 USA

The Haworth Information Press® is an imprint of The Haworth Press, Inc., 10 Alice Street, Binghamton, NY 13904-1580 USA.

This edition published 2012 by Routledge

Taylor & Francis Group, 711 Third Avenue, New York, NY 10017
Taylor & Francis Group, 2 Park Square, Milton Park, Abingdon, Oxon OX14 4RN

Moving Beyond the Presentation Layer: Content and Context in the Dewey Decimal Classification (DDC) System has been co-published simultaneously as *Cataloging & Classification Quarterly*®, Volume 42, Numbers 3/4 2006.

The development, preparation, and publication of this work has been undertaken with great care. However, the publisher, employees, editors, and agents of The Haworth Press and all imprints of The Haworth Press, Inc., including The Haworth Medical Press® and Pharmaceutical Products Press®, are not responsible for any errors contained herein or for consequences that may ensue from use of materials or information contained in this work. With regard to case studies, identities and circumstances of individuals discussed herein have been changed to protect confidentiality. Any resemblance to actual persons, living or dead, is entirely coincidental.

The Haworth Press is committed to the dissemination of ideas and information according to the highest standards of intellectual freedom and the free exchange of ideas. Statements made and opinions expressed in this publication do not necessarily reflect the views of the Publisher, Directors, management, or staff of The Haworth Press, Inc., or an endorsement by them.

DDC, Dewey, Dewey Decimal Classification, OCLC, WebDewey, and WorldCat are registered trademarks/service marks of OCLC Online Computer Library Center, Inc. The Dewey Decimal Classification system is Copyright 2003-2006 OCLC Online Computer Library Center, Inc. Used with permission.

Cover design by Jennifer M. Gaska.

Library of Congress Cataloging-in-Publication Data

Moving beyond the presentation layer : content and context in the Dewey decimal classification (DDC) system / Joan S. Mitchell [and] Diane Vizine-Goetz, editors.
     p. cm.
     "Co-published simultaneously as Cataloging & classification quarterly, volume 42, numbers 3/4."
     Includes bibliographical references and index.
     ISBN-13: 978-0-7890-3452-6 (alk. paper)
     ISBN-10: 0-7890-3452-2 (alk. paper)
     ISBN-13: 978-0-7890-3453-3 (pbk. : alk. paper)
     ISBN-10: 0-7890-3453-0 (pbk. : alk. paper)
     1. Classification, Dewey decimal. I. Mitchell, Joan S. II. Vizine-Goetz, Diane. III. Cataloging & classification quarterly.
Z696.D7M68 2006
025.4'31–dc22
                  2006021354

Moving Beyond the Presentation Layer: Content and Context in the Dewey Decimal Classification (DDC) System

CONTENTS

CONTENT AND CONTEXT: A WEB PERSPECTIVE

ABOUT THE EDITORS

Joan S. Mitchell, MLS, is editor in chief of the Dewey Decimal Classification (DDC) system at the OCLC Online Computer Library Center, Inc. She has been closely affiliated with the DDC since 1985, where she became a member of the Decimal Classification Editorial Policy Committee. Ms. Mitchell chaired the committee from 1992 until her appointment as Dewey Editor in 1993.

Ms. Mitchell has been a member and/or chair of a variety of committees working in the fields of cataloging and classification in the American Library Association. In 2005, she was awarded the Melvil Dewey Medal by ALA. Ms. Mitchell serves on the editorial board of Knowledge Organization, and is a member of the Scientific Advisory Council of ISKO. She is also a member of the University of North Texas School of Library and Information Sciences Board of Advisors.

Prior to joining OCLC in 1993, Ms. Mitchell was director of educational technology at Carnegie Mellon University and an adjunct professor in the School of Information Sciences at the University of Pittsburgh. She has also held various positions in technical and public services in academic and special libraries. Ms. Mitchell has written and spoken extensively in the area of knowledge organization, and has a special interest in localization and interoperability in classification systems.

Diane Vizine-Goetz, PhD, is a research scientist at OCLC Online Computer Library Center, Inc. She joined OCLC in 1983 to continue research on database quality she began as a doctoral student. She has conducted research on the application and use of controlled vocabularies and contributed to the development of Dewey classifier tools and classification-based browsing interfaces such as the OCLC DeweyBrowser. Diane Vizine-Goetz and Lois Mai Chan were the 1999 recipients of the Best of LRTS Award for their article titled "Toward a Computer-Generated Subject Validation File: Feasibility and Usefulness," *Library Resources & Technical Services* 42 (1): 45-60.

Dr. Vizine-Goetz is currently lead researcher on the Terminology Services research project. In this project, OCLC researchers are using Web services to provide access to controlled vocabularies for libraries, museums, and archives to create consistent metadata for their collections. Dr. Vizine-Goetz is also a member of the OCLC team conducting research involving the Functional Requirements for Bibliographic Records (FRBR) model.

Preface

In this special volume, a group of authors drawn broadly from the knowledge organization community explores the Dewey Decimal Classification (DDC) system from a number of perspectives. In doing so, each peels away a bit of the "presentation layer"–the familiar linear notational sequence–to expose the content and context offered by the DDC.

In the physical environment, the Dewey notation provides part of the shelf address in open stack, classified arrangements. On the shelves, the access mechanism and the documents are part of the same system–the Dewey context is integrated with the physical content. In the electronic environment, there is frequently a disconnect between the access mechanism and the documents themselves in terms of integration of content and granularity of representation. Often, a description of the document and not the document itself is linked to the Dewey notation. The broad summary of the DDC is frequently used as an online browsing/informational tool, but the explicit mention/absence of topics at the three-digit level obscures the richness of DDC categories and relationships at deeper levels.

As the DDC is considered for new uses, the question arises–can Dewey evolve to meet the needs of the complex emerging information environment? Is the DDC a rigid, hierarchical structure best suited to a physical information environment, or a polymorphic one that can meet a

[Haworth co-indexing entry note]: "Preface." Mitchell, Joan S., and Diane Vizine-Goetz. Co-published simultaneously in *Cataloging & Classification Quarterly* (The Haworth Information Press, an imprint of The Haworth Press, Inc.) Vol. 42, No. 3/4, 2006, pp. xxiii-xxv; and: *Moving Beyond the Presentation Layer: Content and Context in the Dewey Decimal Classification (DDC) System* (ed: Joan S. Mitchell, and Diane Vizine-Goetz) The Haworth Information Press, an imprint of The Haworth Press, Inc., 2006, pp. xvii-xix. Single or multiple copies of this article are available for a fee from The Haworth Document Delivery Service [1-800-HAWORTH, 9:00 a.m. - 5:00 p.m. (EST). E-mail address: docdelivery@haworthpress.com].

variety of physical and virtual needs? How can the content and context offered by Dewey be used effectively in the electronic information environment? What improvements need to be made to the DDC?

These questions and others are explored as the authors look beyond Dewey's presentation layer in this publication. The issue is divided into three parts: an introduction, an international perspective, and a web perspective. These are categories of convenience and are not mutually exclusive–every author has an international perspective, and nearly every author mentions the impact of the Web on current and future developments and uses of the classification. In the introductory section, three distinguished professors with a long history of teaching and research in classification take an in-depth look at the DDC in terms of its role in online uses of classification, the nature of the Relative Index, and the challenges of teaching the system to new librarians, respectively. In Markey's review of forty years of classification online, she laments the field's failure to embrace classification in online systems for end users and concludes with recommendations to ensure the viability of the DDC and other classification systems in a time of mass digitization. Miksa explores the development of the Relative Index over the twenty-two editions of the DDC, and notes its considerable power in representing concepts in the system and providing context to those concepts. Taylor reviews the various methods employed by her and others to teach the DDC. She concludes that it is worth teaching about classification in general and the DDC in particular because there is a need to categorize recorded knowledge and the DDC is a satisfying tool for that purpose.

In the next section ("An International Perspective"), the authors look at special issues related to the use of the DDC in several countries (Trinidad and Tobago, Switzerland, and Germany, respectively). This is a small slice of Dewey's worldwide usage (the DDC is currently used in 138 countries), but the papers highlight a number of issues related to localization and interoperability of the system that can be generalized to other areas. Nero outlines the challenges faced by classifying the music of Trinidad and Tobago, where local literary warrants outstrips the general literary warrant used as the basis for development of the standard English-language edition of the DDC. Landry discusses the return (after nearly ninety years) of use of the DDC in the National Library of Switzerland and as the organizing tool for the Swiss national bibliography. Heiner-Freiling discusses use of the DDC in an environment in which Dewey has not been (and will not likely be) used for physical location and explores the implications for assignment of multiple numbers and parts of notation.

In the final section ("A Web Perspective"), authors associated with projects in virtual locations in Europe and North America discuss the content and context offered by Dewey on the Web. In each of the projects, the DDC is used as the underlying browsing mechanism for resource discovery. Koch, Golub, and Ardö describe user browsing behavior in Renardus, a service originally funded by the European Union for searching across subject gateways. Nicholson, Dawson, and Shiri discuss using Dewey as the spine for an end-user terminology service in a JISC-funded project in the UK. Zeeman and Turner describe using Dewey to manage Web resources related to Canada and Canadian culture, and note some challenges related to localization. Co-editor Vizine-Goetz reports on a prototype multilingual browser based on the DDC and linked to a variety of demonstration databases (including the DDC itself). When reading the four papers in this final section, one cannot help but wonder if current social classifications are just another set of vocabularies for which a language-independent international standard such as the DDC might provide a useful underlying switching language.

We wish to thank the authors who helped us "move beyond the presentation layer" in exploring the past, present, and future of the Dewey Decimal Classification. We are grateful to Julianne Beall, Michael Cantlon, and Winton E. Matthews, Jr., for comments on selected papers. We also thank Robert Bolander, Robin Cornette, and Carol Hickey for their invaluable assistance in producing this volume.

Joan S. Mitchell
Diane Vizine-Goetz

CONTENT AND CONTEXT:
AN INTRODUCTION

Forty Years of Classification Online:
Final Chapter or Future Unlimited?

Karen Markey

SUMMARY. This paper examines the forty-year history of online use of classification systems. *Enhancing subject access* was the rationale for

Karen Markey is Professor, School of Information, University of Michigan, 1085 South University Avenue, 304 West Hall, Ann Arbor, MI 48109-1107 (E-mail: karen. markey@umich.edu).

The author would like to express special thanks to Joanna Axelrod, Master's Candidate in the School of Information, U-M, who assisted with identifying and assembling relevant papers, books, and conference proceedings, and Professor Dwayne Overmyer, Professor, School of Art & Design, U-M, who supplied relevant citations for diagrams.

[Haworth co-indexing entry note]: "Forty Years of Classification Online: Final Chapter or Future Unlimited?" Markey, Karen. Co-published simultaneously in *Cataloging & Classification Quarterly* (The Haworth Information Press, an imprint of The Haworth Press, Inc.) Vol. 42, No. 3/4, 2006, pp. 1-63; and: *Moving Beyond the Presentation Layer: Content and Context in the Dewey Decimal Classification (DDC) System* (ed: Joan S. Mitchell, and Diane Vizine-Goetz) The Haworth Information Press, an imprint of The Haworth Press, Inc., 2006, pp. 1-63. Single or multiple copies of this article are available for a fee from The Haworth Document Delivery Service [1-800-HAWORTH, 9:00 a.m. - 5:00 p.m. (EST). E-mail address: docdelivery@haworthpress.com].

Available online at http://ccq.haworthpress.com
doi:10.1300/J104v42n03_01

obtaining support to conduct research in classification online and for incorporating classification into online systems. Catalogers have been the beneficiaries of most of the advances in classification online and operational online systems are now able to assist them in class number assignment and shelflisting. To this day, the only way in which most end users experience classification online is through their online catalog's shelflist browsing capability. The author speculates on the reasons why classification online never caught on as an *end user's* tool in online systems. Both the information industry and the library and information science community missed the opportunity to lead the charge in the organization of Internet resources; however, OCLC, the publisher of the Dewey Decimal Classification, has made substantial improvements to the scheme that have increased its versatility for organizing Internet resources. Because mass digitization projects such as Google Print will solve the problem of subject access, the author makes recommendations for classification online to solve these vexing problems of end users: staging of access, retrieving the *best* material in response to user queries, and automatic approaches to finding additional relevant information for an ongoing search. doi:10.1300/J104v42n03_01 *[Article copies available for a fee from The Haworth Document Delivery Service: 1-800-HAWORTH. E-mail address: <docdelivery@haworthpress.com> Website: <http://www.HaworthPress.com> © 2006 by The Haworth Press, Inc. All rights reserved.]*

KEYWORDS. Classification online, DDC, DDC Online Project, Dewey Decimal Classification, LCC, Library of Congress Classification, machine-readable classification data

1. THE IMPETUS FOR CLASSIFICATION ONLINE

The story of classification in online systems truly begins with Ed Brownrigg's assertion at the 1982 Midwinter Meeting of the American Library Association, "Sacred cows are being strewn all over the landscape!"[1] Brownrigg's remark referred to the unexpected findings about subject access–the high percentage of subject searches, the large number of users who expressed difficulties conducting subject searches, and many users' preference for improvements to online catalogs that pertained to subject access–that were being reported in the professional literature as a result of the Council on Library Resources (CLR)-sponsored Nationwide Survey of Online Catalogs.[2]

Survey findings hardly went unnoticed. CLR responded almost immediately by hosting the invitational "Subject Access Meeting" to help its program officers "identify fruitful areas for study and action"[3] in the area of subject access. At this meeting, Pauline Atherton Cochrane[4] briefed invitees about the potential of library classification in online systems especially its ability to enhance subject access. Meeting invitees' deliberations resulted in a list of recommended subject access projects on which CLR should take a leadership role and two projects specifically addressed classification online.[5] Not long after the Meeting, CLR awarded OCLC a grant to study the Dewey Decimal Classification as an online user's tool for subject access, browsing, and display.

There are at least three important reasons why research and development in classification online *took off* following the Nationwide Survey. First, survey findings represented a paradigm shift[6] for the field of library and information science that had focused its attention on descriptive cataloging and known-item for a long time. Now there was empirical evidence in hand that underlined the importance of subject searching to end users and how difficult it was for them to conduct subject searches in online systems. Second, the technology[7] was ready for the development and deployment of information retrieval systems that end users of libraries could search on their own without significant intermediation by a librarian. Third, a key source of funding–the Council on Library Resources–was instrumental in setting the research agenda and funding important needed research.[8]

Fifteen years earlier, when Robert R. Freeman and Pauline Atherton demonstrated AUDACIOUS,[9] a prototype online system for searching and browsing the Universal Decimal Classification (UDC), there were few operational online retrieval systems in existence and fewer (if any) operational online retrieval systems available to end users. In fact, the evaluation of AUDACIOUS required a system operator who was familiar with the system's arcane Boolean-based command language and conducted searches on behalf of interested observers.[10] Despite the AUDACIOUS Project's positive findings about the UDC and online retrieval, the technology of the day was neither ready for classification online nor for end users. Subsequent studies of classification and computer-based systems were limited to the production of printed, offline subject indexes to library collections.[11] Related research that addressed subject augmentation, specifically, promising research findings about the benefits of augmenting library cataloging records with table-of-contents terms and back-of-the-book indexes,[12] was also largely ignored because of the exorbitant cost of storing and searching augmented rec-

ords using the technology of the day and the field's long-standing beliefs about the primacy of known-item searches. Only very recently has
the technology come of age for such subject augmentation and have the
agreements between publishers and search system suppliers been struck
to make online browsing of tables of contents and back-of-the-book index a reality.[13]

2. THE DDC ONLINE PROJECT

2.1 Securing Forest Press Participation in the Project

Because OCLC was one of five recipients of CLR grants for conducting the Nationwide Survey, its Office of Research staff were privy to
preliminary findings about subject access. Research Scientist Karen
Markey was charged with reporting OCLC's administration of self-ad-
ministered surveys and focused-group interviews.[14] Recognizing the
need for subject searching improvements in online catalogs and CLR's
interest in funding subject-access research, Markey and fellow Office
of Research staff strategized about launching a project to study classification online. When they learned that the printed 19th edition of the
Dewey Decimal Classification (DDC) had been produced by computer-
ized photocomposition,[15] they seized the opportunity to secure the print
tapes as the foundation for a classification-enriched online system.
They called on OCLC's Distinguished Scholar Pauline Cochrane, who
was dividing her time between OCLC in Dublin, Ohio, and the Library
of Congress in Washington, DC, to visit Dr. John Comaromi, DDC's
Editor and Chief of the Decimal Classification Division, at his Library
of Congress (LC) office, and inquire about the availability of the print
tapes for research purposes. OCLC received a positive reply from him
and later from the DDC's publisher, John Humphry, Executive Director
of Forest Press. In January 1984, with the support of CLR and Forest
Press, OCLC's Office of Research initiated a study of the Dewey Decimal Classification as a library user's tool for subject access, browsing,
and display.[16]

2.2 Project Objectives

Four features of the DDC[17] were employed in the DDC Online Project to help online catalog searchers match their terminology with an online catalog's terminology: (1) the subject terminology in the DDC
Schedules, such as captions, scope notes, including notes; (2) the sub-

ject terminology in the DDC Relative Index; (3) the hierarchical arrays of related terminology in the DDC Schedules; and (4) class numbers in the DDC Schedules and Relative Index. Through these subject terminologies, online catalog users would have much more subject information than was presently available in online catalogs, i.e., subject headings and title terms from bibliographic records, to match their search terms and to browse for better terms to express their topics. The DDC Online Project team successfully achieved these four project objectives:[18]

1. Use the consensus of experts in the DDC to determine strategies for searching and display of the DDC in an online catalog
2. Demonstrate the DDC as an online searcher's tool for subject access, browsing, and display in an online catalog
3. Test the effectiveness of the DDC as such an online searcher's tool in an experimental online catalog
4. Evaluate the demonstration and test results of the DDC as an online searcher's tool and disseminate the results of the research project

2.3 System Development

The project team built an experimental online catalog from three data sources:[19] (1) machine-readable cataloging (MARC) records from four participating libraries, (2) the 19th edition of the DDC Schedules, and (3) the Relative Index. Each participating library contributed between 8,000 and 15,000 MARC records in one or more subject areas selected by the library:

1. Library of Congress (LC): Economics (330-339), commerce (380-382), and management (658)
2. New York State Library (NYSL): New York State geography (917.47-917.4799), United States colonial history (973.1-973.2), and New York State history (974.7-974.799)
3. Public Library of Columbus and Franklin County (PLCFC): Sports, recreation, and performing arts (790-799)
4. University of Illinois at Urbana-Champaign (UIUC): Mathematics (510-519)

The experimental online catalog's database was actually composed of two online catalogs: (1) the Dewey Online Catalog (DOC) and (2) the Subject Online Catalog (SOC). SOC had the traditional subject searching capabilities of online catalogs, namely, subject heading, subject keyword, and class number searching.[20] DOC had both the traditional subject searching capabilities of SOC and enhanced subject searching capabilities because the DDC Schedules and Relative Index had been incorporated into DOC.[21]

At the time, the DDC Online Project team felt that they were flying solo in terms of the design of online displays and system functionality connected with the DDC because the experimental DOC system was the *first* implementation of a library classification in an online catalog that would be used and evaluated by end users; however, the team received inspiration and feedback from the project's consultants, Decimal Classification Division editors, interested staff at participating libraries, and active researchers who were writing about classification online.[22]

2.4 System Evaluation

The evaluation demonstrated that the DDC enhanced subject access to libraries' bibliographic records.[23] It provided new and fruitful subject searching capabilities that were not possible through the alphabetical and keyword searching permitted by existing online catalogs.[24] Two of every three relevant items retrieved and displayed by end users in a DOC search for a given topic were unique and were not retrieved and displayed in a SOC search for the same topic; thus, DOC was responsible for retrieving a substantial proportion of additional records that SOC did not retrieve.[25] Furthermore, the DDC not only enhanced the display of subject-rich information in bibliographic records, it was a significant contributor of unique terms that were not found in bibliographic records title and subject heading fields.[26]

To achieve the best results in subject searches, online catalogs should have the combined subject searching functionality of SOC and DOC.[27] Yet, SOC or DOC alone was capable of directing users to relevant items on a topic, and the success rates of end users in retrieving and displaying relevant records were virtually the same in both catalogs. The DDC Online Project team performed an extensive failure analysis of every search conducted by end users who participated in the evaluation to determine reasons for success and failure. They documented their analysis in the published literature so that it was accessible to designers who implemented DOC's classification-enriched features[28] in their online systems, specifically, DOC's alphabetical search using the DDC Relative Index,[29] DOC's subject outline search using the DDC Schedules,[30] DOC's direct search using keywords from the DDC Schedules and Relative Index, subject headings, and titles,[31] DOC's class number search using the DDC Schedules,[32] and the DDC Tables.[33]

2.5 Setting the Research and Development Agenda for Classification Online

At the conclusion of the DDC Online Project, CLR sponsored an invitational conference "to review . . . findings and explore the potential for future use of classification schedules in OPACs."[34] In addition to findings from the DDC Online Project, conferees were also knowledgeable of findings from two related projects. The experimental BROWSE System used the tree structure of the Computing Reviews classification as the framework for menu-based browsing.[35] BROWSE did not allow users to select the part of the classification in which they were most interested. Rather, users had to travel from the most general to the most specific classification captions to find relevant retrievals.

Geller and Lesk's[36] experimental online catalog at Bell Labs also used a classification scheme for menu-based browsing. Tests of the Bell Labs catalog demonstrated that users wanted to select a specific area of the classification for browsing by entering a query rather than traveling through many successive levels of a subject outline to arrive at a specific topic. Because the system's designers had no machine-readable DDC in hand at Bell Labs, they forced the most frequently-occurring Library of Congress Subject Headings (LCSH) in a class to represent the class in the deep levels of the DDC hierarchy, i.e., when a DDC number exceeded three digits. Using frequently-occurring subject headings in this way was problematic, just as it was in DOC's subject outline search, because both systems did not take into account the postings for these same subject headings in other DDC classes. Markey and Demeyer[37] analyzed failed subject outline searches in search of an alternative approach. In a redesigned subject outline search, they suggested replacing first-listed subject headings with "common subject headings," that is, first-listed subject headings that are high-posted in the class at hand and not in other classes.

CLR chose Carol Mandel, a practicing academic library administrator, to summarize invitational conference proceedings and to characterize the next broad steps for classification online. At the time of the conference, many OPACs lacked *basic* subject searching functionality so it was not surprising that two of the conference's six recommendations specified improvements to subject searching in online catalogs generally without mentioning classification online specifically. Another two recommendations called for machine-readable authority files for classification data. Although the two remaining recommendations specifically addressed classification online, Mandel was circumspect about the future, encouraging the field "to continue to explore" and "improving on" classification-based displays and functionality.[38]

In this review's sections 3 and 4, readers will learn that when classification online figures into system development, the beneficiaries have been classification editors and online cataloging staff. DOC's classification-enriched functionality was never built into operational OPACs as an end user's tool. Despite thirty-five years of research, the way in which today's end users search classification online in OPACs is through simple shelflist browsing. And shelflist browsing has not changed since its initial implementation in the first OPACs, a half decade before the DDC Online Project. It is possible that the hesitation that characterized those six carefully-worded recommendations from the CLR conference was responsible for the field's failure to embrace classification online wholeheartedly and incorporate it into online systems as an end user's tool for subject access, browsing, and display.

3. MACHINE-READABLE CLASSIFICATION DATA

3.1 Developing a USMARC Format

On the heels of the completed DDC Online Project, Nancy J. Williamson led the charge in the development of a USMARC format for classification data.[39] Library practitioners and other researchers had speculated on such a format's content and on the difficulties of converting the Library of Congress Classification (LCC).[40] Williamson also learned from the experience of Mary Micco, a researcher who was experimenting with LCC as an end user's tool at the same time she was developing the format.[41] Analyzing LCC as the basis for format development, Williamson's[42] approach enlisted three steps: (1) developing a tentative record format for LCC; (2) selecting pages at random from such diverse LC schedules as N (Fine Arts), PQ Part 2 (Italian, Spanish and Portuguese Literature), B-BJ (Philosophy, Psychology), KK-KKC (Law of Germany) and HM-HX (Social Science, Sociology) and coding several hundred records; and (3) analyzing coded results to identify specific requirements for the format.

Library of Congress staff[43] benefited from Williamson's efforts in their formulation of the USMARC Format for Classification Data. LC published the new format in 1991.[44] Rebecca Guenther[45] of LC's Network Development and MARC Standards Office urged the field to utilize formatted classification data: "Designers of future retrieval systems for classification records need to utilize online classification as a powerful tool for subject access, the maintenance of classification schedules, machine-assisted classification, and validation of assignment of numbers in bibliographic records. In our age of increasing use of networked information resources, classification data can provide an alternative approach to the retrieval of information, using a subject oriented approach and thus ensuring that language is not a barrier to finding needed information."

3.2 Editorial Support Systems for DDC and UDC

AUDACIOUS Project researchers[46] were the first to recognize the value of automation for managing a classification system. A half decade before the publication of the *USMARC Format for Classification Data*, Forest Press, DDC's publisher, commissioned Inforonics, Inc., to develop an Editorial Support System (ESS) for online maintenance of the current DDC edition and production of the next one(s).[47] When the *USMARC Format for Classification Data* was published, Decimal Classification Division (DCD) editorial staff had no intention of switching to an entirely new ESS; instead, they made "systematic changes . . . to solve the problems in converting ESS records to USMARC records, in analyzing synthesized DDC numbers by computer and providing access to component parts of synthesized numbers, and in tracking hierarchical relationships not expressed by the DDC notation."[48] Today, DDC editors use an ESS that is three generations removed from the original Inforonics-built system built twenty years ago.[49] Although Ia McIlwaine[50] does not mention the USMARC format specifically, she discusses the Master Reference File (MRF) that is the machine-readable version of the Universal Decimal Classification (UDC) and how publishers, national networks, libraries, and interested researchers can obtain MRF through a licensing agreement.

3.3 Synthesized Classification Numbers

The DDC Online Project team concluded that even more urgent than the development of a machine-readable format for classification data was "the identification and implementation of a coding scheme for the individual elements of a synthesized class number in libraries' bibliographic records."[51] If such coding was added to synthesized numbers, system developers could add DDC Table terms to libraries' bibliographic records for enhanced subject access and display and they could add the Tables into online systems for browsing. In the absence of such coding, browsing and subject access were limited to a classification's schedules.

Arnold Wajenberg[52] proposed such a coding scheme for use in the classification number field (082 and 092) of bibliographic records, but it was never implementd in the MARC format. More than a decade later, Liu[53] described a machine solution to the problem of decomposing synthesized DDC numbers. Based on an analysis of the instructions for synthesizing numbers in the DDC's Arts (700) Schedules and Tables, Liu defined 17 decomposition rules, 13 covering Add Notes and 4 rules covering Standard Subdivisions. He decomposed 1,701 DDC synthesized numbers in a computer system called DND (Dewey Number Decomposer). He randomly selected 600 of them, gave them to three judges, and reported a decomposition success rate of 100%. Additionally, classification notation interested Liu and he also reported on his Flexible Faceted Notation System (FFNS) to facilitate both the creation and use of an online classification.[54] He contended that his notation could be used to generate class numbers automatically, fulfill the hospitality canon, produce short and brief numbers, and facilitate retrieval.[55]

4. CLASSIFICATION AS AN ONLINE CATALOGER'S TOOL

4.1 Early Visions

More than a decade before successful development efforts, Clement Jewitt[56] envisioned functionality that would facilitate class number assignment by library catalogers. His proposed Subject Indexing Engine (SIE) would be "a DDC number builder, intended to take an input consisting of DDC notation pieces representing the facets of the subject of the information item, relate that input to a file of DDC notation pieces and number synthesis rules, and output a correctly constructed DDC number."[57] A key member of the Inforonics team that built DDC's first ESS, John Finni collaborated with Peter Paulson to envision functionality for "a Cataloguer's Work Station (CWS)" in which catalogers could browse classification schedules, tables, and indexes for number assignment.[58]

4.2 DDC As a Cataloger's Tool

The occasion of the publication of the *USMARC Format for Classification Data* in 1991 brought the field closer than ever to realizing online CWS functionality for library classifiers. A year later, OCLC researchers led by Diane Vizine-Goetz reported on their efforts to develop a prototype Electronic DDC (EDDC).[59] Vizine-Goetz[60] and her research team "enhanced DDC records by including: (1) DDC hierarchies, (2) Library of Congress Subject Headings with frequency of usage data, and (3) sample bibliographic records." They were inspired by the notion of common subject headings[61] in their efforts to generate subject heading frequency data. EDDC's user interface was a modified version of OCLC's Search CD450 product, retrieval software for OCLC's CD-ROM reference database series.[62]

Joan S. Mitchell, Editor-in-Chief of several recent DDC editions, described EDDC's transformation into Dewey for Windows and the challenges facing editors due to the DDC's migration from a predominantly print environment to various electronic forms.[63] Julianne Beall,[64] assistant editor, showed how Dewey for Windows offers classifiers a wide variety of strategies for identifying candidate class numbers so they can "select approaches depending on the nature of the topic, on their own familiarity or unfamiliarity with a particular part of the Schedule and on their own individual preferences."

Today, OCLC offers online catalogers WebDewey through its OCLC Connexion Service.[65] Catalogers can use WebDewey to browse and search the DDC, LC subject headings that are intellectually and statistically mapped to DDC class numbers, and the links from mapped LC subject headings to the corresponding LCSH authority records. Catalogers can also add their own notes to WebDewey and display them in context, which allows them to both record valuable information about local classification practices and have it available for ready reference. To facilitate shelflisting, catalogers can use the Dewey Cutter Program, a software program that automatically provides Cutter numbers from the OCLC Four-Figure Cutter Tables.[66]

OCLC researcher Diane Vizine-Goetz and her research team have played a major role in the evolution of the DDC online from its first CD-ROM version to its current manifestation on the Web[67]–establishing statistical associations between classification numbers and subject headings, generating ranked lists of DDC numbers as candidates for assignment to a document in a classifier's hand, and extracting relevant terminology from recent documents as candidates for new classes by

DDC editors. Dewey research projects have involved "developing cus-
tomized views of the DDC, enhancing links to other thesauri, improving
links to DDC editions in other languages, transforming the captions into
end-user language, and decomposing numbers and using component
parts for improved access."[68] Applying solutions from her DDC online
activity to related work, Vizine-Goetz used statistical techniques to produce *People, Places & Things*, a list of popular LC subject headings and
their corresponding DDC numbers. "The goal of the project is to produce a list of popular LC subject headings with DDC numbers. In this
project, we are exploring the feasibility of identifying candidate headings for inclusion in the Popular LCSH list by applying the research
findings on subject heading accuracy of Lois Mai Chan and exploring
the use of techniques borrowed from corpus linguistics processing to
associate DDC numbers with these headings. If successful, the application of these two approaches should produce a high-quality list
that requires minimal human review."[69] Vizine-Goetz is also leading
OCLC's Terminology Services Project, with the goal of making "concepts in knowledge organization schemes and the relationships within
and between schemes more accessible to people and computer applications."[70]

4.3 LCC As a Cataloger's Tool

Hardly five years after finalizing the Classification Format, LC completed the conversion of LCC in 1996. In 1995 and 1996, LC released
the Windows-based Classification Plus on CD-ROM based on Folio
software and updated it quarterly for subscribers. Classification Plus is
a cataloger's tool for LCC number discovery and assignment. Lois Mai
Chan and Theodora L. Hodges described the functionality of Classification Plus; they also enumerated changes to LCC that were a result of the
LCC conversion and listed recommendations about LCC generally that
were a result of Chan's consultation with Cataloging Policy and Support Office staff on the future of LCC.[71]

When interest shifted to the Web, LC released Classification Web, a
web-based cataloger's tool for LCC number discovery and assignment.
"The conversion to electronic form . . . was an especially important development for LCC. That it greatly improves internal operating efficiency goes without saying. It enables much more efficient production
of the print schedules, which continue to be produced. More important,
it facilitates revision, not only of whole schedules but also of tables and
indexes. Finally and significantly, it makes it possible to develop and is-

sue LCC in electronic formats, such as Classification Plus, a full-text, Windows-based CD-ROM tool updated quarterly, and Classification Web, a web-based tool updated weekly. These tools contain not only LCC but also include the full text of Library of Congress Subject Headings (LCSH), with links between LC subject headings and LCC numbers where appropriate. Furthermore, built into the Classification Web are also links to cataloging databases with sophisticated search options."[72]

Classification Web offers catalogers several functions[73] such as browsing the Library of Congress Classification Schedules, browsing the Library of Congress Subject Headings, and finding subject heading and classification number correlations. Like WebDewey, Classification Web is a full-featured cataloger's tool for finding and assigning class numbers and provides catalogers with a rich toolkit of sophisticated features such as Boolean searching, browsing hierarchical arrays of Schedule and Table captions, accessing the subject authority file, writing notes, and saving hotlinks. Although shelflisting has not yet been incorporated into Classification Web, researchers prototyped an expert system for LCC shelflisting using the Mahogany Professional expert systems application in which the system was enlisted as an intelligent job aid.[74]

4.4 UDC As a Cataloger's Tool

Experiments with classification online began with UDC.[75] UDC was the first of the encyclopedic library classifications to be converted to machine-readable form.[76] Subscribers can now search the latest version of the UDC on the Web. "The official text of the UDC is the Master Reference File (MRF), the database created and maintained by the UDC Consortium. It is updated at the end of every year in accordance with agreed amendments. The amendments are also published in the annual Extensions and Corrections to the UDC. In January 2002, the MRF contained 65,931 entries."[77]

5. CLASSIFICATION AS AN ONLINE END USER'S TOOL

The researchers who conducted the DDC Online Project were thorough in their reporting of project findings and so specific about their recommendations for enhancements to the several search DOC capabilities that utilized a library classification that the documentation they produced could be considered system specifications.[78] They expected other researchers and online library systems developers to continue where they had left off, that is, embrace library classification online and build it into enhanced operational online systems as an end user's tool for subject access, browsing, and display. Something very different happened and the subsections that follow tell the story.

5.1 End Users and the Classified Approach to Seeking Information

Several researchers observed library patrons engaged in information-seeking behavior that indicated that patrons would benefit from searching a classified catalog. Focused-group interview participants described the usefulness of a "subject tree" for exploring their topics of interest and for finding related ones by browsing leaves of the tree.[79] Willard and Teece[80] interviewed over 200 library users and found almost half of them came to the library to browse. "These figures are particularly interesting if one reflects that libraries have traditionally been arranged in the classified order most useful for the seekers of specific materials."[81] Using protocol analysis, Markey[82] observed several end users whose searches began at the card catalog where they found call numbers of promising items and continued at the bookshelves where they browsed for additional materials on nearby shelves. Hancock[83] concluded that of the 42 catalog users who had initiated known-item searches at the card catalog, 15 users pursued the bookshelf-browsing approach by browsing the shelves where the known item was or should have been found.

5.2 Promoting Classification Online As an End User's Tool

Throughout the 1980s, researchers speculated on the benefits of searching classification online. Svenonius[84] cited eight uses of classification in future online retrieval systems:

In areas of knowledge admitting of natural taxonomies, classification can be used to improve recall and precision and to save the time of the user in keying in search terms. In other areas of knowledge, perspective hierarchies can be used to contextualize the meaning of vague search terms, enabling the computer to simulate in part the negotiation of a search request carried on by reference librarians. An important use . . . is to provide a framework for meaningful browsing, . . . for the representation and retrieval of

> non-bibliographic information, e.g., statistical data. Automatic classification can be used to collocate citations in ways not possible in manual systems, e.g., by similarity of linguistic features . . . In short, not only does classification have a place in online systems of the future; it likely has such an important place that we should prepare for a resurgence of interest in both its theory and its practice.

Markey[85] reviewed research findings to date that served as inspiration for the development and testing of an experimental online catalog enhanced with a library classification. Chan[86] enumerated the strengths of the Library of Congress Classification as an end user's subject searching tool and described needed changes to overcome its many weaknesses. "Our most pressing need is not simply for more . . . keywords from text . . . Rather, we need additional *kinds* of access points, additional *ways* of approaching knowledge. Classification schemes can provide a fresh approach. Making use of them would be tantamount to reintroducing the advantages of the classed catalog information retrieval."[87]

Although Hildreth did not explicitly promote classification online, he has been a staunch advocate of browsing for online retrieval.[88] "Browsing is essentially visual and depends more on recognition than on recall or a priori formulations of need. A good browsing tool, source, or system exploits the human ability to recognize items of interest, a cognitive ability that is faster and easier than juggling concepts to specify a need and describing relevant items in advance."[89] Williamson[90] is also a strong proponent of browsing, "The direct access to citations through Boolean search must be supplemented and complemented by search mechanisms which permit and encourage systematic browsing of these systems. Classification and classificatory structure of some kind will support this function in retrieval."

By the end of the decade of the 1980s, textbook treatments were being given to classification online.[91]

5.3 Classification Online for End Users

Classification online for end users has evolved very differently from classification as a cataloger's tool. Classification online is a tool that thousands of catalogers use on a daily basis in North American libraries and elsewhere through OCLC's WebDewey, LC's Classification Web, and the UDC Consortium's UDC on the Web. The opposite is true of classification online for end users. With the exception of ETHICS,[92] the online catalog for the library (ETH-Bibliothek) of the Swiss Federal Institute of Technology, classification online in systems for end users has been and remains experimental. Classification online has usually figured into research projects that limited system use to subjects recruited for evaluation. After the research projects ended, so did use of the system. In this section are reviewed experimental online systems that end users searched using various classification-based search capabilities.

Let's begin with ETHICS, the operational OPAC for ETH-Bibliothek, one of the largest technical libraries in Europe. ETHICS development began in 1983 and by 1988, its menu-driven interface was available in German and French, and an English interface was planned. ETHICS developers formulated descriptors for UDC numbers and added them to the system's searchable indexes.[93] In response to user queries, the system produced browsing lists of descriptors in the alphabetical neighborhood of the user-entered term.[94] Users could also obtain logical arrangements of descriptors ordered by UDC numbers and display cataloging records.

At Washington University in St. Louis, Huestis[95] recognized the need for an improved browsing capability for the OPAC's call number search because few end users searched the OPAC with this index. He generated a composite DDC-LCC index and LCC cluster index based on the OPAC's bibliographic database records and LCC number ranges that he entered manually into a data file and distributed the indexes to library staff.[96]

Whereas most researchers were looking at classification online as an opportunity for increasing the OPAC's entry vocabulary, Ray R. Larson[97] took an entirely different tack. He examined the potential of the classification for replacing Boolean search methods with the probabilistic partial-match search methods that have long characterized information retrieval (IR) research. Using his CHESHIRE experimental online catalog, he used terms from the subject-rich fields of bibliographic records, e.g., titles, subject headings, content notes, to represent a cluster for an individual LCC number. Retrieval tests demonstrated particular probabilistic model matching techniques that yielded the best average precision and recall for sample queries. "The major advantage of these methods is that the catalog user need not be trained in the use of Boolean logic or LCSH to obtain good search results."[98] Although today's web search engines do not use Larson's notion of classification clusters for retrieval, their retrieval algorithms are based on the same underlying principles that characterized probabilistic matching in

Larson's CHESHIRE system. In fact, he predicted the migration away from deterministic, exact matching of indexed terms to "a more exploratory and heuristic form of search" in his comprehensive review of subject searching in the online catalog."[99] Reviewing recent trends in subject access in OPACs a year later, Husain and O'Brien,[100] intimate much the same thing, "[t]he real answer . . . lies in developing 'user friendly novel interfaces' and also in designing 'knowledge based systems,' wherein users would not be expected to learn query formulation or even to be familiar with the indexing language of the system."

Mary Micco's[101] Interactive Library Subject Access (ILSA) Project enlisted a library classification to improve subject access in an experimental OPAC. Instead of building her system from scratch, she used the TOMUS online catalog of Carlyle Systems, Inc. She automatically grouped similar books into clusters by subject and used the DDC to produce hierarchical arrays so that users could browse the arrays to broaden or narrow their searches as needed.

Songqiao Liu and Elaine Svenonius developed "a model system, the Dewey Online Retrieval System (DORS), . . . as an interface to an online catalog for the purpose of experimenting with classification-based search strategies and generally seeking further understanding of the role of traditional classifications in automated information retrieval."[102] The guiding principle for DORS development was chain indexing. "A chain index to the *DDC* schedules was created automatically by extracting significant phrases from the schedule captions and the *DDC* 'Relative Index' and then constructing them into chains based on their hierarchical relationships."[103] DORS' Focus Term search served a disambiguating function and favored precision; its Perspective Term search served a collocating function and favored recall.[104] Human intervention in the production of chain indexes from the machine-readable DDC was minimal.[105] Using LCC in the new *USMARC Format for Classification Data*, Broadbent[106] created a chain index to LCC and an index using LC subject headings to LCC. Scanning these indexes, "the catalog user can immediately see which subject headings have been used in connection with which classification numbers and vice versa. This index would also assist the cataloger when assigning subject headings and classification numbers."[107]

Developers of the Okapi online catalog experimented with three different Okapi representations[108] in retrieval tests with end users: (1) Okapi with best-match, probabilistic searching only; (2) Okapi with best-match, probabilistic searching and query expansion; and (3) Okapi with best-match, probabilistic searching, query expansion, and shelflist browsing. With regard to the third Okapi representation, Okapi responded with a prompt to display the online shelflist every time a user gave a relevant rating to a retrieved record.[109] The researchers interviewed subjects about their searching experiences and asked them to compare the systems. The researchers concluded that shelflist browsing was relatively inefficient–users who enlisted the shelflist browsing looked at 17 brief records for every one chosen for full display.[110] Although Okapi researchers were not enthusiastic about results for shelflist browsing, they made recommendations for improving future systems with such a feature. For example, they suggest that the system should be "silently retrieving records and checking whether they would score reasonably highly if they had been retrieved by a query expansion search . . . Other clues, perhaps more practical, include the existence of some, but not too many, other records classified identically to the pivot record, or, in a system which collects relevance information, the fact that several selected records have the same classification."[111]

Charles R. Hildreth's[112] study of an experimental enhancement to the Tinman database management and retrieval software was similar to the Okapi experiment. Because Tinman employed an entity-relationship database structure which permitted linking of any field in the stored bibliographic field to any other field, it allowed for a rudimentary form of hypertext that the researcher used to test online shelflist browsing. In an evaluation, the online pivot feature from retrieved records to shelflist browsing was useful for increasing recall for one of the two tasks that the researcher assigned subjects. Subjects who commented on shelflist browsing "found it novel and they were pleased that they could actually browse the shelves at the online catalog, many expressed the wish that this kind of searching could be done on any OPAC, and those who didn't do [it] . . . said they didn't have enough time but would have liked to have done it."[113]

Borgman's Science Library Catalog (SLC) was a component of Project SEED, a collaborative effort of multiple institutions to design and support opportunities for hands-on science in the elementary schools.[114] In preparation for building an interface in a retrieval system that children could search, SLC investigators gave children a sorting task to determine whether children could sort words into categories.[115] Although SLC investigators experimented with three different SLC interfaces, they were partial to a Hypercard interface in which the governing metaphor was a set of bookshelves that had smaller bookshelves on them in addition to books. "When a set of the small bookshelves is selected, it 'grows,' revealing that it in turn holds still smaller bookshelves, along with books. On the Biology set of shelves, for example, there would be both general books on biology and smaller sets of bookshelves labeled Plants, Animals, etc. If the Plants bookshelf is selected, it grows to show general books on Plants along with smaller bookshelves labeled Flowers, Crops, Trees, and so on."[116] SLC investigators chose the bookshelves metaphor and enlisted the DDC to label the subjects of books on the bookshelves so that children could browse hierarchically, choose amongst broader to more specific subjects, and display bibliographic records for selected subjects.[117]

SLC investigators evaluated the Science Library Catalog with 10-, 11-, and 12-year olds and concluded that children could utilize a simple information retrieval interface with a reasonable success rate. Children at all three ages levels were able to locate relevant material on 77.5% of the six topics they were given with no explicit instruction and only about three minutes of practice time.[118] In a follow-up study, SLC researchers compared the Hypercard-based Science Library Catalog with ORION, a command-based OPAC deployed at university research libraries. Twelve-year olds had significantly greater success using ORION than 10-year olds, children liked the two systems about the same, younger children preferred the Science Library Catalog and older children preferred ORION. SLC investigators concluded that "a browsing, direct-manipulation interface for children is a superior general approach to information retrieval, as it is more generally usable and liked across the upper elementary school population, and less sensitive to computer experience."[119]

The efforts to include end users in the development and evaluation of the AMP-classification for fiction is well documented by Annelise Mark Pejtersen and her Danish colleagues.[120] AMP-Classification "has four independent, facet-like main categories called 'dimensions' . . . These range from reference to the authors' goals, their value criteria, their choice of book content and their level of communication with the reader to the publisher's choice of physical representation of the document."[121]

Pejtersen and her colleagues built the Book House OPAC.[122] With regard to its searching capabilities, they left no stone unturned allowing users to search by analogy, browse pictures, perform analytic searches, and browse book descriptions. Users could also specify their preferences for time period, geographic setting, the emotional experience that reading the book should provide, plot, actors, the author's intention, front-page pictures and colors, genre, readability, and the author's name. The Book House was evaluated at a public library over a six month period by everyday users from 7 to 70 years of age, and was evaluated later in school libraries. "The system received an overwhelmingly positive response from users of all ages, as well as from librarians, and it increased the end-user searches and the use of the book stock."[123]

Pejtersen was a strong advocate of her approach to the design of information retrieval systems that was based on "an analysis of the properties of the work domain, the task situation, and user characteristics."[124] Her colleagues echoed her sentiments in this regard: "The library should be an active participant in the production of knowledge, and this role can be effected by the development of classificatory structures that can support the needs of a diverse information technology consisting of a complex web of interacting agents, users, and technologies. Within such an information ecology, a classificatory structure cannot follow a one-size-fits-all paradigm but must evolve in cooperative interaction between librarians and their user groups."[125]

Inspired by Marcia J. Bates'[126] vision of a future interface for an online retrieval system, Khoo and Poo[127] described how an expert system could be used to select a strategy for reformulating an end user's search. The expert system would have to have knowledge of the initial retrieval size and the precision of retrieved results. For example, to broaden the search, the expert system could choose amongst several approaches such as omitting the least important concept group from the search formulation, omitting the concept group consisting only of keywords, converting the Boolean operator from AND to OR, or using a class number to find similar books. A team of students at the National University of Singapore built a demonstration prototype that "showed that a front-end with a repertory of heuristic procedures can provide a user with substantial help in doing subject searches."[128]

Cochrane and Johnson[129] incorporated the DDC and Legislative Indexing Vocabulary (LIV) into a hypertext environment to demonstrate how easy it is to point and click for browsing, to explore broader and narrower relationships, and to display retrieved records.

Gorman[130] asserts that "[t]he problem with classification lies in the attempt to carry out its two conflicting purposes–subject retrieval and the arrangement of individual items–using only one instrument. The solution requires separating the two purposes [and] [i]ntelligent use of computers is the key to the separation and the solution." The need for a single relative physical position for library materials on bookshelves will diminish over time as print collections yield to electronic collections in size, currency, and convenience to the user, making it possible for faceted classifications to come into their own. When designing classification online in an experimental OPAC, a group of University of Huddersfield researchers, led by Steven Pollitt, acknowledged that library classifications would have to sweep the problem of physical arrangement[131] aside before their proposed view-based searching interface could take hold. Huddersfield researchers designed their system's interface so that the screen would be divided into four separate windows to show arrays of DDC captions for the separate facets of synthesized numbers that interest the end user.[132] "A view-based searching interface can provide a very high number of alternative arrangements and combinations to best suit a user's perspective and information need."[133]

5.4 Critics of Classification Online for End Users

The story of classification online as an end user's tool in an online catalog appears to wane in the mid 1990s. Cochrane and Johnson[134] chide the library community and online library system developers for failing to heed the findings of OPAC use and user studies and make significant system improvements that affect subject searching:

> More than a decade has gone by since the first results came in about user difficulties with OPACs . . . Had we taken these findings seriously and begun the suggested improvements then, maybe we would not find the situation still as bad as ever. In our opinion, the technologies at our disposal at the time were not sufficiently advanced to provide the functionalities required. What is frustrating now is to find that system designers today, with better technologies, have learned little or nothing from those early OPAC user studies, from the analytical papers on preparing classification and thesauri for use online . . . , from the early attempts to mount thesauri and classification systems into retrieval/search systems . . . Neither the continuous stream of international conferences of classification research . . . , nor the numerous Subject Access Conferences sponsored by the Council on Library Resources . . . have delivered the message that library users need more help than they are receiving from current designs of OPACs and other retrieval systems and that presenting classification information may help.

No system developer ever stepped forward to develop full functionality for classification online in their systems. Mary Micco's[135] approach of enlisting Carlyle's TOMUS online catalog for her research was a step in the right direction. A follow-up and a more deliberate step would have been a collaboration between OCLC (DDC's publisher) and an online library system developer to bring classification online to life in an operational turnkey system. It never happened.

To this day, the only way in which most online catalog users experience classification online is through their OPAC's shelflist browsing search. We have known since the first online catalog use studies that few users enter class or call numbers directly through their OPAC's shelflist browsing capability[136] because they do not know the meaning of the numbers. That is why bookshelf browsing was such a popular end user strategy.[137] The technology of today's web-based OPACs has simplified shelflist browsing. The call numbers in retrieved records are hyperlinks on which users can click to initiate the OPAC's shelflist browsing feature. Although shelflist displays could benefit from the inclusion of classification captions to summarize the subject content of listed titles,[138] hyperlinks have certainly increased the efficiency of the shelflist browsing search.

Impressed with the DDC Online Project and the ability of DDC to be a user's tool for subject access, browsing, and display, McAllister-Harper[139] surveyed North Carolina libraries about their OPACs' handling of classification. Of the 29 surveyed libraries, 11 had OPACs but only one catalog featured online shelflist browsing. She recognized that to incorporate classification in an OPAC, several developments were necessary—a machine-readable format for classification data, OCLC or some other company to provide software, and a classification database. "The DDC has limited use in online search today" was how she summed up the situation.[140]

High[141] felt that public services librarians and skilled users would find searching classification schedules "delightful," occasional and regular users of the online catalog would find it "too sophisticated for their needs," but for "novice users," he "fear[ed] this capability would be totally beyond their abilities." He[142] got "nervous" thinking about end users "discovering the full potential" of shelflist browsing because they might "want to print large sections of the shelflist to take home." Especially vociferous are Shoham and Yitzhaki[143] who never witnessed any online shelflist browsing in their academic library's OPAC. They criticized both DDC Online Project and CHESHIRE research because "these projects are very complicated and expensive and their effectiveness very much in doubt."[144] In conclusion, they assert that investing "in enriching the catalogs by words from table[s] of contents . . . can contribute to meeting our most pressing requirements in . . . subject search."[145] Yet, they fail to acknowledge previous efforts in this regard[146] and the reasons why these initiatives were not embraced by the library and systems development communities.

Perhaps the lukewarm reception that critics gave to classification online was to blame for the field's failure to embrace classification in online systems for end users. Earlier, this paper's author commented on the less-than-enthusiastic review that Carol Mandel gave to the DDC Online Project in her report to the Council on Library Resources. The failure could have been due to the inadequate technology that Markey, Svenonius, Micco, Hildreth, and other researchers were using that was unable to give end users simultaneous views of classification schedules and tables for complex queries. The library community's failure to partner with integrated library systems staff in the development of classification online could have also been a contributing factor.

At the close of the 1990s, McIlwaine and Williamson[147] were right on the mark with their observation that "[w]ith few exceptions, there has been little team effort . . . Many researchers are working alone and it is difficult to find cumulative research which building on the work of others. As a result, much of the output from conferences focuses on small projects of individual interest."

The field seemed to stop dead in its tracks a few years after the release of the *USMARC Format for Classification Data.* We embraced a "build it and they will come" mentality, that is, we built the classification format but they–the integrated library systems developers–never did come. Perhaps classification online got lost in the frenzy of enhancing the functionality of online library systems with name and subject authority data, first for cataloging efficiency and later for increasing the OPAC's entry vocabulary for end users. Whether it is too late to recoup what we lost in failing to secure the support of integrated library systems vendors in the development of classification as an end user's tool depends on the extent to which classification online fits into the field's new priorities (see section 7).

5.5 Classification As a Web User's Tool

The story of classification online as a user's tool picks up in the mid 1990s with the advent of the Web. Dahlberg[148] assessed the impact of "the Karen Markey Shock of 1984 . . . classification was brought back into the minds of doubtful librarians and of all those who thought they would not need it any longer." Her[149] response was to propose "a new universal ordering system which more adequately represents and mediates the world of our present-day knowledge." A starting point could be the unfinished Information Coding Classification[150] (ICC) and Svenonius' desiderata[151] of an ideal online classification. Instead of a universal scheme, Baswas and Smith[152] advocated the development of discipline-based Classauri. Gödert's[153] response was to emphasize the superiority of faceted classifications and expressive notation. At least one reviewer of classification in the United States did "not foresee the invention of any new schemes in the near future."[154]

Not long after its inception, the Web grew at an astoundingly rapid pace. By 1992 were published the earliest calls for "effective directories of networked information resources."[155] None of the proposals from classification theorists served as inspiration or a foundation for new universal schemes that were created to organize web resources *and* have stood the test of time in terms of surviving to the present day. Now that the dust has settled, Yahoo! has emerged as the most comprehensive web directory and the one scheme to which other schemes compared themselves. Vizine-Goetz[156] compared 50 most popular categories in Yahoo! to DDC and LCC including the hierarchical levels at which these categories reside in these two universal classifications. She cited features of DDC and LCC that "would make them suitable for providing subject access to Internet resources . . . [they are:] general classification schemes, with hierarchical structures and notation that orders classes, they contain links to other subject schemes, and links to translations in other languages (presently DDC only)." Vizine-Goetz urged the keepers of these older library-based schemes to make the following improvements:

1. Evaluate DDC and LCC captions for expressiveness and currency
2. Decompose and code class number components to identify the specific subject and aspects represented
3. Continue to add new terminology as index terms even if each is not supplied with its own number
4. Expand links to other controlled vocabularies
5. Expand definitions of literary warrant to include Internet resources
6. Build demonstration systems

Up to the present day, Vizine-Goetz and her OCLC-based research team have immersed themselves in making these improvements to the DDC. She[157] analyzed the DDC numbers assigned to Internet resources in bibliographic records from OCLC's NetFirst database, discovered how unevenly DDC's ten main classes were applied to Internet resources, and identified both manual and automatic approaches to elevating high-posted classes to top levels. Her OCLC research team's efforts[158] to increase the DDC's entry vocabulary for end users who are searching databases of Internet resources is well documented as are their efforts to revise DDC captions for currency and expressiveness. After over a half decade of active enhancement of the DDC, Vizine-Goetz[159] revisited her 1996 comparison of Yahoo!, DDC, and LCC in 2002. Using Wheatley's[160] estimates of the number of categories and postings at various levels of the subject trees of the major Internet directory services, Vizine-Goetz compared the enhanced DDC with Yahoo! and LookSmart and concluded that they had much in common. "Overall, the findings suggest that the prospects are very good for developing effective DDC-based browsing structures to large collections."[161] Additionally, she acknowledged that critics of the DDC targeted the constraints its notation imposed on browsing. "In reality [the notation] can provide a great deal of flexibility. [It] can be manipulated to elevate whole branches of the tree to higher levels for display."[162]

A group of Huddersfield researchers[163] acknowledged the improvements that OCLC researchers made to DDC and urged them and the keepers of other traditional classification schemes to cast off the characteristics that placed so much emphasis on making a logical arrangement of physical materials on library bookshelves. When it comes to Internet resources, assigning multiple class numbers to items, increasing the scheme's faceted nature, adding more specificity to classes, and taking user needs into account in interface development are more important than shelf arrangement.[164] The Huddersfield researchers[165] demonstrated the DDC in their view-based searching OPAC that provided simultaneous browsing of DDC's hierarchical structure for topical subjects in the Schedules and geographic areas in the Tables and direct selection of formats and year of publication.

Dodd[166] enlisted both LCC and DDC in his analysis of Internet directories. He compared the main categories in several directories such as Yahoo!, Magellan, and the Whole Internet Catalog (WIC) to the main classes in LCC and DDC and made some concluding remarks about browsing versus direct searching with keywords. Woodward[167] summarized the library community's efforts to organize web resources through traditional classification (i.e., DDC, UDC, LCC) and cataloging (i.e., USMARC) standards. Chan[168] examined how the nature of the Web and characteristics of networked resources affects access, specified requirements for effective indexing and retrieval tools for these resources, and cited the many ongoing research efforts that were making improvements to traditional tools for organizing Internet resources. She concluded that traditional tools had complementary strengths on which future systems could and should capitalize. Hudon[169] criticized web directories for "their lack of standardization, lack of consistency in arranging categories, disregard for theoretical principles of knowledge organization, lack of specificity, and lack of true and sound relational structures." She[170] called on traditional classification schemes to study users, determine what they really want, and respond accordingly with improvements to their schemes for handling Internet resources.

Koch et al.[171] summarized advantages and disadvantages of the various universal, national, special, and homegrown classification schemes that have been used to organize web resources, and surveyed web sites that used these schemes in this way. Saeed and Chaudry[172] limited their survey to the DDC, LCC, and UDC, remarking on the wide-ranging research agenda that OCLC implemented for improving the DDC's ability to handle Internet resources. Instead of a survey, Zins[173] took a different tack to characterize the organization of Internet resources. He sought the classificatory models that were the inspiration for the organization of Internet resources at a variety of web portals and classified directories and arrived at eight such models:[174] "subjects, objects, applications, users, locations, reference sources, media, and language." He suggested that these models could evolve into an integrated faceted classification scheme[175] in which developers could utilize eight, some, or one of the models.

5.6 Automatic Classification for Information Retrieval

A discussion of classification online would not be complete without reference to automatic classification because its future success has important implications for keeping up with the unprecedented growth of the Internet and the information explosion generally. Separate studies by SLC and OCLC researchers demonstrate how automatic classification can be an editor's tool for expanding traditional classifications with new classes or entirely new hierarchies. SLC researchers[176] enlisted automatic classification in their search for a solution to the problem of high-posted DDC classes. They selected bibliographic records from high-posted classes, submitted them to automatic classification, and, in most cases, the automatic clustering was successful in creating coherent categories while in others it produced nonsensical groupings. "Part of the difficulty can be attributed to the choice of some stop words that were context-dependent."[177] For example, words that would be considered stop words in some contexts, e.g., when the word "explore" meant "examine" or "investigate," would be meaningful and content-bearing in other contexts, e.g., when the word "explore" was used in nature, outdoor, or geography contexts. The end result of their automatic classification was the creation of more discrete categories than existed for high-posted DDC classes.

Vizine-Goetz and Beall[178] report the results of an exploratory study to determine literary warrant for new topics in DDC's Mathematics and Natural Sciences (500 to 559) classes. They examined three electronic sources–BUBL, Canadian Information by Subject, and KidsClick!–for literary warrant and expanded the classification to match by creating entirely new Relative Index entries.

The earliest automatic classification experiments[179] were done almost a half century ago to automatically assign documents to broad predefined classes using terms from the documents' abstracts. In the earliest review of classification online, Robert R. Freeman[180] anticipated significant research progress in automatic classification. In this paper are covered a small fraction of exemplary experiments that are carrying on the tradition of finding an optimum solution to the problem of automatically assigning documents to clusters or to broad predefined classes that are drawn from a classification scheme using subject headings from bibliographic records or from the documents themselves.

Enser[181] used a small test collection of 250 books from six DDC classes and submitted the books' titles, table of contents, and back-of-the-book indexes to several different automatic classifications. For example, in one classification, books gathered into four clusters that also characterized four of the original DDC classes, three clusters bearing books from several of the original DDC classes, and two clusters bearing only one book each.[182] The author[183] concluded that automatic classifications of the book collection were achieved, the majority of which proved to be more effective . . . than the manual classification . . . from which it was drawn."

Travis[184] and Vleduts-Stokolov[185] described a natural-language text-processing system as an automatic aid for subject indexers at BIOSIS. Using information in the titles of biology documents, the system assigned index categories in preparation for subsequent review by a human indexer. Irving[186] introduced CAIT, Computer-Assisted Indexing Tutor, that was used at the National Agricultural Library to train novice indexers and described how novice indexers used it to learn how to apply AGRICOLA Subject Category codes to the documents they indexed. Masand, Linoff, and Waltz[187] describe how Dow Jones editors assigned about eight from a list of 350 distinct codes to the hundreds of new stories that they reviewed on a daily basis. Automatic assignment of these codes was considered as an alternative to time-consuming and costly manual assignment. Based on a test of a memory-based reasoning method for automatic classification, the researchers[188] concluded that automatic assignment "offers significant advantages in terms of ease of development, deployment, and maintenance."

Larson conducted an experiment in which 60 variant methods for automatic classification were tested on a set of 283 new books records and sums up his findings as follow:[189] "These results, while quite good considering the size and diversity of the LCC scheme, indicate that fully automatic classification may not be possible. However, semiautomatic classification (where the classifier selects the most appropriate classification from among those given high ranks by the automatic methods described) appears to be effective."

Jacob, Mostafa, and Quiroga[190] used the set of major MeSHs (Medical Subject Headings) to cluster a set of documents from the Medline database into 29 clusters. Comparing the human-classified set with the automatically-assigned set resulted in a homogeneity rating for class assignment of 61%. The researchers'[191] ultimate goal was "to develop a set of analytic tools that will facilitate evaluation of scheme generation techniques more effectively than the traditional relevance-based measures of recall and precision."

Curran and Thompson[192] performed automatic classification experiments on statutory legal materials and concluded that "a substantial proportion of index features are highly amenable to automatic assignment, others can be assigned accurately with some manual intervention, and a few resist automatic assignment even with considerable manual intervention." Dolin et al.[193] trained an automatic classification algorithm using 1.5 million bibliographic records from a major academic library's database. They then automatically classified 2,500 newsgroups into top-level science classes from LCC's Q outline. The researchers posed queries to LCC and retrieved candidate newsgroups. They performed a failure analysis to explain why some queries worked and others did not work. Using automatic classification to assign LCC numbers to documents in the INFOMINE directory of web sites, Frank and Paynter[194] reported that the correct classification appeared among the top 15 predictions about 80% of the time. Liddy[195] reported on the Standard Connection Project in which her research team will develop a middleware tool to automatically assign content standards and benchmarks from the *Compendium of Standards and Benchmarks*.

For almost a decade, a team of OCLC researchers[196] have conducted research through the Scorpion Project "to address the challenge of applying classification schemes and subject headings cost effectively to electronic information." Because class integrity is a highly desirable property for the knowledge base of any classification tool, an early Scorpion experiment tested DDC's class integrity using automatic classification methods. Tests results led the researchers[197] to conclude that the DDC demonstrated a high degree of class integrity. When users of OCLC's CORC database invoke its automatic metadata assignment feature, the system relies on Scorpion technology[198] to automatically assign DDC numbers.

OCLC researchers have been relentless in their pursuit of a satisfactory automatic classification feature for OCLC's CORC and its Connexion Service. Godby and Rieghart[199] have fine tuned the sophisticated word extraction routines that identify key phrases in text. Their objective was to ensure that automatic classification yielded class numbers that were exact or very close to the numbers that a human classifier would choose during manual classification. Scorpion technology is also an important component of OCLC's Taxonomy Server.[200] The intended service, which was never implemented as a stand-alone service separate from Connexion, proposed a publicly accessible automatic metadata creation tool that returns metadata encoded in XML. Metadata includes automatically-assigned DDC classes. Scorpion does the automatic classification. During the automated classification process, a set of terms is extracted from the resource being cataloged and used to retrieve a ranked list of DDC numbers from the terminology-enhanced database. The ranking is based on relative frequency of occurrence of terms and other criteria relating to associations found in the DDC. Highest ranking DDC numbers are inserted into the preliminary metadata record. Editorial review of automatically-generated DDC numbers is still suggested.[201]

Prior to initiating automatic classification experiments, DESIRE Project researchers[202] at Lund University, Sweden, underlined the importance of this technology and assessed the outcomes of previous research: "Automatic classification processes are a necessity if large robot-generated services are to offer a good browsing structure for their documents." DESIRE researchers have collaborated with GERHARD researchers at Oldenburg University, Germany, and Scorpion Project researchers at OCLC to test automatic classification technology on database records in the Electronic Engineering Library, Sweden (EELS).[203]

EELS editors[204] assigned thesaurus terms and classification codes using the Ei Thesaurus and DESIRE Project staff[205] enlisted Scorpion and GERHARD to automatically assign DDC and UDC captions, respectively. Researchers tested DESIRE's automatic assignment of Ei terms with subject experts' manual assignment of Ei terms, found varying degrees of correct classifications: 75.5% for Information Science, 61.5% for Biochemistry, and 37.0% for Concrete and tell reasons why failures occurred.[206] Comparing Ei, DDC, and UDC, DESIRE researchers reported that both DDC and UDC have more classes for Engineering than Ei, a specialized classification for engineering information.

5.7 Classification As a Switching Language

The assignment of three classifications to DESIRE database records will increase the database's entry vocabulary. It will also give users three different logical approaches for exploring the topics that interest them–perhaps users will want to switch between languages when the specificity of the language at hand does not have the depth that suits their needs, when they want an approach that matches their understanding of the field, or when they want an approach that structures the field differently. The idea of a switching language has a long history that involves both computer assistance[207] and editorial review[208] to effect the mapping between vocabularies. Classifications such as ICC[209] and the Broad System of Ordering[210] have been proposed as the chief switching language that would govern the many controlled vocabularies that are now used to organize print and web resources. Mai[211] asserted that the purpose of general classification schemes is to facilitate interoperability among different IR systems and that the purpose of special classification schemes is to give access to the material at a greater level of exhaustivity and specificity. Iyer and Giguere[212] suggested expert systems would play an important role in switching. Over thirty years ago, Robert R. Freeman,[213] a pioneer in classification online research, concluded his review with the prediction that "the matter of switching among existing classification and indexing languages . . . will continue to be the subject of considerable effort." His words ring true today. Expect research in switching languages to surge in the years to come as researchers explore solutions to the problem of finding relevant information as a result of an ever-expanding Internet.

6. ACCOMPLISHMENTS TO DATE

To summarize accomplishments to date, I have enlisted the list that Pauline Cochrane[214] formulated to characterize the direction of classification vis-à-vis electronic information resources on the occasion of the closing of the 36th Allerton Institute entitled "New Roles for Library Classification in the Electronic Age." Section 6 cites all but one of Cochrane's dozen directions. In parentheses are the numbers of this paper's sections that describe research and development activity pertaining to each direction.

> Exploit technology for (a) adding class numbers to materials in digital form, (b) linking subject access systems like LCSH and DDC, and (c) providing navigation and retrieval tools based on outlines of knowledge within classification schedules. Improve the presentation of information in library classification schedules including more lead-in vocabulary, more scope notes, better captions, etc.

When it comes to systems for catalogers, the field has exceeded expectations in this regard. WebDewey (4.2), Classification Web (4.3), and UDC Online (4.4) enable catalogers to search, browse, and display classification indexes, schedules, and tables. These web-based tools include bibliographic databases so that catalogers can search for materials that are comparable to the item they have in hand and use retrievals to facilitate the selection of candidate classes and subject headings. OCLC has been especially proactive in the establishment of thousands of additional editorial and statistical links between the DDC and subject headings in bibliographic records to streamline both class number and subject heading assignment (4.2). At the click of a button, OCLC users can invoke Scorpion's automatic classification capability in OCLC's Connexion Service to retrieve a list of candidate class numbers (5.6).

> Extend the use of library classification to Internet resources.

Both the information industry and the library and information science community missed the opportunity to lead the charge in this regard. When it comes to choosing a web directory, web users start with Yahoo! which built a hierarchical system for organizing web resources. OCLC's DDC has made up ground. LCC and UDC are not far behind DDC but all three have been left in the dust by Yahoo!, LookSmart, and other web-based commercial ventures (5.5).

Share development strategies among and between various classification systems and thesauri, creating the ability to link with one another including multilingual and specialized systems.

The medical community[215] joined forces for the purpose of building a unified vocabulary. If a comparable effort is in the offing for universal and discipline-based vocabularies, it could start with an expansion of the DESIRE Project (5.6 and 5.7).

Conduct more end-user research to determine the utility of library classification systems–new and improved. Build bridges from the past (e.g., library collections classified by DDC, LCC, etc.) to the future (e.g., digitized full text collections).

Following on the heels of the DDC Online Project is a long list of research projects–Larson's CHESHIRE, Micco's ILSA, two separate but complementary chain indexing initiatives by Svenonius and Broadbent, Walker's Okapi, Hildreth's browsing in Tinman, Borgman's Science Library Catalog, Pejtersen's Book House, Cochrane's Visual Dewey, Huddersfield's view-based searching–that demonstrated the value of classification for partitioning the search space, enhancing subject access, and introducing the classified approach to searching that is not possible through title keyword and subject heading searches (5.3). These projects are not without critics who question the value of classification online and their hesitation may have made the integrated library systems community waver in terms of enhancing their systems with functionality for classification online (5.4). Although critics have targeted inconsistencies in the hierarchical structure of Yahoo!'s web-based scheme for organizing Internet resources, its success can be measured in terms of the millions of users who search this directory on a daily basis. Library classifications may remain in the shadow of Yahoo! for some time to come but OCLC researchers have been especially proactive in terms of improving the DDC–enhancing its entry vocabulary, reformulating outdated terminology, and encouraging the field to use it to classify web resources (5.5).

Work with vendors of online catalogs so that these systems will include features where classification systems and thesauri can be used for file partitioning, navigation, and retrieval.

No system developer ever stepped forward to develop full functionality for classification online in their systems. Subsection 5.4 speculates on several reasons why shelflist browsing is the only type of classification searching and browsing in today's online catalogs.

> Reach out to other professions for ideas, stimulation, collaboration, and convergence.

Some critics took researchers to task because they were working alone on small projects of individual interest (5.4). Perhaps these solitary efforts were to blame for the failure of integrated library systems vendors to implement classification functionality in their systems. Only two researchers used turnkey systems; Micco used TOMUS from Carlyle Systems and Hildreth used the TINMAN database management system. Neither enhanced these systems with classification online beyond the usual shelflist browsing that was a feature in the earliest online catalogs (5.3). The field's wake-up call in this regard should be its failure to play a major role in the development of web directories and web search engines. Future success, for example, in the development of switching languages, will depend on collaboration and sharing across the disciplines (5.7).

> Organize the classification schemes differently for the end-user than for the classifier and provide more than one scheme for users to browse and navigate before and after retrieval.

Universal classification schemes have hardly cast off the objective of relative physical arrangement of library material on bookshelves (5.3); however, when these classifications are used to organize networked resources, their expressive notation is useful for promoting and demoting classes as needed (5.5). Switching languages could make it possible for users to browse more than one scheme. Monitor the progress of the DESIRE Project that is making inroads in this regard (5.7). Lin and Chan[216] have gone in an entirely different direction, building an information-organizing framework and interface to help individual researchers and serious information seekers retrieve, organize, and manage electronic resources for individual use in their personal computers.

> Educate consumers, administrators, and practitioners about the value of library classification systems beyond mere shelf arrangement. Make the classification schemes more educational so that

the user can be guided to see relationships and cognate information they might not otherwise have known.

Had we done a better job educating administrators and practitioners about the value of library classification systems, I believe that today's integrated library systems would feature functionality for classification online making it possible for everyone to search the classification directly and browse arrays of schedule and table captions. While we waited for the *USMARC Format for Classification Data* to be published, administrators and practitioners focused on completing retrospective conversions of their shelflists, enhanced their library systems with name and authority control functionality, and added other online databases to their integrated library systems (5.4). Perhaps classification online got lost during the Internet craze which began just as the format was published in the early 1990s. Is it too late to recoup our losses?

I am especially skeptical about educating end users about classification online or just about anything that pertains to system use. The field has known about the difficulty of reaching end users since the Nationwide Survey of Online Catalogs. Users did not give high ratings to the availability of help messages, instruction manuals, "cheat sheets," workshops, etc.; instead, they wanted to be able to use OPACs right from the get-go.[217] The point-and-click *web* interface made self-service possible and by the turn of the century, most OPACs had migrated to a web-based interface. By that time, the OPAC was just one of many online databases available to end users through their library's gateway. Meanwhile, end users' attention was focused on the Web. At the same time librarians were educating users about the need to question the trustworthiness of web-based information, librarians were coaxing end users to come back to the library gateway and search for high-quality information in its databases.

7. CLASSIFICATION ONLINE IN THE NEXT DECADE

7.1 The Google Shock of 2004

Predicting the direction of classification online in the next decade cannot be done without putting the Google Mass Digitization Initiative front and center. On December 14, 2004, Google and the University of Michigan (U-M) announced an agreement to digitize the complete text of all seven million volumes in the library's collection. "Besides digitizing U-M's massive collection, Google plans to scan parts of other research libraries, including those at Harvard, Stanford, Oxford University in England, and the New York Public Library [but these] projects are much smaller in scope than Google's plans for U-M."[218] Ten years from now in 2015, the text of all English-language texts are likely to be available online. By that time, solutions to intellectual property problems will have been found because so many interested parties stand to benefit from the groundswell of demand from everyday people for access to digital information.

Enhancing subject access in online public access catalogs (OPACs) was the rationale for incorporating classification online in this new form of the library catalog. The Google mass digitization initiative will make this benefit of classification online a moot point because people will be able to search full texts–their tables of contents, back-of-the-book indexes, and everything in between–for the subjects that interest them. Traditional approaches to subject analysis–assigning subject headings and classification numbers–may be doomed because library administrators will question why they need to continue supporting armies of catalogers to assign metadata to bibliographic records when Google will supply their systems with every word and phrase in the world's great library collections.

If classification online is to thrive and succeed in the post massdigitization era, it must go into new directions that enable it to parallel the development of mass digitization and enrich future search engines in ways that complement Google's full-text searching. In the sections that follow, the author makes three recommendations for the future of classification online: (1) revisiting chain indexes for producing brief, sound-bite-sized phrases to serve as the briefest document representations in the staging of access to lengthier document representations, (2) building new dimensions in a classification to retrieve the *best* digital information for the topics that interest people, and (3) building information search tactics into web search engines that execute automatically to find additional material based on the end user's assessment of retrieved documents.

7.2 Revisiting Chain Indexes

7.2.1 Awash in Digital Information

As a result of a completed Google Initiative, end users will be awash in digital information. Recall the problems that Rosenberg and Borgman[219] reported regarding the varying contexts of texts that transformed content-bearing words in one context to stop words in a different context. This problem will be compounded ten times, one hundred times, maybe tens of thousands of times for the users who will be searching the full-text databases that are the end result of Google's mass digitization.

The solution to this problem just may be the end product of traditional subject analysis–the assignment of classification numbers, category codes, subject headings, descriptors, to discrete information artifacts–because these devices have the ability to consolidate the subject contents of lengthy text-based documents such as books, journal articles, and conference papers, into simple bite-size statements. They are comparable to the sound bites that news reports utilize to summarize the several different viewpoints in an analysis of a complex issue.

7.2.2 Staging of Access

When Marcia Bates[220] introduces the idea of staging of access, she describes research conducted by Dolby and Resnikoff[221] who discovered that the devices we use to summarize document contents and judge relevance (e.g., titles, subject headings, abstracts, etc.) vary in length in a very systematic way. We human beings, knowingly or unknowingly, have devised staging of access to conform to a 30:1 ratio. For example, the briefest document representations–titles, subject headings, classification captions, and category codes–are about 1/30th the size of the table of contents, the table of contents is about 1/30th the size of the back-of-the-book index, the index is about 1/30th the length of the book's text, etc.[222] Did Google knowingly apply this rule when it announced that it would limit the display of retrievals for in-copyright materials to three lines of text (about 30 times the size of a book's title)?

In the post mass-digitization era, we need to build staging of access mechanisms in our systems that are in keeping with "the Resnikoff-Dolby 30:1 Rule." And we can turn to the end product of traditional subject analysis because classification numbers, category codes, subject headings, descriptors, etc., have the ability to consolidate the subject contents of lengthy text-based documents into simple bite-size statements. However, a few changes are in order based on four decades of research findings on users and online searching.

7.2.3 Chain Indexes for Staging of Access

Here is the approach I suggest for moving ahead with classification online. Instead of building logical arrays of classification captions and alphabetical lists of index entries into future systems, let's enlist the perspective terms and focus terms that Elaine Svenonius built for her experimental DORS system.[223] Like titles and subject headings, these terms would describe documents in simple, sound-bite-sized phrases, and be about 30 times shorter than tables of contents or abstracts, i.e., document representations that would be next in the staging of access. If users do not understand how to "read" perspective terms and focus terms, let's invite linguists, computer scientists, and artificial intelligence experts to help us automatically convert them into English-language phrases that everyday people can understand. When people scan these converted terms in brief displays of retrieved material, we want them to be able to understand them in a split second. Because perspective and focus terms preserve some of the DDC hierarchy, the system could use them to drill down deeper or expand into broader ideas, concepts, and areas of inquiry in a discipline. I am *not* suggesting that systems display arrays of perspective or focus terms to users and ask them to do the exploration. Future systems have to invoke these strategies automatically at a push of a button or the switch of a gear shift. (See section 7.4.)

7.2.4 Precoordinated Subject Headings for Staging of Access

Here is my prognosis for subject headings. We know that users have difficulty understanding the long precoordinated subject heading strings that are the result of applying Library of Congress Subject Headings.[224] Let's keep these strings intact and again invite experts from related fields to help us automatically convert them into English-language phrases that everyday people can understand. When people scan converted subject headings in brief displays of retrieved material, we want them to be able to understand them in a split second. Subject headings are direct and specific and the syndetic structure of LC subject headings could be used to broaden or narrow the search. Again, I am *not* suggesting that systems display arrays of alphabetically-arranged subject headings to users and ask them to do the exploration. Future systems have to invoke these strategies automatically at a push of a button or the switch of a gear shift. (See section 7.4.)

7.2.5 Weighting Chain Indexing Terms and Subject Headings

Being awash in the subject information of millions of books, the builders of future natural language retrieval systems could enlist chain indexing terms and subject headings prominently in weighting and ranking algorithms because these devices characterize the entire contents of a discrete information artifact, not just a single page, paragraph, or an even smaller unit. Let me emphasize that I am not suggesting that future systems use chain indexing terms or subject headings to build alphabetical or hierarchical arrays of terms for end user browsing. Victor Rosenberg[225] forewarned that "[t]he preference for a given method [of information retrieval] reflects the estimated ease of use of the method rather than the amount of information expected." The plethora of research findings demonstrating that end users conduct simple, direct searches and hardly use an information retrieval system's advanced functionality[226] are compelling evidence regarding the futility of implementing browsing approaches in online systems for end users. My recommendations regarding perspective terms, focus terms, and subject headings pertain to their ability to increase the precision of search results when used for weighting and ranking retrievals.

7.3 Dimensions for Partitioning the Knowledge Space

7.3.1 Classification Online for Partitioning the Knowledge Space

Partitioning the knowledge space was the underlying principle in Larson's experimental CHESHIRE system.[227] His clustering algorithms gathered documents into clusters. Cluster membership was based on the extent to which documents shared the same characteristics (such as words in titles, in subject headings, etc.) with other documents in the cluster. When users submitted a query to CHESHIRE, the system compared the characteristics of the query to characteristics of clusters. Clusters having the most in common were ranked higher than clusters sharing few characteristics. Because users are likely to find a satisfactory amount of useful information in high-ranking clusters, low-ranking clusters might not even figure into a search.

The Google Mass Digitization Initiative will put a Mount Everest of information at the fingertips of everyday users of information systems. Let's consider using this same clustering approach to partition the digital knowledge space that results from the Google's Initiative.

7.3.2 New Dimensions for Classification Schemes

Partitioning has great potential for accomplishing three important missions:

- Increasing the efficiency and precision of end user searches
- Identifying candidate documents and document collections to which catalogers would assign subject headings and chain indexing terms
- Sidelining remaining documents and document collections for automatic classification and the assignment of chain indexing terms and subject headings

We could apply existing universal classifications to partition the digital knowledge space but they would not do much more than divide it by discipline. Depending on the classification, sometimes facets for form, geography, and classes of persons would enter in the mix. A new starting point could be the eight models that Zins[228] used to characterize web directories and portals, i.e., subject, objects, application, users, geography, form, media, and language. Let me suggest additional models, facets, points of view, or dimensions based on my many years studying information-seeking models, my knowledge of user studies, and my experience as an information seeker. For now, I will call them dimensions:

- Authority. Divide the search space according to the most respected experts writing in their area of expertise.
- Popularity. Use citation patterns to divide the search space. Traditional footnotes and references and web links are popularity indicators.
- Level of difficulty. Rate information at the level of expertise that the author expected of the reader on a continuum from novice to expert.
- Audience. Identify the class of people and the level of expertise for which authors are writing.
- Reading level. Assign a reading level to the text at hand.
- Discovery currency. Characterize the content on a continuum from the latest, most up-to-date, cutting-edge discoveries, advances, or leaps forward in a discipline to a repackaging of long accepted and well documented knowledge.

I am sure that others would like to add their favorite dimensions to my list and delete ones they do not like. Let's also involve users in the identification of these dimensions. Such activities would be worthwhile ones in preparation for prototyping new dimensions in a classification for partitioning the digital knowledge space. Additionally, I would like to think that we could generate computer algorithms to automatically classify the digital knowledge space for most of these dimensions. We may have to invite experts in other disciplines to help us accomplish this. For example, "authority" is an area on which scholars in social networking and bibliometrics could collaborate. Some researchers in the former area have generated complex graphs to indicate the most active researchers in a discipline or multidisciplinary area of inquiry. I bet we could benefit from their methods and use them to represent the "authority" dimension. "Audience" may be very difficult to accomplish automatically; however, many authors of books cite their intended audience in their introductions and prefaces. Could artificial intelligence experts help us to identify audience statements in texts? "Reading level" is a dimension that my word processing software accomplishes automatically right now. Just highlight the text, select an option from the software's pulldown menu, and the software rates the highlighted text.

7.3.3 How Would a Classification's Dimensions Work?

How would a classification's dimensions work? Robots could be enlisted to partition the digital knowledge space. When robots place documents or collections of documents into a certain combination of dimensions, for example, in a scholarly discipline, at a high level of authority, and at a high level of difficulty, they would be candidates for the assignment of perspective terms, focus terms, and subject headings using teams of editors, catalogers, and indexers. When robots place documents or collections of documents in a different combination, for example, in a popular culture subclass, at a low level of popularity, and a low level of difficulty, they would be handled by automatic classification instead of given to professional teams for special treatment. To keep automatic classification algorithms sharp, digital resources to which professional teams of indexers assign dimensions would become training-database fodder for the latter.

Partitioning of the knowledge space would never be "done." Updating dynamic and volatile dimensions such as authority, popularity, discovery currency, would be needed. New material would always be added to the digital knowledge space.

Users could query digital knowledge space using natural language terms, just like they search today's web search engines. Under search, certain dimensions would always be set at a default level, for example, medium to high levels of authority, medium to high levels of popularity, high levels of currency, etc., for users who merely want to type their queries into a dialogue box, much like Google users do today.

Users wanting higher levels of precision could choose a detailed query-entry form on which they could set dimensions of interest at levels that suit their particular needs. During search, choosing and setting dimensions must be very simple–perhaps as simple as pulling a control bar up and down to indicate how much users care about a particular dimension–because of the plethora of research that demonstrates the simple, unsophisticated searches that end users conduct (see section 7.2.5). Choosing a high level for "authority," "popularity," and "currency" would mean that the system would omit documents or collections at medium or low levels of authority, popularity, and currency. Choosing a low level for any one of these three dimensions would mean that the system would not take them into consideration when choosing clusters. Setting a few dimensions might warrant browsing hierarchically-arranged terms and phrases. "Disciplines," "Audience," and "Application" may be candidates for such browsing. In the event of too few retrievals, the system could always move upwards in the hierarchy to increase retrievals. The dimensions that users select would result in clusters to which user query would be submitted for the retrieval of documents or collections of documents.

When I think of an image to depict partitioning for digital knowledge space partitioning and information retrieval, I envision a magician at a circus who locks a human being in a box, closes the box, and pierces the box with swords or daggers. When the magician opens the box, the human being is no longer (or hopefully no longer) inside the box. Instead, what remains are the areas where several swords intersect or come close to intersecting. Consider these areas to be candidate high-ranking clusters of documents and collections that have the greatest likelihood of bearing relevant information for (1) human indexing in the form of perspective terms, focus terms, and subject headings and (2) probabilistic matching of user queries.

7.4 Where Should the Person Stop and the Information Search Interface Start?

"When people look up a term and do not find anything under it that suits them, they assume the library does not have anything on the subject. Almost never do they assume that they need to try another term . . . The average user identifies their search term with their whole subject query. It does not occur to them that it might be called other things by the catalog."[229] Belkin called this phenomenon the "anomalous state of knowledge."[230] How can systems help such users find useful information for the topics they have in mind but find so hard to express in words?

The title of a paper by Marcia J. Bates is "Where Should the Person Stop and the Information Search Interface Start?"[231] I have given her paper's title to this section because it is the inspiration for what I have to say in this regard. In her article, Bates breaks system involvement in the user's ongoing search into 5 categories:[232] "(0) no system involvement, all search activities are done manually, (1) displays possible activities, the system lists search activities when asked, (2) executes activities on command, (3) monitors search and recommends only when searcher asks for suggestions or always when it identifies a need, and (4) executes automatically and then informs the searcher or does not inform the searcher." When Bates wrote the article, most extant systems fell into categories 0, 1, and 2. Now we have systems that fall into all five categories including web search engines that are at level 4–they are executing automatically and not informing the searcher. The overwhelming popularity of web search engines and the simple searches that people conduct are compelling evidence that they want more of the same.

Bates listed information search tactics that online systems could invoke on their own to further the search based on numbers of hits or the user's assessment of the effect that their search terms were having on the search.[233] While her suggested search tactics are still valid, recent findings about the low levels of metacognitive knowledge that end users have about their ongoing searches may indicate that this may not be the right way to proceed.[234] Instead, users should be asked to assess the retrievals they have in hand because they can usually recognize what is relevant and what is not.

To register user assessments, we need to find alternatives to the prompts and feedback mechanisms we have used in the past. Let's partner with information design experts and experiment with "diagrams" that the user can manipulate to express the closeness of retrievals to their needs. A working definition of "diagrams" comes from *Webster's Third New International Dictionary*:[235] "A graphic design that explains rather than represents: a drawing that shows arrangements and relations (as often parts of a whole, relative values, origins and development, chronological fluctuations, distribution)." Diagrams may be viewed as unique graphic forms of schematic notation, distinct both from text and from more pictorial forms of representation; they are a means of giving visual form to otherwise non-visual information and making structural and logical relations apparent.[236]

In a short period of time, the cell phone's strength-of-signal diagram has become a familiar icon.[237] It is a staple in television ads, in magazine ads, on roadside billboards, and on posters to indicate the dependability of a cell phone provider's service. Why can't our field arrive at a comparable strength-of-retrievals indicator? Based on a user's manipulation of the indicator, the system would automatically invoke one or more information search tactics. Some of these search tactics–SUB, SUPER, NEIGHBOR, RELATE, PARALLEL, and PINPOINT–would enlist perspective terms, focus terms, or some other subject-access device to further the search.

7.5 Next Steps for Classification Editors and System Designers

Some readers may be tempted to conclude that continued development of traditional classification schemes is no longer necessary now that Google is about to solve the problem of in-depth subject access to scholarly materials. Traditional classification schemes are likely to continue to be used for organizing specific collections by discipline (e.g., psychology, engineering, biology), by form (e.g., web sites, books, journal articles), or by genre (e.g., newspaper articles, patents, dissertations). In the middle of the next decade, mass digitization efforts are likely to come to a successful end and access to digital collections will probably take precedence over physical library collections. Classification will finally be free of its long-standing obligation to effect a single relative physical position for library materials on bookshelves. Between now and then, classification editors may want to consider increasing the faceted nature of their classifications. Perhaps they will introduce new facets and dimensions such as objects, application, and audience and experiment with automatic approaches to assigning others. Full faceting would finally free today's traditional classification schemes from the discipline facet that has long been their underlying organizational principle. During search, users could change the ordering of facets or dimensions and effect an entirely different classification of the collection at hand or the retrievals in hand, perhaps a classification that is more in keeping with their own point of view, knowledge, or understanding of their field.

Traditional classification schemes are the most likely source of chain-indexing terms that would describe documents in simple, sound-bite-sized phrases for the purpose of staging access. Classification editors could get started on the production of chain indexes immediately, demonstrate the usefulness of these terms to online cataloging system suppliers, and urge suppliers to add routines to their systems that prompt catalogers to choose from a list of chain-indexing terms based on the class number(s) assigned to the bibliographic record in hand and insert selected terms into it. In a few years, when the physical arrangement of library materials is a moot point, catalogers could add chain-indexing terms to bibliographic records from sources that are not necessarily the same as their library's choice of classification.

Traditional classification schemes could benefit from a modicum of automatic classification and visa versa. Let's take Grokker[238] as an example of a web-discovery tool that uses automatic classification. In response to the searcher's entry of a few keywords, Grokker clusters retrievals, enlists a type of semantic analysis to characterize retrievals in a few words and phrases, and presents them in the form of a three-dimensional topical map. The map's visual devices such as color, shape, position, and size, are exceedingly efficient at conveying relationships between topics such as importance, frequency of occurrence, and currency in a cursory glance.

I can imagine Grokker and a traditional classification working together. When a traditional classification's organization of a subdiscipline is not satisfactory to searchers, they could call on Grokker to effect a different organization, one that is more in keeping with their point of view or immediate objectives. Additionally, traditional classifications may benefit from the visual maps that Grokker produces to display their retrievals to end users.

Because Grokker produces clusters that are a mixture of different topics, facets, and dimensions, it could call on a traditional classification to sort these clusters, then use the sorted results to produce visual maps that are governed by the one or more cluster types that most interest the user. Grokker already utilizes traditional classifications to cluster retrievals–if retrievals can be characterized using a pre-existing classification, then Grokker uses this classification instead of semantic analysis results to cluster retrievals. Switching languages and mappings between multiple controlled vocabularies would lessen Grokker's reliance on semantic analysis to an even greater extent; however, given the rapid proliferation of digital content, the inability of catalogers to manually apply traditional classification schemes to each and every document, and the desire of end users to perform cross-database searching, clustering, automatic classification, and semantic analysis will become increasingly important approaches to knowledge organization in the future.

The time is right for system designers to incorporate information search tactics into their search engines. Because so many users are content with using a search engine's basic functionality, these engines must be equipped with tools that make searching effortless, otherwise, end users will not use such functionality. In the previous section, I suggested experimenting with simple graphic devices to give visual form to how information search tactics could further the ongoing search. Let's enlist graphic designers in the search for the most appropriate graphics or ones that are particularly successful conveying their objective to the searchers. How a search engine executes a particular search tactic depends upon the formal structures and logical relations that are present in individual database records and shared across one or more databases. For example, the SUPER tactic described in section 7.4 could be accomplished by using class numbers from a traditional classification scheme for the retrievals in one database or by using broader terms from a controlled vocabulary for the retrievals in another database. In databases in which these formal mechanisms are absent, the SUPER tactic could be effected by the system's execution of a follow-up search in which one or more concepts in the user's original query has been eliminated.

8. CONCLUSION

Enhancing subject access in online public access catalogs (OPACs) was the rationale for incorporating classification online in this new form of the library catalog. The Council for Library Resources (CLR) provided funding that enabled this paper's author to lead a research team in the development and evaluation of an experimental online system that was enhanced with the Dewey Decimal Classification (DDC) as an online user's tool for subject access, browsing, and display. Positive findings spurred the Library of Congress to define the new *USMARC Format for Classification Data.* The publishers of universal classification systems responded with web-based systems to assist catalogers in class number assignment. OCLC has been especially proactive in terms of making improvements to the DDC to streamline the classification process. In fact, OCLC's Connexion Service now provides catalogers with an automatic classification button that they can push to retrieve a ranked list of candidate DDC classes.

Despite the efforts of a long list of individual researchers to demonstrate the usefulness of classification as an online user's tool, no system developer ever stepped forward to develop full functionality for classification online in a turnkey integrated library system. To this day, the only way in which most online catalog users experience classification online is through their OPAC's shelflist browsing capability. The author speculates on the reasons why classification online never caught on as an *end user's* tool in OPACs.

When the World-Wide Web began to grow at an unprecedented rate in the mid 1990s, the story of classification online as a user's tool picks up again. Amongst the earliest attempts to organize web resources were Yahoo!, Argus Clearinghouse, and the Whole Internet Catalog (WIC), and their creators developed their own hierarchical approaches to organizing web resources instead of enlisting an existing universal classification scheme. OCLC recognized an opportunity, introduced improvements to the DDC for organizing web resources, encouraged librarians to assign metadata to cataloging records, and add them to its NetFirst database. Today, web directories that use DDC to organize web resources far outnumber the other universal classification schemes. OCLC is now partnering with other research teams to experiment with automatic classification and experiment with classification as a switching language.

Today's challenge is the Google Mass Digitization Initiative. When the next decade begins, people will be able to access a considerable proportion of the world's knowledge through Google and other search engines. The rationale for classification online–enhancing subject access–will be a *moot point* because mass digitization will enable users to search the world's great library collections from cover to cover. Library administrators will question the need for traditional subject analysis–assigning subject headings and classification numbers–because Google will supply their systems with the full digitized texts of books which their library users will search through Google or some other search engine.

Recognizing the need to go in an entirely new direction, this paper's author gives three recommendations for classification online. These recommendations will enable classification online to parallel the development of mass digitization and enrich future search engines in ways that complement Google's full-text searching. The time is right to: (1) revisit the idea of chain indexes for consolidating a book's contents in the form of brief, sound-bite sized phrases that would serve as the first document representations that users would see prior to lengthier representations such as book jacket blurbs, tables of contents, introductions, and prefaces; (2) build new dimensions in a classification that would partition digital knowledge space so that end users retrieve the *best* digital information for the topics that interest them, information that is trustworthy, authoritative, precise, and in keeping with their level of expertise and knowledge of a discipline; and (3) build information search tactics into web search engines that execute automatically to find additional relevant material based on the end user's assessment of the retrieved documents. The review concludes with the next steps that classification editors and system designers should take to ensure the viability of classification online in the era of mass digitization.

9. POSTSCRIPT

Every ten years, I find that I am asked to review the literature of subject access. In 1984, I reviewed *Subject Searching in Library Catalogs* in my book bearing this title. In 1995, I reviewed "Online Catalog User Needs and Behavior" for the Reference and Adult Services Division's *Think Tank on the Present and Future of the Online Catalog*.[239] Now, in 2005, I find myself reviewing "Classification Online" for this special volume.

When Google announced the mass digitization of the University of Michigan's library collection, the slogan "This changes everything!" from a recent television advertising campaign came to mind because it aptly describes the impact that mass digitization will have on the information industry, libraries, library education, the people who write scholarly publications, and the people who read them. The impact will be deep and systemic, far more profound than the major technological advances that have preceded it such as the MARC format, shared online cataloging systems, and OPACs.

If history is any indication, in 2015, I will be asked to write another review. For me personally, it will likely be the final chapter in my professional career. Between now and then, the information industry and the library and information science community must *think deeply* about the impact that mass digitization will have on classification online, subject and descriptive cataloging, and technical services generally, and on just about everything else libraries do, and *act immediately and swiftly* on new developments that parallel and complement mass digitization initiatives. We must sow the seeds *now* for a *future unlimited*.

REFERENCES

1. Larry Besant, "Early Survey Findings: Users of Public Access Catalogs want Sophisticated Subject Access," *American Libraries* 13, no. 3 (1982): 160.

2. Nationwide Study Findings are published in a number of publications including Rosemary Anderson et al., *Library of Congress Online Public Access Catalog Users Survey*. ED 231384 (Washington, D.C.: Office of Planning and Development, Library

of Congress, 1982); Douglas Ferguson et al., "The CLR Public Online Catalog Study: An Overview," *Information Technology & Libraries* 1, no. 1 (1982): 84-97; Ray R. Larson, *Users Look at Online Catalogs; Part 2: Interacting with Online Catalogs; Final Report to the Council on Library Resources.* ED 231401 (Berkeley, Calif.: Office of the Assistant Vice President, Library Plans and Policies, University of California, 1983); Gary S. Lawrence, *Users Look at Online Catalogs: Results of a National Survey of Users and Non-Users of Online Public Access Catalogs.* ED 231395 (Berkeley, Calif.: Division of Library Automation and Library Research and Analysis Group, University of California, 1982); Karen Markey, *Online Catalog Use: Results of Surveys and Focus Group Interviews in Several Libraries.* OCLC/OPR/RR-83/3 (Dublin, Ohio: OCLC Online Computer Library Center, 1983); and Joseph Matthews et al., *Using Online Catalogs: A Nationwide Survey* (New York: Neal-Schuman, 1983).

3. Keith W. Russell, editor, *Subject Access: Report of a Meeting Sponsored by the Council on Library Resources* (Washington, D.C.: Council on Library Resources, December 1982), p. 1.

4. Pauline Cochrane, "Classification as an Online Subject Access Tool" in *Subject Access: Report of a Meeting Sponsored by the Council on Library Resources* edited by Keith W. Russell (Washington, D.C.: Council on Library Resources, December 1982): 35-39.

5. Russell, *Subject Access,* p. 1.

6. Pauline A. Cochrane, "A Paradigm Shift in Library Science," *Information Technology & Libraries* 2, no. 1 (1983): 3-4.

7. Charles R. Hildreth, *Library Automation in North America* (Munich: K. G. Saur, 1987), pp. 14-19.

8. Russell, *Subject Access,* p. 18.

9. Several publications report on the AUDACIOUS Project: Robert R. Freeman, *Evaluation of the Retrieval of Metallurgical Document References Using the Universal Decimal Classification in a Computer-Based System.* Report no. AIP/UDC-6 under National Science Foundation Grant GN-433 (New York: American Institute of Physics, 1 April 1968); Robert R. Freeman and Pauline Atherton, *AUDACIOUS–An Experiment with an Online, Interactive Reference Retrieval System Using the Universal Decimal Classification as the Index Language in the Field of Nuclear Science,* Report no. AIP/UDC-7 (New York: American Institute of Physics, 25 April 1968); Robert R. Freeman and Pauline Atherton, "AUDACIOUS–An Experiment with an Online, Interactive Reference Retrieval System Using the Universal Decimal Classification as the Index Language in the Field of Nuclear Science," *ASIS Proceedings* (April 1968): 193-199; Robert R. Freeman and Pauline Atherton, "File Organization and Search Strategy Using DDC in Mechanized Reference Retrieval Systems," *Mechanized Information Storage, Retrieval, and Dissemination Proceedings of the FID/IFIP Joint Conferences* (Amsterdam: North-Holland, 1968): 122-152; and Robert R. Freeman and Pauline Atherton, *Final Report of the Research Project for the Evaluation of the UDC as the Indexing Language for a Mechanized Reference Retrieval System,* Report no. AIP/UDC-9 (New York: American Institute of Physics, 1 May 1968).

10. Freeman & Atherton, "AUDACIOUS–An Experiment," p. 26.

11. Malcolm Rigby, *Computers and the UDC: A Decade of Progress 1963-1973.* FID Publication 523 (The Hague: International Federation for Documentation, 1974); Malcolm Rigby, *Automation and the UDC, 1948-1980.* FID Publication 565. 2nd ed. (The Hague: International Federation of Documentation, 1981); and S. P. Dufton and

R. Talbot, "The Computerised production of Dewey Subject Indexes for the Libraries of HERTIS," *Program* 14, no. 1: 24-35.

12. Pauline A. Atherton, *Books are for Use: Final Report of the Subject Access Project to the Council on Library Resources.* ED 156131 (Syracuse, N.Y.: Syracuse University, School of Information Studies, 1978), pp. 84-89; Irene Wormell, "Subject Access Project: The Use of Book Indexes for Subject Retrieval System in Libraries," *International Forum on Information and Documentation* 6, no. 4 (1981): 24-28; Alex Byrne, "Life Wasn't Meant to be Whimsical: Painless Subject Augmentation," *Australasian College Libraries* 4, no. 2 (June 1986): 83-90; and Alex Byrne and Mary Micco, "Improving OPAC Subject Access: The ADFA Experiment," *College & Research Libraries* 49, no. 5 (September 1988): 432-441.

13. Joseph Janes, "Books are for Use," *American Libraries* 34, no. 1, (January 2004): 92.

14. Markey, *Online Catalog Use;* Karen Markey, "Thus Spake the OPAC User," *Information Technology and Libraries* 2, no. 4 (1983): 381-387; and Karen Markey, *Subject Searching in Library Catalogs: Before and After the Introduction of Online Catalogs.* OCLC Library, Information, and Computer Science Series 5 (Dublin, Ohio: OCLC Online Computer Library Center, 1984).

15. Melvil Dewey, *Dewey Decimal Classification and Relative Index* edited by Benjamin Custer. 19th ed. (Albany, N.Y.: Forest Press, 1979), vol. 1, p. xii.

16. Karen Markey and Anh N. Demeyer, *Dewey Decimal Classification Online Project: Evaluation of a Library Schedule and Index Integrated into the Subject Searching Capabilities of an Online Catalog.* OCLC/OPR/RR-86/1 (Dublin, Ohio: OCLC Online Computer Library Center, 1986), p. 3.

17. Markey and Demeyer, *Dewey Decimal Classification Online Project,* pp. 27-52.

18. Markey and Demeyer, *Dewey Decimal Classification Online Project,* p. 3.

19. Markey and Demeyer, *Dewey Decimal Classification Online Project,* pp. 27-28.

20. Markey and Demeyer, *Dewey Decimal Classification Online Project,* pp. 54-62.

21. Markey and Demeyer, *Dewey Decimal Classification Online Project,* pp. 63-78; Karen Markey, "The Dewey Decimal Classification as a Library User's Tool in an Online Catalog," *Proceedings of the 47th ASIS Annual Meeting* 21 (White Plains, N.Y.: Knowledge Industry Publications, Inc., October 1984), pp. 121-125; Karen Markey and Anh N. Demeyer, "Dewey Decimal Classification Online Project: Integration of a Library Schedule and Index into the Subject Searching Capabilities on an Online Catalogue," *International Cataloguing* 14, no. 3 (1985): 31-34; and Karen Markey and Anh N. Demeyer, "Searching the Dewey Decimal Classification in an Online Catalog," *Proceedings of the 48th ASIS Annual Meeting* edited by Carol A. Parkhurst, 22 (White Plains, N.Y.: Knowledge Industry Publications, Inc., October 1985), pp. 262-265.

22. Markey and Demeyer, *Dewey Decimal Classification Online Project,* pp. 22-25; Janet Swan Hill, "Online Classification Number Access: Some Practical Considerations," *Journal of Academic Librarianship* 10, no. 1 (1984): 17-22; Elaine Svenonius, "Use of Classification in Online Retrieval," *Library Resources & Technical Services* 27, no. 1 (January/March 1983): 76-80; and Pauline Cochrane, "Classification as a User's Tool in Online Public Access Catalogs" in *Universal Classification, Proceedings of the Fourth International Study Conference on Classification Research,* (Frankfurt: Indeks Verlag, 1982): 382-390.

23. Markey and Demeyer, *Dewey Decimal Classification Online Project*, p. XLIII.

24. Markey and Demeyer, *Dewey Decimal Classification Online Project*, p. 327.

25. Markey and Demeyer, *Dewey Decimal Classification Online Project*, p. 146.

26. Markey and Demeyer, *Dewey Decimal Classification Online Project*, pp. 303-316; and Karen Markey and Karen Calhoun, "Unique Words Contributed by MARC Records with Summary and/or Contents Notes," *Proceedings of the 50th ASIS Annual Meeting* edited by Ching-chih Chen, 24 (Medford, N.J.: Learned Information, Inc., October 1987), pp. 153-162.

27. Markey and Demeyer, *Dewey Decimal Classification Online Project*, pp. 375-378.

28. Karen Markey and Anh N. Demeyer, "Findings of the Dewey Decimal Classification On-line Project," *International Cataloguing* 15, no. 2 (1986): 15-19; Karen Markey and Anh N. Demeyer, "Library Classification as a Subject Searcher's Tool in an Online Catalog" in *Information, Communication, and Technology Transfer* edited by E. V. Smith and S. Keenan (Amsterdam: North-Holland, 1987), pp. 477-483; and Karen Markey, "Subject Searching Strategies for Online Catalogues Through the Dewey Decimal Classification" in *The Online Catalogue* edited by Charles R. Hildreth (London: Library Association, 1989), pp. 61-83.

29. Markey and Demeyer, *Dewey Decimal Classification Online Project*, pp. 231-260; and Karen Markey, "Alphabetic Searching in an Online Catalog," *Journal of Academic Librarianship* 14, no. 6 (1989): 353-360.

30. Markey and Demeyer, *Dewey Decimal Classification Online Project*, 202-230; Karen Markey, "Searching and Browsing the Library Classification Schedules in an Online Catalogue," in *Online Public Access to Library Files: Second National Conference* edited by Janet Kinsella (Oxford: Elsevier, 1986): 49-66; and Karen Markey, "Searching and Browsing the Dewey Decimal Classification in an Online Catalog," *Cataloging & Classification Quarterly* 7, no. 3 (spring 1987): 37-67.

31. Markey and Demeyer, *Dewey Decimal Classification Online Project*, pp. 190-201; and Karen Markey, "Keyword Searching in an Online Catalog Enhanced with a Library Classification" in *Classification of Library Materials* edited by Betty G. Bengtson and Janet Swan Hill (New York: Neal-Schuman Publishers, Inc., 1990), pp. 99-125.

32. Markey and Demeyer, *Dewey Decimal Classification Online Project*, pp. 261-268; and Karen Markey, "Class Number Searching in an Experimental Online Catalog," *International Classification* 13, no. 3 (1986): 142-150.

33. Karen Markey Drabenstott, "Experiences with Online Catalogs in the USA Using a Classification System as a Subject Searching Tool," *Advances in Knowledge Organization, Tools for Knowledge Organization and the Human Interface, Proceedings of the 1st International ISKO Conference* edited by Robert Fugmann, 1 (Frankfurt: Indeks Verlag, 1990): 35-46.

34. Carol A. Mandel, *Classification Schedules as Subject Enhancement in Online Catalogs* (Washington, D.C.: Council on Library Resources, October 1986), p. 1.

35. Mark S. Fox and Andrew J. Palay, "Machine-assisted Browsing for the Naïve User" in *Public Access to Library Automation: Clinic on Library Applications of Data Processing* edited by J. L. Divilbiss (Urbana, Ill.: Graduate School of Library and Information Science, University of Illinois at Urbana-Champaign, 1981), 77-97.

36. V. J. Geller and M. E. Lesk, *How Users Search: A Comparison of Menu and Attribute Retrieval Systems on a Library Catalog* (Murray Hill, N.J.: Bell Laboratories, September 27, 1981).

37. Karen Markey and Anh N. Demeyer, "The Concept of Common Subject Headings in Subject Online Searching," *Classification Theory in the Computer Age: Conversations Across the Disciplines, Proceedings from the Conference* (Albany, N.Y.: Rockefeller College Press, 1989), pp. 46-57.

38. Mandel, "Classification Schedules," pp. 19-20.

39. Nancy J. Williamson, "The Library of Congress Classification: Problems and Prospects in Online Retrieval," *International Cataloguing* (October/December 1986): 45-48.

40. Hill, "Online Classification Number Access," p. 21; and Pauline A. Cochrane and Karen Markey, "Preparing for the Use of Classification in Online Cataloging Systems and in Online Catalogs," *Information Technology and Libraries* 4, no. 2 (1985): 100-108.

41. Mary Micco, "Suggestions for Automating the Library of Congress Classification Schedules," *Classification Research for Knowledge Representation and Organization, Proceedings of the 5th International Study Conference on Classification Research* edited by Nancy J. Williamson and Michele Hudon (Amsterdam, Elsevier: 1992), pp. 285-294.

42. Nancy J. Williamson, "The Library of Congress Classification and the Computer: Research in Progress," *International Cataloguing and Bibliographic Control 18* (January/March 1989), 8-12; Nancy Williamson, "The Library of Congress Classification in the Computer Age" in *Classification Theory in the Computer Age: Conversations Across the Disciplines, Proceedings from the Conference* (Albany: Rockefeller College Press, 1989), pp. 58-64; and Nancy J. Williamson, "The Library of Congress Classification: Preparation for an Online System," *Advances in Knowledge Organization* 2 (1991): 210-218.

43. Rebecca S. Guenther, "The Development and Implementation of the USMARC Format for Classification Data," *Information Technology and Libraries* 11, no. 2 (1992): 120-131; Rebecca S. Guenther, "The USMARC Classification Format Experiment," *ALCTS Newsletter* 3, no. 3 (1992): 25-27; Rebecca S. Guenther, "The USMARC Format for Classification Data: Development and Implementation," *Classification Research for Knowledge Representation and Organization, Proceedings of the 5th International Study Conference on Classification Research* edited by Nancy J. Williamson and Michele Hudon (Amsterdam: Elsevier, 1992), pp. 235-245; Rebecca S. Guenther, "The Library of Congress Classification in the USMARC Format," *Knowledge Organization* 21, no. 4 (1994): 199-202; Rebecca S. Guenther, "Bringing the Library of Congress Classification into the Computer Age: Converting LCC to Machine-Readable Form," *Advances in Knowledge Organization, Knowledge Organization and Change, Proceedings of the 4th International ISKO Conference* edited by Rebecca Green, 5 (Frankfurt: Indeks Verlag, 1996), pp. 26-32; and Jolande E. Goldberg, "Library of Congress Classification: Does Organization of Knowledge Need a Shelf?" *Advances in Classification Research, Proceedings of the 7th ASIS SIG/CR Classification Research Workshop* edited by Paul Solomon, 7 (Washington, D.C.: Information Today, October 1996), pp. 55-68.

44. Library of Congress, Network Development and MARC Standards Office. *USMARC Format for Classification Data: Including Guidelines for Content Designation* (Washington, DC: Cataloging Distribution Service, 1991).

45. Guenther, "Bringing the Library of Congress Classification," p. 32.

46. Robert R. Freeman, "The Management of a Classification: Modern Approaches Exemplified by the UDC Project of the American Institute of Physics," *Journal of Doc-

umentation 23, no. 4 (December 1967): 312-314; Freeman and Atherton, *Final Report of the Research Project for the Evaluation of the UDC*, p. 4.

47. John J. Finni and Peter J. Paulson, "The Dewey Decimal Classification Enters the Computer Age: Developing the DDC Database and Editorial Support System," *International Cataloguing* 16, no. 4 (October/December 1987): 46-48.

48. Julianne Beall, "Editing the Dewey Decimal Classification Online: The Evolution of the DDC Database," *Classification Research for Knowledge Representation and Organization, Proceedings of the 5th International Study Conference on Classification Research* edited by Nancy J. Williamson and Michele Hudon (Amsterdam: Elsevier, 1992), pp. 36-37.

49. Joan S. Mitchell, Personal Communication with the Author. (15 February 2005).

50. Ia C. McIlwaine, "Preparing Traditional Classifications for the Future: Universal Decimal Classification," *Cataloging & Classification Quarterly* 21, no. 2 (1995): 49-58.

51. Markey and Demeyer, *Dewey Decimal Classification Online Project*, p. 323.

52. Arnold S. Wajenberg, "MARC Coding of DDC for Subject Retrieval," *Information Technology and Libraries* 2, no. 3 (September 1983): 250.

53. Songqiao Liu, "Decomposing DDC Synthesized Numbers," *62nd IFLA General Conference Proceedings* (August 1996). http://www.ifla.org/IV/ifla62/62-sonl.htm.

54. Songqiao Liu, "Online Classification Notation: Proposal for a Flexible Faceted Notation System (FFNS)," *International Classification* 17, no. 1 (1990): 14-20.

55. Liu, "Online Classification Notation," p. 20.

56. Clement Jewitt, "A Subject Indexing Engine," *8th International Online Information Meeting* (Oxford, N.J.: Learned Information, Inc., December 1984), pp. 154-160.

57. Jewitt, "A Subject Indexing Engine," p. 154.

58. Finni and Paulson, "The Dewey Decimal Classification Enters the Computer Age," p. 47.

59. OCLC acquired Forest Press and the Dewey Decimal Classification on July 28, 1988 so future DDC research and development rested in OCLC's hands.

60. Diane Vizine-Goetz, "The Dewey Decimal Classification as an Online Classification Tool," in *Classification Research for Knowledge Representation and Organization, Proceedings of the 5th International Study Conference on Classification Research* edited by Nancy J. Williamson and Michele Hudon (Amsterdam: Elsevier, 1992), p. 376.

61. Markey and Demeyer, "The Concept of Common Subject Headings in Subject Online Searching," pp. 51-56.

62. Vizine-Goetz, "The Dewey Decimal Classification as an Online Classification Tool," p. 379.

63. Joan S. Mitchell, "DDC 21 and Beyond: The Dewey Decimal Classification Prepares for the Future," *Cataloging & Classification Quarterly* 21, no. 2 (1995): 37-47.

64. Julianne Beall, "Dewey for Windows," in *Advances in Knowledge Organization, Knowledge Organization and Change, Proceedings of the 4th International ISKO Conference* edited by Rebecca Green (Frankfurt: Indeks Verlag, 1996), p. 404.

65. OCLC, "Using WebDewey: An OCLC Tutorial." (2004). http://www.oclc.org/dewey/resources/tutorial/.

66. OCLC, "Speed Your Classification Efforts." (2004). http://www.oclc.org/dewey/support/program/.

67. Diane Vizine-Goetz and Jean Godby, "Library Classification Schemes and Access to Electronic Collections: Enhancement of the Dewey Decimal Classification with Supplemental Vocabulary," *Advances in Classification Research, Proceedings of the 7th ASIS SIG/CR Classification Research Workshop*, edited by Paul Solomon, 7 (Washington, D.C.: Information Today, Inc., 1996), pp. 127-135.

68. Joan S. Mitchell and Diane Vizine-Goetz, "A Research Agenda for Classification," (2002). http://digitalarchive.oclc.org/da/ViewObject.jsp?objid=0000003953.

69. Diane Vizine-Goetz, "Subject Headings for Everyone: Popular Library of Congress Subject Headings with Dewey Numbers," *OCLC Newsletter* no. 233, (1998).

70. Diane Vizine-Goetz, "Making Knowledge Organization Schemes More Accessible to People and Computers." (2004): http://www.oclc.org/news/publications/newsletters/oclc/2004/266/research.html.

71. Lois Mai Chan and Theodora L. Hodges, "The Library of Congress Classification," in *The Future of Classification* edited by Rita Marcella and Arthur Maltby (Brookfield, Vt.: Gower, 2000): 105-127.

72. Lois Mai Chan, "Library of Congress Classification in a New Setting." (2004). http://www.loc.gov/cds/chanarticle.html.

73. Karen Selden, "What is Classification Web?" *Technical Services Law Librarian* 26, 3/4 (March/June 2001). http://www.aallnet.org/sis/tssis/tsll/26-0304/26-0304.htm.

74. Karen Markey Drabenstott, Leslie C. Riester, and Bonnie A. Dede, "Shelflisting Using Expert Systems," *Classification Research for Knowledge Representation and Organization, Proceedings of the 5th International Study Conference on Classification Research* edited by Nancy J. Williamson and Michele Hudon (Amsterdam: Elsevier, 1992), pp. 200-206.

75. Robert R. Freeman, "Computers and Classification Systems," *Journal of Documentation* 20, no. 3 (September 1964): 137-145.

76. Freeman and Atherton, *AUDACIOUS–An Experiment*, pp. 6-7.

77. UDC Consortium, "About UDC Online." (2002). http://www.udc-online.com/about.html.

78. Markey and Demeyer, *Dewey Decimal Classification Online Project*, pp. 327-363.

79. Neal K. Kaske and Nancy P. Sanders, "Online Subject Access: The Human Side of the Problem, *RQ* 20, no. 1 (1980): 56.

80. Patricia Willard and Viva Teece, "The Browser and the Library," *Public Library Quarterly* 4, no. 1 (spring 1983): 60-62.

81. Willard and Teece, "The Browser and the Library," p. 60.

82. Karen Markey, *The Process of Subject Searching in the Library Catalog: Final Report of the Subject Access Research Project*, OCLC/OPR/RR-83/1 (Dublin, Ohio: OCLC Online Computer Library Center, 1983), pp. 35, 38, 41.

83. Micheline Hancock, "Subject Search Behaviour at the Library Catalogue and at the Shelves: Implications for Online Interactive Catalogues," *Journal of Documentation* 43 (December 1987): 308.

84. Svenonius, "Use of Classification in Online Retrieval," p. 80.

85. Karen Markey, "Subject-Searching Experiences and Needs of Online Catalog Users: Implications for Library Classification," *Library Resources & Technical Services* 29, no. 1 (January/March 1985): 34-42.

86. Lois Mai Chan, "Library of Congress Classification as an Online Retrieval Tool: Potentials and Limitations," *Information Technology and Libraries* (September 1986): 181-192; Lois Mai Chan, "Library of Congress Class Numbers in Online Catalog Searching," *Reference Quarterly* (Summer 1989): 530-536; Lois Mai Chan, "The Library of Congress Classification System in an Online Environment," *Cataloging & Classification Quarterly* 11, no. 1 (1990): 7-25.

87. Chan, "Library of Congress Classification as an Online Retrieval Tool," p. 191.

88. Charles R. Hildreth, *Intelligent Interfaces and Retrieval Methods for Subject Searching in Bibliographic Retrieval Systems*, Advances in Library Information Technology 2 (Washington, D.C.: Cataloging Distribution Service, 1989), pp. 83-98.

89. Charles R. Hildreth, "Extending the Online Catalog: The Point of Diminishing Returns," in *Emerging Communities: Integrating Networked Information into Library Services* edited by Ann P. Bishop (Urbana-Champaign, Ill.: University of Illinois at Urbana-Champaign, 1993), p. 97.

90. Nancy J. Williamson, "The Role of Classification in Online Systems," *Cataloging & Classification Quarterly* 10, no. 1/2 (1989): 99.

91. Pauline A. Cochrane, *Improving LCSH for Use in Online Catalogs: Exercises for Self-help with a Selection of Background Readings* (Littleton, Colo.: Libraries Unlimited 1986), pp. 69-81; and Rao Aluri, D. Alasdair Kemp & John J. Boll, *Subject Analysis in Online Catalogs* (Englewood, Colo.: Libraries Unlimited, 1991), pp. 157-209.

92. Annette Weber and Rudolf Noethiger, "ETHICS: ETH Library Information Control System," *ABI-Technik* 8, no. 4 (1988): 385-388.

93. Klaus Loth and Herbert Funk, "Subject Search in ETHICS on the Basis of the UDC" in *The UDC: Essays for a New Decade* edited by Alan Gilchrist and David Strachan (London: Aslib, 1990): 43-44; Hannes Hug and Meta Walser, "Retrieval in the ETH Database Using the UDC," *Advances in Knowledge Organization, Dynamism and Stability in Knowledge Organization, Proceedings of the 1st International ISKO Conference* edited by Clare Beghtol, Lynne C. Howarth, and Nancy J. Williamson, 1 (Würzburg, Germany: Ergon Verlag, 1990): 218; Weber and Noethinger, "ETHICS," p. 386.

94. Weber and Noethinger, "ETHICS," p. 387.

95. Jeffrey C. Huestis, "Clustering LC Classification Numbers in an Online Catalog for Improved Browsability," *Information Technology and Libraries* 7, no. 4 (December 1988): 383.

96. Huestis, "Clustering LC Classification Numbers," pp. 386-391.

97. Ray R. Larson, "Managing Information Overload in Online Catalog Subject Searching," *Proceedings of the 52nd ASIS Annual Meeting* edited by Jeffrey Katzer and Gregory B. Newby, 26 (Medford, N.J.: Learned Information, Inc., October/November 1989), pp. 129-135; Ray R. Larson, "Between Scylla and Charybdis: Subject Searching in the Online Catalog," in *Advances in Librarianship* edited by Irene P. Godden, 15 (San Diego: Academic Press, Inc., 1991), pp. 175-236; Ray R. Larson, "Classification Clustering, Probabilistic Information Retrieval and the Online Catalog," *Library Quarterly* 61 (1991): 133-173; Ray R. Larson, "Evaluation of Advanced Retrieval Techniques in an Experimental Online Catalog," *Journal of the American Society for Information Science* 43, no. 1 (1992): 34-53.

98. Larson, "Evaluation of Advanced Retrieval Techniques," p. 47.

99. Larson, "Between Scylla and Charybdis," p. 227.

100. Shabahat Husain and Ann O'Brien, "Recent Trends in Subject Access to OPACs: An Evaluation," *International Classification* 19, no. 3 (1992): 140.

101. Mary Micco, "Report on Linking Subject Headings to LC Classification Numbers and Suggestions for Automating the Classification Schedules for the Explicit Purpose of Improving Subject Access in Online Public Access Catalogs," *Advances in Classification Research, Proceedings of the 1st ASIS SIG/CR Classification Research Workshop*, (November 1990), pp. 107-118; Mary Micco, "The Next Generation of Online Public Access Catalogs: A New Look at Subject Access Using Hypermedia," *Cataloging & Classification Quarterly* 13, no. 3/4 (1991): 103-132; Mary Micco and Xiangyu Ju, "Improving Intellectual Access to Material: An Online Browser for the Dewey Decimal Classification System," *Advances in Classification Research, Proceedings of the 3rd ASIS SIG/CR Classification Research Workshop* edited by Raya Fidel, Barbara H. Kwasnik, and Philip J. Smith, 3 (Medford, N.J.: Learned Information, Inc., 1992), pp. 115-127.

102. Songqiao Liu and Elaine Svenonius, "DORS: DDC Online Retrieval System," *Library Resources & Technical Services* 35, no. 4 (1991): 359.

103. Liu & Svenonius, "DORS," p. 361.

104. Liu & Svenonius, "DORS," p. 366.

105. Elaine Svenonius, Songqiao Liu, and Bhagi Subrahmanyam, "Automation of Chain Indexing," *Classification Research for Knowledge Representation and Organization, Proceedings of the 5th International Study Conference on Classification Research* edited by Nancy J. Williamson and Michele Hudon (Amsterdam, Elsevier, 1992), pp. 351-365.

106. Elaine Broadbent, "Classification Access in the Online Catalog," *Cataloging & Classification Quarterly* 21, no. 2 (1995): 119-141.

107. Broadbent, "Classification Access in the Online Catalog," p. 127.

108. Stephen Walker and Rachel De Vere, *Improving Subject Retrieval in Online Catalogues; 2. Relevance Feedback and Query Expansion*, British Library Research Paper 72 (London: The British Library Research and Development Department, 1990), p. 19.

109. Walker and De Vere, *Improving Subject Retrieval in Online Catalogues*, p. 37.

110. Walker and De Vere, *Improving Subject Retrieval in Online Catalogues*, p. 65.

111. Walker and De Vere, *Improving Subject Retrieval in Online Catalogues*, p. 79.

112. Charles R. Hildreth, "End Users and Structured Searching of Online Catalogues: Recent Research Findings," *Advances in Knowledge Organization, Tools for Knowledge Organization and the Human Interface, Proceedings of the 1st International ISKO Conference* edited by Robert Fugmann, 2 (Frankfurt: Indeks Verlag, 1991), pp. 9-24.

113. Hildreth, "End Users and Structured Searching of Online Catalogues," p. 18.

114. Christine L. Borgman et al., "Children's Use of an Interactive Catalog of Science Materials," *Proceedings of the 53rd ASIS Annual Meeting* edited by Diane Henderson, 27 (Medford, N.J.: Learned Information, Inc., 1990), p. 56.

115. Christine L. Borgman, Mark H. Chignell, and Felix Valdez, "Designing an Information Retrieval Interface Based on Children's Categorization of Knowledge: A Pilot Study," *Proceedings of the 52nd ASIS Annual Meeting* edited by Jeffrey Katzer and Gregory B. Newby, 26 (Medford, N.J.: Learned Information, Inc., October/November 1989), pp. 81-95.

116. Christine L. Borgman et al., "From Hands-On Science to Hands-On Information Retrieval," *Proceedings of the 52nd ASIS Annual Meeting* edited by Jeffrey Katzer and Gregory B. Newby, 26 (Medford, N.J.: October/November 1989), p. 99.

117. Borgman et al., "Children's Use of an Interactive Catalog of Science Materials," pp. 56, 61.

118. Borgman et al., "Children's Use of an Interactive Catalog of Science Materials," p. 59.

119. Christine L. Borgman, Virginia A. Walter, and Jason Rosenberg, "The Science Library Catalog Project: Comparison of Children's Searching Behavior in Hypertext and a Keyword Search System," *Proceedings of the 54th ASIS Annual Meeting* edited by José-Marie Griffiths, 28 (Medford, N.J.: Learned Information, Inc., October 1991), p. 169.

120. Annelise M. Pejtersen, "Design of Classification Scheme for Fiction based on an Analysis of Actual User-librarian Communication, and Use of the Scheme for Control of Librarians' Search Strategies," in *Theory and Application of Information Research* edited by O. Harbo and L. Kajberg (London: Mansell, 1980), pp. 167-183; Annelise Mark Pejtersen and Jutta Austin, "Fiction Retrieval: Experimental Design and Evaluation of a Search System Based on Users' Value Criteria (Part 2)," *Journal of Documentation* 40, no. 1 (March 1984): 230-246.

121. Annelise Mark Pejtersen, Hanne Albrechtsen, Ringa Sandelin, Lena Lundgren, and Riitta Valtonen, "The Scandinavian Book House: Indexing Methods and OPAC Development for Subject Access to Scandinavian Fiction Literature," *Advances in Classification Research, Proceedings of the 6th ASIS SIG/CR Classification Research Workshop* 6 (1995), p. 103.

122. Annelise Mark Pejtersen, "Icons for Representation of Domain Knowledge in Interfaces," *Advances in Knowledge Organization, Tools for Knowledge Organization and the Human Interface* edited by Robert Fugmann, 2 (Frankfurt: Indeks Verlag, 1991), pp. 175-193.

123. Annelise Mark Pejtersen, "A New Approach to Design of Document Retrieval and Indexing Systems for OPAC Users," *Online Information, 17th International Online Information Meeting Proceedings* edited by David I. Raitt and Ben Jeapes (Oxford: Learned Information, Inc., December 1993), p. 286.

124. Annelise Mark Pejtersen, "A Framework for Indexing and Representation of Information Based on Work Domain Analysis: A Fiction Classification Example," *Advances in Knowledge Organization, Knowledge Organization and Quality Management, Proceedings of the Third International ISKO Conference* edited by Hanne Albrechtsen, 4 (Frankfurt: Indeks Verlag, 1994), p. 251.

125. Hanne Albrechtsen and Elin K. Jacob, "The Dynamics of Classification Systems as Boundary Objects for Cooperation in the Electronic Library," *Library Trends* 47, no. 2 (Fall 1998): 293.

126. Marcia J. Bates, "Where Should the Person Stop and the Information Search Interface Start?" *Information Processing & Management* 26, no. 5 (1990): 575-591.

127. Christopher S. G. Khoo and Danny C. C. Poo, "An Expert System Approach to Online Catalog Subject Searching," *Information Processing & Management* 30, no. 2 (1994): 223-238.

128. Khoo and Poo, "An Expert System Approach to Online Catalog Subject Searching," p. 236.

129. Pauline Atherton Cochrane and Eric H. Johnson, "Visual Dewey: DDC in a Hypertextual Browser for the Library User," *Advances in Knowledge Organization,*

Proceedings of the Fourth International ISKO Conference, Rebecca Green, ed. 5, (Frankfurt: Indeks Verlag, 1996), pp. 95-106.

130. Michael Gorman, "The Longer the Number, the Smaller the Spine," *American Libraries* (September 1981): 498.

131. A. Steven Pollitt, "The Application of Dewey Classification in a Searching OPAC," *Advances in Knowledge Organization, Proceedings of the Fifth International ISKO Conference* edited by Widad Mustafa el Hadi, Jacques Maniez, and Steven A. Pollitt, 6 (Würzburg, Germany: Ergon Verlag, 1998): 181.

132. A. Steven Pollitt and Amanda J. Tinker, "Enhanced View-Based Searching Through the Decomposition of Dewey Decimal Classification Codes," *Advances in Knowledge Organization, Dynamism and Stability in Knowledge Organization, Proceedings of the Sixth International ISKO Conference* edited by Clare Beghtol, Lynne C. Howarth, and Nancy J. Williamson, 7 (July 2000), pp. 288-294.

133. Pollitt, "The Application of Dewey Classification in a Searching OPAC," p. 181.

134. Cochrane and Johnson, "Visual Dewey," p. 95.

135. Micco, "Report on Linking Subject Headings," p. 109.

136. Christine L. Borgman, *End User Behavior on The Ohio State University Libraries' Online Catalog: A Computer Monitoring Study*, OCLC/OPR/RR-83/7 (Dublin, Ohio: OCLC Online Computer Library Center, 1983), p. 17; John E. Tolle, *Current Utilization of Online Catalogs: Transaction Log Analysis*, OCLC/OPR/RR-83/2 (Dublin, Ohio: OCLC Online Computer Library Center, 1983), pp. 55, 71; and Markey, *Subject Searching in Library Catalogs*, p. 77.

137. Willard and Teece, "The Browser and the Library," pp. 60-62; and Hancock, "Subject Search Behaviour at the Library Catalogue and at the Shelves," p. 308.

138. Markey, "Class Number Searching in an Experimental Online Catalog," pp. 147-149.

139. Desretta McAllister-Harper, "Dewey Decimal Classification in the Online Environment: A Study of Libraries in North Carolina," *Cataloging & Classification Quarterly* 11, no. 1 (1990): 49.

140. McAllister-Harper, "Dewey Decimal Classification in the Online Environment," p. 45.

141. Walter High, "Library of Congress Classification Numbers as Subject Access Points in Computer-Based Retrieval," *Cataloging & Classification Quarterly* 11, no. 1 (1990): 39.

142. High, "Library of Congress Classification Numbers as Subject Access Points," p. 42.

143. Snunith Shoham and Moshe Yitzhaki, "Classification Systems and the Online Catalog," *Advances in Knowledge Organization, Proceedings of the Third International ISKO Conference* (Frankfurt: Indeks Verlag, 1994), p. 317.

144. Shoham and Yitzhaki, "Classification Systems and the Online Catalog," p. 316.

145. Shoham and Yitzhaki, "Classification Systems and the Online Catalog," p. 318.

146. Atherton, *Books are for Use*; Wormell, "Subject Access Project," pp. 24-28; Edwin Posey and Charlotte A. Erdman, "An Online Unix-based Engineering Library Catalog: Purdue University Engineering Library," *Science & Technology Libraries* 6 (Summer 1986): 31-43; Alex Byrne, "Life Wasn't Meant to be Whimsical: Painless Subject Augmentation," *Australasian College Libraries* 4, no. 2 (June 1986): 83-90; and Byrne and Micco, "Improving OPAC Subject Access," pp. 83-90.

147. Ia C. McIlwaine and Nancy J. Williamson, "International Trends in Subject Analysis Research," *Knowledge Organization* 26, no. 1 (1999): 25.

148. Ingetraut Dahlberg, "The Future of Classification in Libraries and Networks, a Theoretical Point of View," *Cataloging & Classification Quarterly* 21, no. 2 (1995): 23.

149. Dahlberg, "The Future of Classification in Libraries and Networks," p. 23.

150. Dahlberg, "The Future of Classification in Libraries and Networks," p. 31; Ingetraut Dahlberg, "Library Catalogs in the Internet: Switching for Future Subject Access." *Advances in Knowledge Organization, Proceedings of the Fourth International ISKO Conference* edited by Rebecca Green, 5 (Frankfurt: Indeks Verlag, 1996), pp. 158-160.

151. Elaine Svenonius, "An Ideal Classification for an On-line Catalog" in *Classification Theory in the Computer Age: Conversations Across the Disciplines, Proceedings from the Conference* (Albany, N.Y.: Rockefeller College Press, 1989), pp. 35-43.

152. Subal C. Biswas and Fred Smith, "Classed Thesauri in Indexing and Retrieval: A Literature Review and Critical Evaluation of Online Alphabetic Classaurus," *Library and Information Science Research* 11 (1989), pp. 109-141.

153. Winfried Gödert, "Facet Classification in Online Retrieval," *International Classification* 18, no. 2 (1991): 98-109.

154. Robert P. Holley, "Classification in the USA," *International Classification* 13, no. 2 (1986): 73-78.

155. Clifford A. Lynch and Cecilia M. Preston, "Describing and Classifying Networked Information Resources," *Electronic Networking* 2, no. 2 (spring 1992): 13-23.

156. Diane Vizine-Goetz, "Using Library Classification Schemes for Internet Resources," Proceedings of the OCLC Internet Cataloging Colloquium (19 January 1996). http://staff.oclc.org/%7Evizine/Intercat/vizine-goetz.htm.

157. Diane Vizine-Goetz, "Online Classification: Implications for Classifying and Document [-like Object] Retrieval," *Advances in Knowledge Organization, Knowledge Organization and Change, Proceedings of the Fourth International ISKO Conference* edited by Rebecca Green 5 (Frankfurt: Indeks Verlag, 1996), pp. 249-253.

158. Carol Jean Godby, "Enhancing the Indexing Vocabulary of the Dewey Decimal Classification," in *Annual Review of OCLC Research 1996* (Dublin, Ohio: OCLC Online Computer Library Center, 1996), pp. 30-33; Diane Vizine-Goetz, "Classification Research at OCLC," in *Annual Review of OCLC Research 1996* (Dublin, Ohio: OCLC Online Computer Library Center, 1996), pp. 27-30; Diane Vizine-Goetz, "OCLC Investigates Using Classification Tools to Organize Internet Data," *OCLC Newsletter* no. 226 (1997): 14-18.

159. Diane Vizine-Goetz, "Classification Schemes for Internet Resources Revisited," *Journal of Internet Cataloging* 5, no. 4 (2002): 5-18.

160. Alan Wheatley, "Subject Trees on the Internet: A New Role for Bibliographic Classification," *Journal of Internet Cataloging* 2, no. 3/4 (2000): 115-141.

161. Vizine-Goetz, "Classification Schemes for Internet Resources Revisited," p. 15.

162. Vizine-Goetz, "Classification Schemes for Internet Resources Revisited," p. 11.

163. Amanda J. Tinker et al., "The Dewey Decimal Classification and the Transition from Physical to Electronic Knowledge Organisation," *Knowledge Organization* 26, no. 2 (1999): 88.

164. Tinker et al., "The Dewey Decimal Classification and the Transition," p. 81.

165. Tinker et al., "The Dewey Decimal Classification and the Transition," p. 92.

166. David G. Dodd, "Grass-Roots Cataloging and Classification: Food for Thought from World Wide Web Subject-Oriented Hierarchical Lists," *Library Resources & Technical Services* 40, no. 3 (July 1996): 275-286.

167. Jeannette Woodward, "Cataloging and Classifying Information Resources on the Internet," *Annual Review of Information Science and Technology* edited by Martha E. Williams, 31 (Medford, N.J.: Information Today, Inc., 1996), pp. 189-221.

168. Lois Mai Chan, "Exploiting LCSH, LCC, and DDC to Retrieve Networked Resources: Issues and Challenges." (2000). http://www.loc.gov/catdir/bibcontrol/chan_paper.html.

169. Michèle Hudon, "Innovation and Tradition in Knowledge Organization Schemes on the Internet, or, Finding One's Way in the Virtual Library," *Advances in Knowledge Organization, Dynamism and Stability in Knowledge Organization, Proceedings of the Sixth International ISKO Conference* edited by Clare Beghtol, Lynne C. Howarth, and Nancy J. Williamson, 7 (Würzburg, Germany: Ergon Verlag, 2000), p. 39.

170. Hudon, "Innovation and Tradition in Knowledge Organization Schemes," p. 40.

171. Traugott Koch et al., "Role of Classification Schemes in Internet Resource Description and Discovery." (1997). http://www.lub.lu.se/desire/radar/reports/D3.2.3.

172. Hamid Saeed and Abdus Sattar Chaudry, "Potential of Bibliographic Tools to Organize Knowledge on the Internet: The Use of Dewey Decimal Classification Scheme for Organizing Web-based Information Resources," *Knowledge Organization* 28, no. 1 (2001): 17-26.

173. Chaim Zins, "Models for Classifying Internet Resources," *Knowledge Organization* 29, no.1 (2002): 20-28.

174. Zins, "Models for Classifying Internet Resources," p. 20.

175. Zins, "Models for Classifying Internet Resources," p. 27.

176. Jason B. Rosenberg and Christine L. Borgman, "Extending the Dewey Decimal Classification Via Keyword Clustering: The Science Library Catalog Project," *Proceedings of the 55th ASIS Annual Meeting* edited by Debora Shaw, 29 (Medford, N.J.: Learned Information, Inc., 1992), pp. 171-184.

177. Rosenberg and Borgman, "Extending the Dewey Decimal Classification Via Keyword Clustering," p. 177.

178. Diane Vizine-Goetz and Julianne Beall, "Using Literary Warrant to Define a Version of the DDC for Automated Classification Services," *Advances in Knowledge Organization, Proceedings of the Eighth International ISKO Conference* edited by Ia C. McIlwaine, 9 (Würzburg, Germany: Ergon Verlag, 2004), pp. 13-16.

179. M. E. Maron, "Automatic Indexing: An Experimental Inquiry," *Journal of the ACM* 8 (1961): 404-417; Harold Borko and M. D. Bernick, "Automatic Document Classification," *Journal of the ACM* 10 (1963): 151-163; Harold Borko, "Measuring the Reliability of Subject Classification by Men and Machines," *American Documentation* 15 (1964): 268-273.

180. Robert R. Freeman, "Classification in Computer-Based Information Systems of the 1970s," *Journal of Documentation* 32 (1976): 195-208.

181. P. G. B. Enser, "Automatic Classification of Book Material Represented by Back-of-the-Book Index," *Journal of Documentation* 41, no. 3 (September 1985): 135-155.

182. Enser, "Automatic Classification of Book Material," p. 152.

183. Enser, "Automatic Classification of Book Material," p. 154.

184. Irene Travis, "Applications of Artificial Intelligence to Bibliographic Classification," in *Classification Theory in the Computer Age: Conversations Across the Dis-*

ciplines, Proceedings from the Conference (Albany, N.Y.: Rockefeller College Press, 1989), pp. 46-57.

185. Natasha Vleduts-Stokolov, "Concept Recognition in an Automatic Text-Processing System for the Life Sciences," *Journal of the American Society for Information Science* 38, no. 4 (1987): 269-287.

186. Holly Berry Irving, "Computer-Assisted Indexing Training and Electronic Text Conversion at NAL," *Knowledge Organization* 24, no. 1 (1997): 4-7.

187. Brij Masand, Gordon Linoff, and David Waltz, "Classifying News Stories Using Memory Based Reasoning," *Annual ACM Conference on Research and Development in Information Retrieval, Proceedings of the 15th Annual International ACM SIGIR Conference on Research and Development in Information Retrieval* (New York: ACM, 1992), p. 59.

188. Masand, Linoff, and Waltz, "Classifying News Stories," p. 64.

189. Ray R. Larson, "Experiments in Automatic Library of Congress Classification." *Journal of the American Society for Information Science* 43, no. 2 (1992): 147.

190. Elin K. Jacob, Javed Mostafa, and Luz Marina Quiroga, "An Approach to the Evaluation of Automatically Generated Classification Schemes," *Advances in Classification Research, Proceedings of the 7th ASIS SIG/CR Classification Research Seminar* edited by Paul Solomon, 7 (Washington, D.C.: Information Today, Inc., 1996), pp. 78-96.

191. Jacob, Mostafa, and Quiroga, "An Approach to the Evaluation," p. 79.

192. Tom Curran and Paul Thompson, "Automatic Categorization of Statute Documents," *Advances in Classification Research, Proceedings of the 8th ASIS CIG/CR Classification Research Workshop* edited by Efthimis N. Efthimiadis, 8 (Washington, D.C.: Information Today, Inc., 1997), p. 30.

193. R. Dolin, "Using Automated Classification for Summarizing and Selecting Heterogeneous Information Sources," *D-Lib Magazine* 4, no. 1 (January 1998): 1-12.

194. Eibe Frank and Gordon W. Paynter, "Predicting Library of Congress Classifications From Library of Congress Subject Headings," *Journal of the American Society for Information Science and Technology* 55, no. 3 (2004): 222.

195. Liz Liddy, "Computer Assisted Content Standard Assignment and Alignment." (N.d.) http://www.cnlp.org/research/project.asp?recid=48.

196. Roger Thompson, Keith Shafer, and Diane Vizine-Goetz, "Evaluating Dewey Concepts as a Knowledge Base for Automatic Subject Assignment," *International Conference on Digital Libraries, Proceedings of the Second ACM International Conference on Digital Libraries* (1997), p. 37.

197. Thompson, Shafer, and Vizine-Goetz, "Evaluating Dewey Concepts," p. 43.

198. Diane Vizine-Goetz, "Dewey in CORC: Classification in Metadata and Pathfinders," *Journal of Internet Cataloging* 4, no. 1/2 (2001): 73-74.

199. Carol Jean Godby and Ray Reighart, "Terminology Identification in a Collection of Web Resources," *Journal of Internet Cataloging* 4, no. 1/2 (2001): 49-66.

200. Joan S. Mitchell and Diane Vizine-Goetz, "DDC Taxonomy Server," *Advances in Knowledge Organization, Dynamism and Stability in Knowledge Organization, Proceedings of the Sixth International ISKO Conference* edited by Clare Beghtol, Lynne C. Howarth, and Nancy J. Williamson, 7 (Würzburg, Germany: Ergon Verlag, 2000), pp. 282-287.

201. Mitchell and Vizine-Goetz, "DDC Taxonomy Server," p. 285.

202. Koch et al., "Role of Classification Schemes in Internet Resource Description and Discovery."

203. Anders Ardö et al., "Browsing Engineering Resources on the Web: A General Knowledge Organization Scheme (Dewey) vs. A Special Scheme (Ei)," in *Advances in Knowledge Organization, Dynamism and Stability in Knowledge Organization, Proceedings of the Sixth International ISKO Conference* edited by Clare Beghtol, Lynne C. Howarth, and Nancy J. Williamson, 7 (Würzburg, Germany: Ergon Verlag, 2000), pp. 385-390; Traugott Koch and Diane Vizine-Goetz, *Automatic Classification and Content Navigation Support for Web Services.* (1998). http://digitalarchive.oclc.org/da/ViewObject.jsp?objid=0000003489.

204. Milstead, Jessica, *Ei Thesaurus*, 4th ed. rev. (Hoboken, N.J.: Engineering Information, 2001).

205. Koch & Vizine-Goetz, *Automatic Classification and Content Navigation Support*.

206. Traugott Koch and Anders Ardo, "Automatic Classification of Full-Text HTML: Documents from One Specific Subject Area." (2000). http://www.lub.lu.se/desire/desire36a-wp2.html.

207. Robert T. Niehoff and Greg Mack, "The Vocabulary Switching System; Description of Evaluation Studies," *International Classification* 12, no. 1 (1985): 2-6; Edward T. O'Neill, Martin Dillon, and Diane Vizine-Goetz, "Class Dispersion Between the Library of Congress Classification and the Dewey Decimal Classification," *Journal of the American Society for Information Science* 38, no. 3 (1987): 197-205.

208. Sara D. Knapp, "Creating BRS/TERM, a Vocabulary Database for Searchers," *Database* 7 (1984): 70-75; Sara D. Knapp, *The Contemporary Thesaurus of Search Terms and Synonyms: A Guide for Natural Language Computer Searching* (Phoenix, Ariz.: Oryx Press, 2000).

209. Dahlberg, "The Future of Classification in Libraries and Networks," p. 31; Dahlberg, "Library Catalogs in the Internet," pp. 158-160.

210. Unesco, *UNISIST Study Report on the Feasibility of a World Science Information System* (Paris: Unesco, 1971); Eric Coates, G. Lloyd & D. Simandl, *The BSO Manual: The Development, Rationale, and Use of the Broad System of Ordering* (The Hague: FID, 1979).

211. Jens-Erik Mai, "The Future of General Classifications," *Cataloging & Classification Quarterly* 37, no. 1/2 (2003): 3-12.

212. Hemalata Iyer and Mark Giguere, "Towards Designing an Expert System to Map Mathematics Classificatory Structures," *Knowledge Organization* 22, 3/4 (1995): 141-147.

213. Freeman, "Classification in Computer-Based Information Systems," p. 205.

214. Pauline Cochrane, "New Roles for Classification in Libraries and Information Networks," *Cataloging & Classification Quarterly* 21, no. 2 (1995): 4.

215. Steven J. Squires, "Access to Biomedical Information: The Unified Medical Language System." *Library Trends* 42, no. 1 (Summer 1993): 127-151.

216. Xia Lin and Lois Mai Chan, "Knowledge Class–A Dynamic Structure for Subject Access on the Web," *Advances in Classification Research, Proceedings of the 8th ASIS SIG/CR Classification Research Workshop* edited by Efthimis N. Efthimiadis, 8 (Washington, D.C.: Information Today, Inc., 1997), pp. 33-42.

217. Markey, *Subject Searching in Library Catalogs*, pp. 123, 129, 140.

218. Mike Wendland, "U-M's Entire Library to be Put on Google: Billion-dollar Project will Move Text of 7 Million Volumes Online," *Detroit Free Press* (14 December 2004): 1.

219. Rosenberg and Borgman, "Extending the Dewey Decimal Classification Via Keyword Clustering," p. 177.

220. Marcia J. Bates, "Task Force Recommendation 2.3 Research and Design Review: Improving User Access to Library Catalog and Portal Information." Final Report 3 (1 June 2003). http://www.loc.gov/catdir/bibcontrol/2.3BatesReport6-03.doc.pdf.

221. J. L. Dolby and Howard L. Resnikoff, "On the Multiplicative Structure of Information Storage and Access Systems," *Interfaces: The Bulletin of the Institute of Management Sciences* 1 (1971): 23-30.

222. Marcia J. Bates, "Indexing and Access for Digital Libraries and the Internet: Human, Database, and Domain Factors," *Journal of the American Society for Information Science* 49, no. 13 (1998): 1198.

223. Liu and Svenonius, "DORS," p. 361.

224. Karen Markey Drabenstott, Schelle Simcox, and Eileen G. Fenton. "End-user Understanding of the Subject Headings in Library Catalogs," *Library Resources & Technical Services* 43, no. 3(1999): 140-160.

225. Victor Rosenberg, *The Application of Psychometric Techniques to Determine the Attitudes of Individuals Toward Information Seeking*, AD 637713 (Lehigh, Pa.: Lehigh University, 1966), p. 19.

226. Amanda Spink et al., "Searching the Web: The Public and their Queries," *Journal of the American Society for Information Science and Technology* 52, no. 3 (2001): 226-234; N. J. Belkin et al., "Iterative Exploration, Design, and Evaluation of Support for Query Reformulation in Interactive Information Retrieval," *Information Processing and Management* 37 (2001): 403-434; Bernard J. Jansen, Amanda Spink, and Tefko Saracevic, "Real Life, Real Users, and Real Needs: A Study and Analysis of User Queries on the Web," *Information Processing & Management* 36 (2000): 207-227; Craig Silverstein et al., "Analysis of a Very Large Web Search Engine Query Log," *SIGIR Forum* 33, no. 3 (1999): 6-12; Bernard J. Jansen et al., "Real Life Information Retrieval: A Study of User Queries on the Web," *SIGIR Forum* 32, no. 1 (1998): 5-17; Lyn Keily, "Improving Resource Discovery on the Internet: The User Perspective," in *Proceedings of the 21st Online Information Meeting* edited by David I. Raitt, Paul Blake and Ben Jeapes (Oxford: Learned Information Europe, 1997), pp. 205-212; Karen Markey Drabenstott and Diane Vizine-Goetz, *Using Subject Headings for Online Retrieval* (San Diego: Academic Press, 1994), pp. 199-200; Thomas Peters et al., "Transaction Log Analysis," *Library Hi Tech* 11 (1993): 37-106; Christine L. Borgman, 1986. "Why are Online Catalogs Hard to Use? Lessons Learned from Information-Retrieval Studies," *Journal of the American Society for Information Science*, 37, no. 6 (Nov. 1986): 387-400; Larson, *Users Look at Online Catalogs*, p. 53; Markey, *Subject Searching in Library Catalogs*, 66.

227. Larson, "Evaluation of Advanced Retrieval Techniques," pp. 48-49.

228. Zins, "Models for Classifying Internet Resources," p. 20.

229. Bates, "Task Force Recommendation."

230. Nicholas J. Belkin, "Anomalous States of Knowledge as a Basis for Information Retrieval," *Canadian Journal of Information Science* 5 (1980): 133.

231. Bates, "Where Should the Person Stop," p. 575.

232. Bates, "Where Should the Person Stop," p. 581.

233. Bates, "Where Should the Person Stop," p. 584.

234. Janette R. Hill and Michael J. Hannafin, "Cognitive Strategies and Learning from the World Wide Web," *ETR&D* 45, no. 4 (1997): 37-64.

235. *Webster's Third New International Dictionary of the English Language* (Springfield, Mass.: Merriam-Webster, 1986), p. 622.

236. Alan Blackwell, "Psychological Perspectives on Diagrams and their Users" in *Diagrammatic Representation and Reasoning* edited by Michael Anderson et al. (London: Springer-Verlag, 2002), pp. 109-123; Manfredo Massironi, *The Psychology of Graphic Images* (Mahwah, N.J.: Lawrence Erlbaum Associates, 2002); Elzbieta Kazmierczak, "A Semiotic Perspective on Aesthetic Preferences, Visual Literacy, and Information Design," *Information Design Journal* 10, 2 (2001), pp. 176-187; James Elkins, *The Domain of Images* (Ithaca, N.Y.: Cornell University Press, 1999); Rudolf Arnheim, "Spatial Aspects of Graphilogical Expression," *Visible Language* 12, no. 2 (1978): 163-169.

237. "Cingular's New Ad Campaign is 'Raising the Bar.'" (2004). http://www.prnewswire.com/mnr/cingular/20359/.

238. Groxis, Inc., "Knowledge Management, Data Mining, and Information Mapping with Grokker: A Picture is Worth 30 Billion Web Pages." (2005). http://www.groxis.com/service/grok/.

239. Karen Markey Drabenstott, "Online Catalog User Needs and Behaviors," in *Think Tank on the Present and Future of the Online Catalog: Proceedings* edited by Noelle Van Pulis, 9 (Chicago: American Library Association, 1991), pp. 59-84.

doi:10.1300/J104v42n03_01

The DDC Relative Index

Francis Miksa

SUMMARY. The "Relative Index" of the Dewey Decimal Classification (DDC) is investigated over the span of its lifetime in 22 editions of the DDC as to its character as a concept indexing system, its provision of conceptual contexts for the terms it lists, and the way in which the index intersects with special tables of categories used in the system. Striking features of the index that are discussed include how the locater function of an index is expressed in it, its practice of including concepts that have not been given specific notational locations in the system, its two methods of providing conceptual contexts for indexed terms (by means of the notation of the system and by the insertion of enhancement terms that portray conceptual context), and how the index has intersected with three types of special tables of categories in the system. Critical issues raised include the indexing of constructed or synthesized complex concepts, inconsistencies in how enhancement terms are portrayed and the absence of them in some instances, the problem of equating conceptual context with disciplinary context, and problems associated with not in-

Francis Miksa is Professor, School of Information, The University of Texas at Austin, Sanchez Building (SZB) 564, 1 University Station D7000, Austin, TX 78712-0390 (E-mail: miksa@ischool.utexas.edu).

[Haworth co-indexing entry note]: "The DDC Relative Index." Miksa, Francis. Co-published simultaneously in *Cataloging & Classification Quarterly* (The Haworth Information Press, an imprint of The Haworth Press, Inc.) Vol. 42, No. 3/4, 2006, pp. 65-95; and: *Moving Beyond the Presentation Layer: Content and Context in the Dewey Decimal Classification (DDC) System* (ed: Joan S. Mitchell, and Diane Vizine-Goetz) The Haworth Information Press, an imprint of The Haworth Press, Inc., 2006, pp. 65-95. Single or multiple copies of this article are available for a fee from The Haworth Document Delivery Service [1-800-HAWORTH, 9:00 a.m. - 5:00 p.m. (EST). E-mail address: docdelivery@haworthpress.com].

Available online at http://ccq.haworthpress.com
© 2006 by The Haworth Press, Inc. All rights reserved.
doi:10.1300/J104v42n03_02

dexing one type of special table. Summary and conclusions are extended
to problems that arise in studying the index. doi:10.1300/J104v42n03_02

*[Article copies available for a fee from The Haworth Document Delivery Ser-
vice: 1-800-HAWORTH. E-mail address: <docdelivery@haworthpress.com>
Website: <http://www.HaworthPress.com>* © 2006 by The Haworth Press, Inc.
All rights reserved.]

KEYWORDS. DDC, Dewey Decimal Classification, Relative Index

INTRODUCTION

A book index is a locater system that ordinarily connects a set of
terms from the text of a book to the page location where they occur in
the book's text. How the terms in such an index correspond to their textual counterparts sometimes varies, of course. Most often the two are
exactly the same, but sometimes an index term will represent variant de-
clensions and cases of its textual partners, and occasionally it will stand
for an idea that does not specifically use the indexed term at all in a
given section of the text, but rather is denoted in the text by some synon-
ymous term.

The DDC Relative Index differs somewhat in both of these matters.
Its terms refer to classification notations and their corresponding category statements[1] as found in the schedule text rather than to page numbers. And the relationship of the index entries to the category statements
found in the schedule at their respective notations has always centered
on matching their conceptual content, not merely on matching strings of
alphabetic characters, although the two aspects often coincide.

The DDC Relative Index has been an essential part of the DDC since
its beginnings in 1876, but it would be erroneous to conclude that it
came into existence fully formed with all of its complexities worked out
right from the start. In reality, the editors of the DDC had to learn how to
make the Relative Index and this took much time, an incredible amount
of energy, not a small number of experiments (some of which had to be
abandoned), and countless adjustments that reflected both how the index entries were to represent concepts in the system and how they were
to be formatted.

The present account is an attempt to trace important features of the
Relative Index that have characterized it over its lifetime. As such, it
arises from my own growing interest in it after having worked with the
DDC system over more than four decades. I began classifying with

DDC 17[2] in a small college library, and during those initial years I approached the Relative Index as many people do in a very intuitive way rather than with any overall sense of its attributes. In the ensuing years, I learned through practice that as an intuitive tool the Relative Index can be used well enough with only a modest number of rules of thumb–for example, that Relative Index terms point to classification numbers not page locations; that one should probably check notations found in the index also in the schedules to see what else is available at the notation location; that when a term points to more than one class number, the class number that most clearly represents the context of its idea in the informational object being classified is likely the best one to use; that if no specific location within an adequate conceptual context matches the object being classified, one probably ought to choose a class location for the item in an appropriate context area anyway rather than an inappropriate one even if doing so means classifying the item at a broad level that does not specify closely the item's content.

What does it mean, however, to approach the Relative Index as something more than simply an intuitive tool with such rules of thumb? In my own experience, this question began to assert itself only when I began to view the DDC as a system of concepts that together form a cohesive whole and not simply as an orderly list of individual classes denoted by numbers. The metaphor of an interwoven fabric with complex threadwork and intricate designs and symbols comes to mind as a way to portray this view of the system. The Relative Index in this view then becomes a guide for finding particular subject patterns, images, and individual threads as concepts within particular environments or contexts rather than merely individual class locations. And, although concepts and their contexts are not always immediately findable or even always intelligible, one goes forward on the assumption that the whole system (including the Relative Index) or some portion of it will help one to make sense of such particular patterns, images, and threads in relationship to the subject content of the item in hand.

But, even this more integrated view of the whole, which began for me as I and my students studied DDC 18 during the 1970s and as I attempted to review DDC 19 in 1980 (Miksa 1980), did not spur me to take a close look at the Relative Index. A close examination only began after I began to study DDC 1 for my 1998 discussion of the DDC (Miksa 1998) and found that even that simple "proto" version of the index was something of much greater complexity and intricacy than I ever before imagined and thus worthy of study in its own right. Since then I have attempted to determine some sensible way to study the index and its most important features systematically without being overwhelmed by its sheer magnitude. The present paper is the result of some small progress in this effort. It is based primarily on spending a good deal of time with the text of the Relative Index itself. And while all of the Relative Index editions have been dipped into, a selection of specially important editions of it (DDC 1, 2, 7, 12, 13, 14, 15, 17, and 22) have received the most attention because of their relationship to significant changes in the life of the DDC.[3] Ultimately, my observations have centered on three questions that deal with critical issues for the index.

1. Given that index terms represent concepts, how do the concepts so listed relate to the system as portrayed in the schedules?
2. Given that one of the stated goals of the Relative Index is to list terms in relation somehow to certain conceptual contexts, how are those contexts represented?
3. Given that the DDC involves categories in special tables as well as in the basic schedules, how has the Relative Index represented the concepts in the special tables?

Accordingly, the sections that follow here will reflect each of these questions in turn. Afterwards, findings will be summarized and implications for the study of the Relative Index will be discussed.

I. CONCEPT REPRESENTATION

The basic task of the Relative Index is to correlate concepts found in the index in the form of verbal terms that are arranged alphabetically with category statements also written in verbal form but arranged systematically in the DDC schedules in the order of their notations. The latter serve as addresses for the index locater function. The basic task of the index as a process of concept correlation is important because of the open-endedness of the system.

System Open-Endedness and Development

Open-endedness refers to the DDC's constant state of development over its lifetime. When Melvil Dewey first published the DDC in 1876 it was mostly undeveloped, consisting at that starting point of a relatively uncomplicated list of 921 category statements, each of which had a notation affixed to it. Each individual notation consisted of two or three digits from among 999 numeric possibilities in a metric based array of numbers expressive of the hierarchical structure of the whole.[4] Today the DDC consists of approximately 26,000 unique category statements with notations as well as another 12,000 or so that consist of "constructed" statements and notations, and instructions for synthesis that have the potential of creating millions of additional notations representing categories. The system could hardly be anything other than open-ended, of course, being an attempt to encompass the whole of human knowledge which itself is forever expanding. At the start, however, most of system's open-endedness was due not to some simpler knowledge structure from an earlier time, but rather to the fact that Dewey simply had neither the time nor the intellectual acumen to develop it such that all areas of knowledge were represented in the system with reasonable fullness. In reality, a significant number of editions (i.e., until DDC 14 in 1942, or nearly three-quarters of a century) would have to be issued before the system had achieved reasonable fullness throughout its parts.

The fact that many parts of the system remained under- or undeveloped for long periods of time would have been disastrous for library use of the system because classifiers would need to know how to classify many acquisitions that fell into such lacunae. A useful example illustrates this point. The potato was a common table vegetable when the system began. And given its common status, one might expect the term **Potato** to occur in the system with a specific notation, most likely in the realm of **Agriculture** (630s). As it turns out, however, the division called **Agriculture** remained essentially undeveloped–a single page of ten category statements at the third digit level (i.e., 630, 631, 632 . . . 639)–for the system's first seven editions. It was subsequently expanded to three pages in DDC 8 (1913), but the concept of potato was not specifically identified in its schedule until DDC 10 in 1919.

Concept Indexing

The lack of system development was less than disastrous for library use because of the DDC's concept indexing. DDC in effect provided a conceptual location for the term **Potato** and for thousands of other terms that could be exploited for non-specific "broad" class entry until such time that the undeveloped classes to which such terms belonged might be divided with specific sub-notations for the "included" concepts that the terms represented. Although informational objects classified in this broad manner would be intermixed with others on similar topics until the schedule's details were worked out, the objects would at least be kept together in cohesive conceptual groups.

This is precisely what happened to the term **Potato**. **Potato** was indexed in the first edition but it was correlated only with **Agriculture**, class 63, rather than with any more specific location inside that class.[5] In DDC 2-DDC 6, **Potato** was correlated with class 633 (**Grains, Grasses, Fibers, Tea, etc.**) but without a specific class notation of its own. In DDC 7, it was correlated with class 635 (**Garden crops**) and in DDC 8-DDC 9 with class 635.2 (**Tubers and bulbs**), a subdivision of **Garden crops**, but still without its own notation. Only in DDC 10 (1919) was it specified distinctly though in this case in two different hierarchies, one at 633.491 in the context of **Field crops**, the other at 635.21 in the context of **Garden crops**. Had the Relative Index been a device that indexed only terms that actually appeared with specific class notations and not also terms conceptually associated with one or another notational locations, representing the concept "potato" in the system would not have been possible.

DDC Concept Indexing Developments

The DDC appears to have extensively practiced this kind of conceptual correlation of terms without specific notations during its earliest periods of development. For example, DDC 1 contained only 921 category statements (consisting of 1,044 unique terms) in its schedules, but its index correlated no less than 2,765 index terms with those notations. In short, the indexed concepts numbered nearly three times the actual schedule categories.[6] As time passed and schedules in the system became more fully developed, the number of concept terms in the index that were of this "included but not specified" kind appears to have diminished greatly although this conclusion has not been tested rigorously. But, if this was indeed the case (and it seems highly likely), their reduction in numbers could perhaps be attributed to the appearance by the time of DDC 7 of increasing numbers of notes in the schedules that discussed what kinds of subtopics a class included without giving the topics mentioned their own specific sub-entries with notations. Notes of this kind, now very numerous in the system, are described in section 7 of the DDC 22 Introduction, especially section 7.18 "Including Notes (Notes that Identify Topics in Standing Room)." Such notes employ various methods of showing included topics for which explicit sub-notations have not been devised. By means of this practice, the Relative Index regularly includes such concepts in much the same manner as the concept "potato" was included in the system's earlier years.

By the time DDC 14 appeared in 1942, the number of concepts in the index that had no specific locations in the system appears to have greatly diminished also because of the extraordinary efforts of the editorial staff to keep expanding the system. During the intervening span of years, the index, having often accommodated terms long before the schedules included them, appears to have had a policy of adding entries but not of removing them readily, the result of which was to support this developmental effort. By DDC 14, therefore, one might conclude that the schedules had nearly caught up with the index, which by then had in excess of 46,000 entries.[7]

DDC 15 (1951/52) represented a definitive break in this progression. It encompassed a severe and in some respects almost disastrous effort to reshape the DDC as a "Standard edition" for small to medium-sized libraries, its schedules being reduced from the approximately 31,000 notations of DDC 14 to only about 4,600 (along with extensive updating of language and many relocations of topics within the system). And the Relative Index (called only "Index" in this edition) was reduced to only about 14,000 entries with notations. The ratio of index entries to class locations (a little more than 3 to 1) was not simply larger than previous editions by a great deal, but was comparable to that of DDC 1. The index included the terms from all of the category statements as well as the terms in all of the edition's extensive notes, the latter possibly being the preponderant of the two kinds.[8] Regardless of the proportions, the overall result of the downsizing was to return the index to something resembling that of DDC 1–many more terms than specific notational locations–but with the critical difference that most, if not all such terms were likely represented verbally in notes. This practice also made the DDC 15 index much more akin to a book index in that the presence of an Index entry seems to have been based on the actual appearance of the verbal terms in the schedules, even if only in a note, and not on the fact that the concept belonged in the system at some given location.

Users of the DDC were not generally satisfied with the changes and this led to the restoration of the system in DDC 16 to something of its previous parameters. With the subsequent growth of the index in succeeding editions up to the present DDC 22, the Relative Index has once again assumed something of the richness in concept indexing that it had developed by DDC 14.

Three other things deserve mention in this discussion of the Relative Index as a concept indexing device, all of them experiments in some respects. The first was the practice of including specific literary and philosophical authors by name (in large numbers as it turned out) in both the schedules and in the Relative Index, a practice begun in DDC 2 that lasted through DDC 14 but was abandoned in DDC 15. Some found its discontinuance a loss of convenience, but others felt it had no place in a system that focused on concept classification. In actuality arguments both for and against its fittingness for the DDC and its Relative Index are possible. For example, since some informational objects are *about* the views of literary or philosophical authors, listing them by name is no different than including any other topic as a subdivision. In contrast, however, since the predominant kind of work related to these people is *by* them rather than *about* them, including their names in the schedules and index specifically more readily supports shelf-listing convenience than concept classification. Further, considering that works about people related to other particular subject areas are ordinarily handled by shelflisting devices such as Cutter's author numbers, there would seem to be no compelling reason to make an exception to that practice in the case of authors of this kind. Finally, as a pragmatic matter, abandoning such listings also contributed to cost savings when making the schedules and Relative Index simply by avoiding the costs of inputting, printing and subsequent updating that including them entailed.

A second matter has to do with the appearance of WebDewey and its correlation of Library of Congress Subject Headings with the DDC. This correlation, which provides the capacity to search for an LSCH term to find whether such a term is correlated with DDC categories, has added in effect an auxiliary index to the system beyond the Relative Index. The operation of the matching system is based on both automated term matching algorithms and matching that comes from formally mapping the LCSH system to the DDC system. In the latter case, the result is not unlike creating a switching or cross-walk mechanism. In either case the product would seem worth pursuing, but only time will tell whether it has been worth the effort.

A third and final matter related to the Relative Index as a concept indexing device is the current rise in the number of entries in it that represent not actual permanent categorical statements and notations found in the schedules of the system, but rather "constructed" categorical statements that exist only in the Relative Index. However, since this matter is also related to the matter of how the Relative Index is related to the categories of special tables, it will be dealt with in the third section.

II. CONCEPTUAL CONTEXTS

A second general characteristic of the Relative Index has to do with how it goes about representing the conceptual context or contexts of any term listed in the main alphabetical sequence of the index, since a basic goal of the index is to portray not only the notational location of an indexed term, but also to do so with contextual cues that provide further meaning to it.[9] For example, indexing the term **Potato** is not simply a matter of expressing where the concept represented by that term is to be found physically as a notation in the actual enumeration of all categories and their notations in the schedules, but also of providing a conceptual context for it such that one can assess the role it plays at a given notational location and thus ascertain some sense of its usefulness for classifying without looking it up in the schedules specifically. Were this not to be done, the Relative Index would consist only of an alphabetical list of terms each of which would have one or more (and sometimes many) separate notations following it with no further information. **Potatoes** in DDC 22 might end up appearing as follows.

Potatoes   583.592; 635.21, 641.352 1; 641.652 1; 664.805 21

The result would be increasingly more difficult to navigate as the number of locations increased, but the chief thing that would make this kind of listing less useful would be the necessity of looking each one up to find out where they belonged conceptually in the classificatory structure of the system. The result would be, in effect, little more than a regular book index that serves as a term locater system, only in this case it would be a classification notation locater. What might enhance such a bare list would be some way to interpret or indicate in a nutshell the conceptual context represented by each notation.

Providing conceptual context in this way is not ordinarily accomplished in many book indexes for the terms they list except when a term is subdivided by some other terms that provide some sort of context. Conceptual context is not regularly supplied, one might assume, either because the indexer thinks most terms are self-defining or, what is more likely, the indexer does not consider providing such context to be part of the indexing task. Not having such context readily available is often not a problem, at least when a term is only listed for at most one or two locations. They can simply be looked up to find out what the context is. But, when a book index term has many locations, determining which one is relevant to a person's search is not always so easy.[10] In the DDC, two means of providing conceptual context of this sort are provided, one having to do with the notation, the other with inserting additional enhancing context terms into specific entries.

Notation As Conceptual Context

The most consistent method by which the Relative Index and the DDC as a system provides conceptual context and one that is intuitive to regular users of the system is simply the act of supplying the class notations from the schedules associated with the term in the index. The notation, being for the most part "expressive" of the hierarchical structure of the system, will reveal the conceptual context of a given term through its numerical values. For example, by being correlated with notation 63 in the DDC 1 Relative Index, the term **Potato** has been correlated with the conceptual context of that notation. The meaning of the notation is

> 6   **Useful arts**
>
> 3   **Agriculture**

It does not matter that **Potato** is not specifically listed at that location. The notation by itself is enough to provide a conceptual context for this listing of the term within the system. It is a very general conceptual context in this case, of course, but it is a conceptual context nonetheless. The effectiveness of having access to conceptual contexts of this kind presupposes, of course, that the user of the index is familiar with the structure of the system, or at least has the Summaries of the system near at hand because one would need them to "interpret" the notation. But, supposing the latter to be true and given that this is the only instance of the term **Potato** in the DDC 1 index, it says in effect that were one classifying an informational object about potatoes, the object should be placed at this notational location.

In the indexes of DDC 2 to DDC 6, the foregoing context was enriched by assigning it to the slightly expanded notation 633, representing not simply agriculture in the context of the useful arts, but also grain, grasses, fibers, tea, etc., in the context of agriculture. Here again, of course, the actual location does not list the concept **Potato** specifically.

> 6   **Useful arts**
>
> 3   **Agriculture**
>
> 3   **Grains Grasses Fibers Tea, etc.**

In the index of DDC 7 this context was changed to 635 and in the 8th and 9th editions to 635.2 (i.e., the context of **Useful arts–Agriculture–Garden crops** for the first, and the context of **Useful arts–Agriculture–Garden crops–Tubers and bulbs** for the second), although again still without specifically listing the actual term **Potato** in either case. Why the shift in context was made, by the way, is not explained although it may well have had something to do with the status of schedule development in the respective sections of 633 and 635, the latter being a little further along than the former.

With the much fuller expansion of sections 631 to 635 in DDC 10, the Relative Index supplied two rather than one conceptual contexts for **Potato** (633.491 and 635.21), each one focusing on the concept as a crop.

6	Useful arts				6	Useful arts	
	3	Agriculture				3	Agriculture
		3	Grains Grasses Fibers Tea, etc.				5	Garden crops
			4	Root crops				2	Tubers and bulbs
				9	Tubers and bulbs				1	Potato
					1	Potato	

The first denoted the concept **Potato** as a **Root crop**, the other as a **Garden crop** or vegetable. This pair of contexts were retained through DDC 14, but in the greatly revised and reduced DDC 15, only the second of the two was retained. When the system was again expanded in DDC 16, the first location was restored, their dual existence continuing to DDC 20 when the entire section related to root crops in 633 was removed so that such crops were located only in the 635.2 context.

The practice of providing conceptual context by means of notation has been a normal aspect of the DDC for all of its 22 editions. The only things that seriously interrupt it from edition to edition are those occasions when the editors of the system change the context of a given term listing by restructuring the relevant part of the system in some way or when the notational structure contains unexpressed and thus hidden hierarchical levels (identified as "Centered headings" since DDC 17) that, were they known, might somewhat alter how the contextual environment is understood. But, one could argue that neither of these interruptions are ultimately fatal to this method of providing conceptual context. Neither of these interruptions cause conceptual context to disappear but rather simply modify it. Furthermore, interruptions caused by incomplete hierarchies are somewhat mitigated by the second provision for conceptual context, the insertion of verbal enhancement terms in Relative Index entries.

Term Enhancement As Conceptual Context

The second way that the Relative Index provides conceptual context for index terms is by providing a verbal indication of conceptual context of an indexed term in addition to a notational indication. The product of this practice could be called an enhanced entry. Again, using the concept of **Potato** already discussed, one will find that in addition to the notational location supplied for the term, the Relative Index also supplied an additional enhancement term for each of its index entries interposed between the index term and its notational location.

Potato	agriculture	6<u>3</u>3	(DDC 2-DDC 6)
Potato	agriculture	6<u>3</u>5	(DDC 7)
Potato	agriculture	6<u>3</u>5.2	(DDC 8-DDC 9)

In each of these entries **Potato** is the index term, and **agriculture** plays the role of an enhancing term that provides a verbal statement of a conceptual context of **Potato**. In the first two examples, the context resides in effect at one hierarchical level above the full notation as listed. In the third example, it resides at two hierarchical levels above. The underscore in each notation identifies the element of the notation that the enhancing term represents.

When dual locations began to be provided for **Potato** as a crop in DDC 10 to DDC 14 and again in DDC 16 to DDC 19 (the latter after the term itself had been changed to the plural form **Potatoes**), the context of **agriculture** was replaced with context enhancement terms closer to the more specific notational level of **Potatoes**, specifically, **field crops** in one case and **garden crops** in the other. In these cases, the conceptual enhancement term represents hierarchical levels one step lower than agriculture.

Editions 10-14			Edition 15			Editions 16-19		
Potato	field crops	63<u>4</u>.491	Potatoes	Culture	63<u>5</u>.2	Potatoes	field crops	63<u>4</u>.491
Potato	garden crops	63<u>5</u>.21				Potatoes	garden crops	63<u>5</u>.21

When DDC 15 returned the term to only a single location at 635.2, it changed the context enhancement term to **Culture**, the latter one may suppose reflecting the edition's change of the name of the third digit level from **Garden crops** to **Horticulture**. Finally, in DDC 20 to DDC 22, not only did the system provide only one location for the term in this specific area of the system; it also resumed using the context enhancement term of **agriculture** for the term.

One common aspect of all these instances is that the conceptual context supplied is hierarchically "broader" than the index term itself with respect to the specific hierarchical "chain" involved.[11] Hierarchically broader terms in this sense are also conceptually broader since they conceptually "include" the content of terms subordinate to them. When reading entries in the Relative Index, therefore, enhancing terms indented under a term in the main alphabetical sequence of the index should be viewed as containing broader conceptual environments than the indexed term itself.

This account of a single term in the Relative Index over many decades of the system may seem vastly oversimplified. It is only one term among thousands in the system, and the contexts reported for it are very limited in terms of other contexts also reported for the same term but not used in this discussion. Furthermore, using this term may also appear confusing insofar as its changes over time may seem unjustified or even nonsensical. But the usefulness of the example resides primarily in its uncomplicated depiction of a basic practice found in the Relative Index that has been part of the system since its beginnings. The Relative Index is, in effect, not simply a term locater system, nor is it even a term-in-context locater system. Rather, it is intended to be a concept-in-context system. As such, this practice provides a basis for the very name of the index–"Relative"–for as each term is enhanced in this way the index searcher is able to view it "relative" (i.e., in relationship) to some broader conceptual context.

One practical way to understand this emphasis is to insert a phrase such as "in the context of" or "in relationship to" into the way one reads a particular term listing and the enhancement terms next to or beneath it. For example, one might construct the following statements as a way to understand two of the **Potato** examples used above.

Potatoes

[in the context of the broader concept] **agriculture** [is found at notation] 635.21

Or again,

Potatoes

> [in the context of the broader concept] **garden crops** [is found at notation] 635.21

The reverse of reading the enhancement terms this way would be to treat them as some sort of subdivisions of the term **Potatoes**. However, besides being nonsensical, approaching them as subdivisions suggests that the Relative Index is some sort of mini-classificatory structure in parallel with the schedules when in fact the Relative Index is in many respects quite the opposite. It is an inverted classificatory structure, at least with respect to the relationship between the indexed term and other enhancement terms indented under it.

The editors of the DDC have added contextual enhancement terms to a significant proportion of all terms in the Relative Index. The practice is followed in order to help users of the system identify how any particular indexed terms fit into the system as a whole. Because many indexed terms fit into multiple locations in the system, this practice helps the classifier compare the various conceptual contexts of such terms. The goal is to determine with some ease which one of them might be appropriate for classifying an informational object in hand, and to do so without having to memorize the notational structure of all parts of the system so as to be able to "interpret" notations of considerable length.

The Relative Index practice of providing conceptual contexts for index terms in its main indexing sequence by supplying them with context enhancement terms has been a notable success. But, its success has not been free of difficulties, four of which seem useful to note in the form of questions. First, why are some single context index terms supplied with an enhancement term to indicate their single conceptual context whereas others are not? In a discussion of enhancement terms indented under main index terms, the introduction to the DDC (DDC 22, section 11.1) suggests that some terms imply their own context. This conclusion might be applied to multiple context index terms in the main sequence of indexed terms, but when applied to single context terms, it appears not to be the case for all of them. This is the case for some single context terms for which no conceptual context is supplied. And even when conceptual context is implied, especially by one word in a multi-word phrase, how one determines which is the context term is not always clear.[12]

Second, how do the indexers determine which hierarchical conceptual level to focus on in relationship to the full hierarchy of conceptual context denoted by a given notation when creating enhancement terms? Any close examination of any portion of the current Relative Index will show quickly that the relationship of enhancement terms to the notations that follow them vary widely when connected to the latter's hierarchical structures.

Third, for complex index entries where many enhancing conceptual context sub-headings are listed (e.g., the term **Copper** lists 22 contexts in which that concept is found in the system) and, further, where some of the context terms themselves have one or more indented terms under them, how is one to understand a second enhancement term indented under the first, or a third indented under the second? While the relationship of a single indented enhancement term to an individual index term may seem clear enough (given that the relationship between the two may be interpreted by interposing "in the context of the broader concept of" between them as described above), this is not easy to do when multiple indentions are included. For example, does a second level enhancement term in such indented structures enhance all terms that precede it (including the index term), or only the term that immediately precedes it?

Fourth, on what basis do the editors of the DDC portray conceptual context as "disciplinary" context when in many instances context enhancement terms do not appear to indicate disciplines at all, at least in the general sense of that term? Some appear to denote what at best might be considered merely some loose sense of a region or topic of study. Some might conclude that attempting to refine more precisely what is meant by conceptual context has the flavor of an abstruse philosophical issue with little practical relevance. But, the position here is that the opposite is actually the case. An attempt to spell out more precisely the relationship between indexing terms and the conceptual context enhancement terms indented under them might well lead among other things to determining how much consistency is desirable in the matter and, given a desire for greater consistency, reformulating the policies for how enhancement terms that spell out conceptual context are to be determined.

These are only four issues that might be mentioned with respect to the practice of supplying enhancement terms that aim to provide conceptual context in the Relative Index. There may well be others. And so while applauding the effort to show conceptual context in this way, it also seems reasonable to conclude that the resulting product merits further systematic scrutiny.

III. THE RELATIVE INDEX AND SPECIAL TABLES

The final section of this discussion concerns other indexible content that comes under the aegis of the Relative Index, and more specifically, how the Relative Index is related to the categorical content of what in the DDC are called special tables–lists of categories that are ordinarily devised to enhance number building in the system by allowing the notations of a table to be added (i.e., attached at the end) to class notations found in the schedule text.

Special tables of categories of these kinds have been an important part of the DDC since DDC 2 in 1885 and have existed primarily in three forms:

1. Tables applicable widely throughout the system but ordinarily set apart from the regular schedules in some special location (e.g., in a special volume since DDC 18).
2. Tables consisting of parts of the regular schedules–that is, in the form of some particular sequence of category statements and their notations that are abstractly identified as tables–of which portions of the notations are used as sources for subdividing categories in other parts of the schedules. Applying this kind of table is ordinarily accomplished by extracting final digits of one or another of the categories in the identified table and attaching them to the notation of a target schedule category, though in one form of this application entire DDC notations may be attached to some given target notation in the schedule.
3. Tables similar to the first but applicable only to a relatively small part of the total system and usually inserted into the schedule text near that location.

The first two types in the above list have been used in the DDC in all editions since the second. The third type is more recent, having come into existence principally since DDC 17. The third type of special table is like the first in being a special table and not simply an abstracted part of the schedules, but also like the second in being found in the schedules rather than in some separated location. For the purposes of the present discussion, only the first and third types of tables are of explicit interest since they represent categories that are essentially "extra" to the schedules, even though used with the schedules. Thus, they represent additional indexible content. The second type of table is essentially part of the content of the schedules, and even though the categories of this kind of table are abstracted from the schedules for use in other schedule locations they have been indexed as part of those schedules. Thus, they do not represent categories "extra" to the schedules and will not be considered in the present discussion.

Special tables are extensive in the DDC and in order to bring some order to a discussion of them from the standpoint of indexing, it will be useful to view them in two groups–Special tables used in DDC 2 to DDC 14 (which all are of the first type), and Special tables used in DDC 15 to DDC 22 (which are of both the first and third type).

Special Tables in DDC 2 to DDC 14

Only three of the following five special tables are found in DDC 2 (at the beginning of the Relative Index), but all five are found in DDC 3 to DDC 14 (at the end of the Relative Index):[13]

1. Geographic Divisions
   (A list of target subjects and their notations taken from the schedules. The notations of these subjects may have geographic subdivision notations attached to them. The actual subdivisions are the names of places and their notations, and these are found both in the schedules in the span 930-999 and in the Relative Index.)
2. Form Divisions
   (A list of form characteristics of publications.)
3. Languages
   (A list of target languages and their notations taken from the schedules in the span 420-499. The notations of these languages may have philological subdivisions attached to them. The actual philological subdivisions are found in Table 4, in the Relative Index, and in the form of exemplar constructions at the 420 division of the schedules of the English language notation plus philological subdivision notations.)
4. Philological Divisions
   (A list of subdivisions related to the character and study of individual languages that may be attached to Language notations as listed in Table 3.)

5. Literatures
   (A list of target literatures and their notations taken from the 800s
   of the schedules. The notations of these literatures may have the
   notations of literary subdivisions attached to them. The actual literary subdivisions are found in the Relative Index and in the form
   of exemplar constructions at the 820 division of the schedules of
   the English literature notation plus literary subdivision notations.)

All five tables are arranged as columns of two-element entries, each
entry consisting of a notation followed by a category name. For example,

912	**Atlases**	(an entry in Table 1)
03	**Encyclopedias**	(an entry in Table 2)
493.2	**Coptic**	(an entry in Table 3)
11	**Alphabet**	(an entry in Table 4)
891.62	**Irish**	(an entry in Table 5)

Three of the tables (1, 3, and 5) have full notations taken from the
schedules, whereas the other two have abbreviated notations that are to
be attached to ends of notations found in the schedules. Each table is organized alphabetically by the terms in the descriptor column of their entry lines rather than numerically by the notational element that begins
each entry. Finally, and in terms of longevity, all five tables remained
exactly the same from DDC 3 to DDC 8 (1888-1913) and although each
thereafter underwent some change, especially in edition 14, much of
that was often not much more than adding additional entries to them.[14]
Each table was relevant to class number building in some way and
because of this the existence of the special tables were indicated in the
Relative Index by placing a correlating superscript number (1 to 5, referring to one of the tables) at the beginnings of index entries found in
the index that served as subdivisions of the kind denoted by the table.
The relationship of superscripted index entries to the actual tables was
of two kinds, however. Because three of the tables (1, 3, and 5) merely
listed target subjects (with their notations) to which subdivision notations could be added, the role of the Relative Index along with other
sources as noted above was to supply the actual subdivisions and their
notations that one could add to the target notations.

The other two tables were actual lists of subdivisions–"form" subdivisions in the case of Table 2 and philological subdivisions in the case of Table 4. Within these two tables, the notations for the respective categories in each table have one, two, or three digits and are to be understood decimally. All the categories were also listed in the Relative Index, but in that location they were simply referenced to their targets in general.

Table 1 listed target subjects from the schedules that could be subdivided geographically. The actual subdivisions (place names and their notations) can be found either in the schedules at 930-999 where they are portions of history notations and are arranged systematically according to their full history notations, or in the Relative Index where they consist of alphabetically listed place names entries each with a history notation following them and each with a superscript [1] preceding them to direct one to the target topics and notations in Table 1 to which they could be attached. For example, given the topic Atlases in the list of entries that comes from Table 1 (**912 Atlases**), should one have an atlas of France it would be sufficient to look up France in the Relative Index to find its notation in the 900s.

France

. . . . .

[1] **History**   944

By removing the "9" from the notation for France (it represents the subject field History) and attaching the remaining digits "44" which represent France to the notation for **Atlases** in Table 1, one would arrive at the notation 912.44 for Atlases of France.

Tables 3 and 5 worked in the same way, except that Relative Index entries for the subdivisions to be added to language and literature notations (e.g., alphabet, or poetry) were represented in the index chiefly as examples applied to English language and to English literature after which an additional line would read "[3] **other languages**" and "[5] **other literatures see Table 5**." The latter was designed to direct the classifier's attention to the tables that held the basic notations for specific languages and literatures.

Table 2 Form divisions and Table 4 Philological divisions, functioned differently. Each consisted of a list of subdivisions rather than a list of target notations to which some sort of subdivision could be attached. Thus, one had to understand for each where its target notations were to be found. Table 2 notations (i.e., 01 to 09 considered as decimals) could be attached to nearly any subject notation in the schedules if the form division notation was not in conflict with some schedule use of the same notational symbols. Table 4 notations (i.e., 1 to 9 considered as decimals, including their notational extensions to as many as three digits) could be attached to any language notation in the 400s. Language notations could be found in Table 3 or in the schedules at the 400s. Table 4 numbers were to be attached in other words to Table 3 language numbers. The categories in each of these two tables were also listed in the Relative Index with superscripted numbers directing the classifier to these tables.[15] Entries in the Relative Index for form divisions–for example, **History**, or **Encyclopedias**, etc.–also had separate lines with messages such as:

[2] special, see subject;   [2] see special subject;   [2] of special topics see subject

These lines directed the classifier's attention not only to Table 2, but to the applicability of its subdivision categories to any subjects.

Regardless of the fact that three of the special tables here were merely lists of target categories and notations to which subdivision notations could be attached, the overall use of the tables plus subdivisions found in these tables and in the Relative Index in this earlier version is not very different than what occurs in the DDC today.[16] The importance of them for this discussion of the Relative Index was how they were represented in it.

Tables in DDC Editions 15-22

Tables in the DDC since the 15th edition differ in two distinct ways from those in earlier editions, and these differences have affected how categories from the tables are related to the Relative Index. The first way they differ is that they consist chiefly of subdivisions and notations useful in class number building, and while they do contain instructions and examples for notational synthesis, they do not consist of systematic lists of target categories and notations culled from the schedules. Further, categories in these more recent tables are always listed in the numerical order of their notations, not in alphabetical order. And, where tables are maintained separately from the schedules (e.g., special tables 1 to 6 in DDC 22, volume 1) long printed dashes have been inserted in front of each notation listed (e.g., —09 History) in order to show that some other notation must precede the special subdivision notation.

The second way that special tables in the more recent era differ from those in the past is in the sheer number of them. At first, DDC 15 all but abandoned special tables. Only form divisions were kept as a formal special table and it contained a bare list of only nine basic categories numbered from —01 to —09. DDC 15 also discussed an informal list of literary forms numbered from —1 to —8 in its Introduction (p. xiii), but although form divisions of this kind were listed in the Relative Index, they were never formally made into a special separate list in their own right.

In contrast, DDC 16 began to resuscitate special tables, principally by expanding the general form divisions table to something approaching the fullness it had achieved in DDC 13 and DDC 14 when the DDC had first adopted some of the form division complexity found in the UDC.

In DDC 17, the table of form divisions, renamed Standard Subdivisions for the first time, was joined by an "Area Table" that listed geographic subdivisions separately from the notations they had always been associated with in the 930-999 array of the History schedule. And in DDC 18, five new special tables were introduced for a total of seven.

1. Standard Subdivisions
2. Areas
3. Subdivisions of Individual Literatures
4. Subdivisions of Individual Languages
5. Racial, Ethnic, National Groups
6. Languages
7. Persons

Subsequently, Table 3 has been expanded to include separate sub-tables (DDC 19-DDC 22) and more recently Table 7 has been discontinued (DDC 22).

In addition to the foregoing, the DDC instituted a new kind of special table beginning in DDC 17–type 2 tables as described earlier that are of limited application and that are placed within the schedules close to where they are to be applied. The first of these (e.g., the tables at 616.1-616.9 or at 617.1-617.9) were of limited extent, but succeeding DDC editions have increasingly resorted to them and in many cases have greatly increased their categories. They have become especially important for sections of the DDC in which faceted structures and notational synthesis has been incorporated (e.g., the tables for 780 Music introduced in DDC 20).

In sum, the overall increase of special tables has been spectacular. This has had the practical effect of adding huge numbers of new categories to the system, if not in actuality in the tables themselves, then at least in the potential they have for increasing the size of the system when applied. Given such increases in the numbers of real or potential categories, how then have the categories they enumerate been handled in the Relative Index? In answer to this question, three separate effects of their presence can be identified.

First, the categories found in all special tables of type 1 (i.e., Tables 1-6 in DDC 22) are regularly included in the Relative Index with the dashed notations that belong to each. In DDC 15 and DDC 16, this amounted to index entries for Form divisions and for literary forms with some sort of preceding explanatory phrase to alert the classifier to the extent of their application.

History	Poetry
see other specific subjects —09	other literatures —1

In DDC 17, entries from the two formal tables that came into existence at that time were labeled with an abbreviation of the tables from which they came.

History	Picardy France area —4426
see also s.s. —09	

In contrast, literary forms continued to be represented in the manner shown above for DDC 15 and DDC 16.

Beginning with DDC 18, all such Relative Index entries have used the simple expedient of citing the table number with the entry.

Picardy (France)   T2—442 6;   Numic languages T6—974 57

The second effect on the Relative Index of the increasing total number of special tables of all kinds in the system has been an increase in entry contexts that arise from constructed notations that do not appear in the schedules by themselves. The following three examples are in the DDC 22 Relative Index.

Nudity	Jade	Jazz
literature 808.803 <u>561</u>	occultism 133.25<u>5 3876</u>	songs 782.42<u>1 65</u>

The first of these arises from using special Table 3C (Table type 1), the second from using internal tables that are primarily extracted from schedule sections (Table type 2), and the third from using special internal tables with their respective instructions (Table type 3). None of the actual entries and their notations can be found in the schedules.

Constructed entries and notations were only very occasionally used in the Relative Index in DDC 2 to DDC 12. They increased greatly in DDC 13 and DDC 14 as the system struggled with influences on it from the UDC. They disappeared almost entirely in DDC 15 and only began to reappear in increasing numbers since DDC 17 until now in DDC 22 they are again numerous enough to have become noticeable. They are justified in the sense that the Relative Index is a concept index as discussed earlier in this paper. In short, the Relative Index includes concepts whether or not they are actually present in the schedules, just as in earlier days it included an entry for **Potato**, even though that entry was not in the schedules. But constructed entries also raise the issue of propriety for they represent concepts absent not only in the schedules in terms of wording but also in terms of the specific notations coordinated with them. Upon what theoretical general principle could one justify any one of them?

The third effect of the rise in the number of tables on the Relative Index is associated with the growing number of type 3 tables–those of limited applicability inserted into the schedules at relevant locations. Some of these are very brief, their categories consisting principally of those that can be built from add instructions drawing notations from regular parts of the DDC schedule (e.g., the tables in the 780s that arise from its faceted structure and that essentially use concepts and categories that appear in the regular parts of the 780s), whereas others are very lengthy and contain unique categories not extracted from elsewhere in the schedules but rather created specifically for the table itself to be applied to a limited range of schedule categories and notations (e.g., the table at 362-363 of subdivisions for "Specific social problems and services").

The chief problem that arises with these kinds of tables for the Relative Index is that their categories are not ordinarily indexed in the Relative Index and therefore they have no presence in it except in the form perhaps of an occasional constructed topic and notation and except as the same subdivisions may have been included in some regular part of the schedules and was thus indexed. For some of these tables, notably those that are parts of faceted sections of the system, the absence of their categories in the Relative Index is not critical because their categories, ordinarily constructed from schedule elements, are already indexed through the latter. Even so, their existence in special tables makes access to them considerably less robust than access to the categories of other special tables. For tables not constructed from schedule elements, as is the case with the 362-363 table mentioned above, their categories simply have no presence in the Relative Index at all, because they are simply not indexed, and this appears to be a significant gap in the coverage of the index.

CONCLUSIONS

The foregoing discussion of the DDC Relative Index has focused chiefly on describing how it has accommodated three issues over the course of its existence: (1) how it has handled concepts as opposed to merely giving location information for terms; (2) how it has handled the idea of conceptual context of terms and (3) how it has handled the indexing of categories that arise apart from the schedules themselves in the form of special tables. It has been demonstrated that the Relative Index is primarily a concept index rather than merely a term location system, that over the years it has provided access to many concepts not formally included in its classificatory structure; that it provides two means of showing the conceptual context of terms (one through notation, the other through specially inserted enhancement terms); and that it has a long history of having entries for table categories. It has also been demonstrated that in each of these three aspects of the Relative Index, some problems have arisen that color the picture of it–for example, that index categories not represented specifically in terms of notational locations have waxed and waned over the decades and now increasingly include the subjects of constructed notations that do not appear in the schedules; that enhancement terms showing conceptual context are not consistently applied or identified and that the idea that they represent "disciplinary contexts" needs clarity and greater consistency in application; and that while the categories of special tables have a long history of being included in the index, type 3 found in DDC 17 to DDC 22 are not so indexed.

Overall, it is easy to conclude that over the years the Relative Index has developed a series of unique strategies for its tasks that while not always successful in their particular applications, have when viewed together contributed to making the Relative Index a tool of considerable uniqueness and power. It has grown robust as a concept index providing considerable contextuality for the concepts included, and that this robustness has been extended to special table categories to a notable extent. That problems also exist with respect to the result simply means that the Relative Index has more developments to look forward to in its future. Given the track record of the DDC editorial staff for adjusting to complexities and difficulties, however, the prospect of facing off to such problems in a systematic way would seem to hold some promise.

One other conclusion is also merited, but this comes from the act of studying the Relative Index over 22 editions, quite apart from the specific findings presented here. The conclusion is that studying the Relative Index will most likely be confined to anecdotal evidence of patterns and practices until better approaches exist for investigating it. In many respects, the findings here consist of observations at the intersection of the DDC schedules and its Relative Index. In many respects, they can also be called anecdotal because they are based on the very time consuming effort of having to go back and forth between the two differently arranged types of enumerations represented by these two different tools, always with the temptation not to be thorough. The reason for the latter is that because one of the two kinds of sequences (the schedules) is arranged systematically in terms of notations and the other (the index) is arranged alphabetically by verbal term, comparing them by finding evidence of an issue in one type of enumeration has depended on checking it out in the other. And given their different arrangement orders and their sheer sizes, this cannot be easily accomplished with robust consistency because of the huge amount of effort involved. The alternative is, of course, to stop such comparisons at the anecdotal level.

A better situation for examining the issues here would be if one of these two kinds of files could be converted to the order of the other. This approach would be helpful if, for example, one wished to find all instances of certain kinds of entries that point to one kind of schedule category statement. In examining the small Relative Index of DDC 1, this problem was overcome by entering all Relative Index entries in a single list and resorting them by class number.[17] For other editions, however, no such comparison is presently possible until they or, what is more likely, a sample of them is treated the same way through OCR and database technology that is now available.[18] If and when that occurs, conclusions might be drawn that have a much firmer foundation in supportive empirical data.

NOTES

1. The phrase "category statement" rather than "class" is used here for the verbal matter that is numbered by notations in the DDC schedules for the simple reason that a class suggests a singular thing, but many of the DDC's so-called classes are plainly multiple rather than singular in their content. Were the plural form "classes" to be used for multiple content "classes," confusion and awkwardness would arise when attempting to distinguish between a single notation with multiple classes and several notations denoting multiple classes. The phrase "category statement" is found preferable because it encompasses both singular and multiple concepts when used for the name of the verbal content that accompanies any particular notation.

2. Since there are 22 DDC editions, and a variety of ways to refer to them, this paper will reduce reference to them to the simple statement of DDC with an edition number–for example, DDC 17 for DDC's 17th edition, DDC 1 for its first edition, etc. A full list of the 22 editions will be found in the Reference List at the end.

3. A brief history of the DDC in which especially important editions are identified and discussed can be found in Miksa (1998). A much longer history that does the same in the context of a review of the first eighteen editions of the system is Comaromi (1976). In a sense all editions are important, but these seem to stand above the others. DDC 1 (1876) began the system and set its general direction. DDC 2 (1885) was the first representation of the system in its fuller form, the first being minuscule in comparison. DDC 7, which came more than 25 years after the groundbreaking 2nd, was notable for being the first comprehensive response to increasing of calls for changes and to the existence of the *Classification Décimale* (i.e., the UDC). DDC 12 is the first one that Dorkas Fellows fully edited and it shows her influence in every part. DDC 13 is the second and last she edited, the last the Melvil Dewey influenced directly, and the first edition to be deeply effected by the *Classification Décimale*. DDC 14 represents the apex of the early development of the system and was the first to be published after the deaths of the systems founders (Melvil Dewey, W. S. Biscoe) and of Fellows. DDC 15 was and remains the 'crisis' edition, a critical turning point in how the system would come to be conceived. DDC 17 is the first in which modern standardized "add devices" and the first to truly strike out in new directions that have persisted. And, of course, Ed 22 is not only the newest edition, but the first that has had to deal with a Web presence.

4. Dewey persisted to the end of his life in referring to DDC notations as combinations of whole numbers with decimal extensions, the latter beginning after the third digit. This contrasts with those who have subsequently described such notations as completely decimal in nature, the decimal point functioning merely as a divider (e.g., DDC 22, "Introduction," p. xl (section 4.16).

5. In the DDC 1 "Introduction" (pp. 3-4), Dewey's explanation of his numbering system, including its 2-digit numbers that represented divisions of a class (i.e., a special "library"), suggests that he really was undecided as to where in **Agriculture** the subject **Potato** should be placed. He could not use 630 because a zero was to be used to indicate a class of general works that applied to the whole of the two digits (i.e., 63) that preceded it. Using it here would suggest that **Potato** was a concept that applied to the entire field of Agriculture. Since he had not decided what more specific section (i.e., 631, 632, etc.) included **Potato** as a concept, he simply left it unspecified in the notation for the class as a whole in the same sense that DDC 22 uses the idea of "standing room." In later editions, after he had decided always to have at least 3 digits in any notation, he most likely would have indexed this work with the notation 630, for the zero in the third

position with no digit following it was rationalized as no longer referring by itself to general works, but rather served only as a filler to get the length of the notation to 3-digits.

6. In Miksa 1998 (p. 6-7), the total number of index entries was said to be 2,612. But, this total failed to take into account multiple class locations listed together for some terms–for example, as in **Perfumery . . . . . 660, 646**. Beginning in DDC 2, multiple listings of this kind were given separate lines. The total of 2,765 unique notations does not include 66 instances in which ranges of notations rather than individual notations are listed for a term. Ranges occur in two varieties–those that describe an explicit range of notations (e.g., **Orders of architecture . . . . 722-724**) and those that describe an implied range of notations (e.g., **Readers . . . . . 418, 428, 438, etc.**). Theoretically, it would be possible to count the explicit notations inferred by either kind, but since the character of the range sometimes appears to be vague and therefore open to interpretation, it was not done. Were they to be included, however, the total number of individual class notation correlations in the index would exceed 3,000.

7. The index term location count for DDC 14 is an estimate calculated on the basis of a sample of its pages. The conclusion that DDC 14 was the apex of this development is partly based on the fact that it was the first edition in which editors made a concerted effort to even out depth of hierarchies and coverage in all parts of the schedules. The conclusion does not preclude the possibility that previous editions had not exceeded it in size. Front matter in each of DDC 12 and DDC 13 listed the total number of "heds" (i.e., headings) in their indexes as 46,000 and 54,500 respectively. But, both of these editions also varied greatly in the full of various parts of the system such that some were very rich in sub-classes and others were not. Since classes that were shallow in their development appear to have been the chief cause of non-specific index entries, at least in the earlier editions, the evenness of DDC 14 in its distribution of sub-classes makes it a better candidate for the conclusion. Ultimately, only rigorous empirical testing will establish what is the truth of the matter.

8. That more index entries were from the notes than from the entries is conjectured but not definitively established. It is based thinly on the analysis of two randomly chosen columns in the index where of the 73 terms coordinated with distinct notational locations, 45 (62%) were from notes and only 25 (34%) were from category statements. [Three (4%) were from neither source.]

9. The idea that "context" of this kind could be described as "disciplinary" was first made explicit in the DDC 17 "Introduction" (p. 10) by its editor, Benjamin A. Custer. In the DDC's earlier years, Melvil Dewey did not refer to the idea of disciplinary context, his explanation of the distribution of subjects in relation to indexed terms being simply that they represented physical phases ("fazes" in his reformed spelling) or aspects of subjects. Custer appears to have struggled with using aspect or discipline when discussing the matter in Relative Index in DDC 17 (p. 34-35) and DDC 18 (p. 18), but by DDC 19 (p. xxxi) appears to have settled on the term "discipline." Subsequent "Introductions" to the DDC by John P. Comaromi (DDC 20, section 4.1) and Joan S. Mitchell (DDC 21-DDC 22, section 4.1 in each) used the term "discipline" exclusively. One might argue whether "discipline" is appropriate to use in the matter in all cases and, in fact, a question is raised about the matter later on in this paper. Because settling on the exact nature of the context is not as important as establishing that conceptual context is a goal when listing terms, the idea of context here is connected only to the less explicit modifier "conceptual" (as in the phrase, 'conceptual context') without pinning the matter down further than that.

10. One not uncommon way to obtain information quickly on the conceptual context of a given book index term is to hold open at the same time both the index of the book and its table of contents. This allows one not simply to locate a term's page location, but to correlate the page location with the chapter containing the page number, the result of the correlation being a way to obtain a quick read on the intellectual setting of the term in that instance.

11. The term "chain" and the phrase "chain relationship," both coined by S. R. Ranganathan, refer to a sequence of terms in which each successive couplet of terms from the beginning of the sequence bears a superordinate to subordinate relationship to each other. Sequences of this kind are commonly displayed by indenting the subordinate terms under the superordinate. Thus, where a multiple term chain exists, it will appear as a cascade of indentions downward toward the right. The notational and category statement listings at the beginning of this section are "chains" in this sense.

12. For example, on a page chosen at random from the DDC 22 Relative Index (p. 650), 30 terms of the 51 indexed terms in the main alphabetical sequence have only one notational location (i.e., conceptual context) listed. Eight of these terms are supplied with a verbal conceptual context by the use of an enhancement term under them next to which is placed the notation. Four other terms (**Positrons, Post exchanges, Post-hypnotic phenomena**, and **Postludes**) have no such enhancement terms and in my opinion do not automatically imply a necessary particular context. The 18 remaining terms have more than one word each in their syntax (e.g., **Postal clerks   383.492; Postal insurance   368.2**) and it seems apparent that one word in each phrase does imply conceptual context. But, in surveying the various two-word phrases, which of the two words actually indicates the appropriate context varies from entry to entry. Of the two phrase terms here, the first word is the key to conceptual context for the first, whereas the second word plays that role for the second.

13. Only three of these tables are formally placed at the beginning of DDC 2 (1, 3, and 4) and they are numbered 1, 3, part 1, and 3, part 2. Form divisions appear only as a paragraph note at the end of Table 1, and consist of nine category terms with their respective notations. It would appear that Dewey had intended to make a formal table of them at that location but was perhaps unable to do so before the second edition went to press. To make matters even more confusing, when table superscript numbers are attached to entries in the Relative Index, the numbers used in the index are 1 to 4 and thus do not correspond to the way the tables are actually numbered. It is possible, of course, that the edition used here was faulty, but this seems doubtful since the actual page numbering of the Relative Index which includes the tables is sequential and shows no gaps. All five tables are at the end of the Relative Index in DDC edition 14, but since two of them (3 and 5) are actually combined, only four tables are actually present even though the four have the whole of the content of all five of the tables as described here.

14. The principal exceptions to this conclusion that change was primarily incidental and additive occurred with Table 2, which was expanded enormously in editions 13 and 14, and Tables 3 and 5 which were combined in edition 14. The latter made both lists equal in their entries, whereas previously, the Literatures table was always shorter than the Languages table, and both tables differed somewhat as to the language groups represented.

15. Unfortunately, the entries in the index for philological divisions were sometimes superscripted with a [3] pointing to the language list and at other times with a [4] pointing to the philological subdivisions list. How could this not have caused some confusion?

16. The only really serious conceptual difference between the earlier period and the present with respect to special tables occurs in the relationship between two subdivision categories–the idea of history (09) as found in the form divisions of Table 1, and the idea of geographic subdivision of a topic that was engineered by adding place names to topics notations listed in Table 1. While modern editions of the DDC allow place division apart from the 09 history number, one is limited in doing so to special instructions at certain points in the schedules. Any other instances of dividing a topic by place must be done by adding places to 09 and the result to the topical number. The correlation of these two concepts in more recent editions of the DDC by adding place notations to the –09 History subdivision of Standard Subdivisions was not apparently present in the DDC in its earlier years. Place division was one thing whereas history division, and even history in a place division was quite a different matter and were apparently treated differently. That is why the early DDC had a Table of topics to be divided by place quite apart from the History subdivision in the Forms table. The merging of these two concepts apparently came about by adopting form division ideas from the *Classification Décimale* (i.e., the UDC) in the 13th and 14th editions. Thereafter, the correlation of the two concepts in the DDC has become standard fare with no indication of its origin or of the conceptual and practical issues it raises. In contrast to the DDC, the Library of Congress Classification system persists in keeping these two concepts separate. This causes me to conjecture that keeping them separate may well have been an essentially 19th century tradition that was put aside in the 20th century by the UDC.

17. I wish especially to thank Dr. Kyung-Sun Kim, now a faculty member at the School of Library and Information Studies at the University of Wisconsin at Madison who, during her Ph.D. studies at the University of Texas School of Information, was chiefly responsible for making this list and re-sorting it.

18. The exception may well be the Relative Index of DDC 22 which likely is available in a database format and thus may well be adaptable to this kind of conversion. However, time has not been available to pursue this possibility.

REFERENCES

DDC Editions

DDC 1 (1876). *A Classification and Subject Index for Cataloging and Arranging the Books and Pamphlets of a Library* [Amherst, Mass.]. Facsimile reprint, Albany, N.Y.: Forest Press, 1976.

DDC 2 (1885). *Decimal Classification and Relativ Index for arranging, cataloging, and indexing public and private libraries and for pamflets, clippings, scrap books, index rerums, etc.* 2nd ed., rev. and greatly enl. Boston: Library Bureau.

DDC 3 (1888). *Decimal Classification and Relativ index for arranging, cataloging, and indexing public and private libraries and for pamflets, clippings, notes, scrap books, index rerums, etc.* 3rd ed., rev. and greatly enl. Boston: Library Bureau.

DDC 4 (1891). *Decimal Classification and Relativ Index for libraries, clippings, notes, etc.* 4th ed., rev. and enl. Boston: Library Bureau.

DDC 5 (1894). *Decimal Classification and Relativ Index for libraries, clippings, notes, etc.* 5th ed. Boston: Library Bureau.

DDC 6 (1899). *Decimal Classification and Relativ Index for libraries, clippings, notes, etc.* 6th ed. Boston: Library Bureau.

DDC 7 (1911). *Decimal Classification and Relativ Index for libraries, clippings, notes, etc.* Edition 7. Lake Placid Club, N.Y.: Forest Press.

DDC 8 (1913). *Decimal Classification and Relativ Index for libraries, clippings, notes, etc.* Edition 8. Lake Placid Club, N.Y.: Forest Press.

DDC 9 (1915). *Decimal Classification and Relativ Index, for libraries, clippings, notes, etc.* [9th ed.] Lake Placid Club, N.Y.: Forest Press.

DDC 10 (1919). *Decimal Classification and Relativ Index for libraries, clippings, notes, etc.* Edition 10., rev. and enl. Lake Placid Club, N.Y.: Forest Press.

DDC 11 (1922). *Decimal Classification and Relativ Index for libraries and personal use, in arranjing for immediate reference books, pamphlets, clippings, pictures, manuscript notes and other material.* Edition 11, rev. and enl. Lake Placid Club, N.Y.: Forest Press.

DDC 12 (1927). *Decimal Clasification and Relativ Index for libraries and personal use, in arranging for immediate reference books, pamflets, clippings, pictures, manuscript notes and other material.* Edition 12, rev. and enl. Semi-centennial ed. Lake Placid Club, N.Y.: Forest Press.

DDC 13 (1932). *Decimal Clasification and Relativ Index for libraries and personal use, in arranging for immediate reference books, pamflets, clippings, pictures, manuscript notes and other material.* Edition 13, revixed and enlarjd by Dorkas Fellows, Editor, Myron Warren Getchell, Associate editor. Memorial ed. Lake Placid Club, N.Y.: Forest Press.

DDC 14 (1942). *Decimal Classification and Relativ Index.* Edition 14. Lake Placid Club, N.Y.: Forest Press.

DDC 15 (1951). *Decimal Classification.* Devised by Melvil Dewey. Standard (15th) edition. Lake Placid Club, N.Y.: Forest Press.

DDC 16 (1958). *Dewey Decimal Classification & Relative Index.* Devised by Melvil Dewey. 16th Edition. Lake Placid Club, N.Y.: Forest Press.

DDC 17 (1965). *Dewey Decimal Classification & Relative Index.* Devised by Melvil Dewey. Edition 17. Lake Placid Club, N.Y.: Forest Press, of Lake Placid Club Education Foundation.

DDC 18 (1971). *Dewey Decimal Classification & Relative Index.* Devised by Melvil Dewey. Edition 18. Lake Placid Club, N.Y.: Forest Press, of Lake Placid Club Education Foundation.

DDC 19 (1979). *Dewey Decimal Classification & Relative Index.* Devised by Melvil Dewey. Edition 19, edited under the direction of Benjamin A. Custer. Albany, N.Y.: Forest Press, a Division of Lake Placid Club Education Foundation.

DDC 20 (1989). *Dewey Decimal Classification & Relative Index.* Devised by Melvil Dewey. Edition 20, edited by John P. Comaromi . . . (et al.). Albany, N.Y.: Forest Press, a Division of OCLC Online computer Library Center.

DDC 21 (1997). *Dewey Decimal Classification & Relative Index.* Devised by Melvil Dewey. Edition 21, edited by Joan S. Mitchell . . . [et al.]. Albany, N.Y.: Forest Press, a Division of OCLC Online Computer Library Center.

DDC 22 (2003). *Dewey Decimal Classification & Relative Index.* Devised by Melvil Dewey. Edited by Joan S. Mitchell . . . [et al.]. Dublin, Ohio: OCLC Online Computer Library Center.

Other Sources

Comaromi, J. (1976). *The Eighteen Editions of the Dewey Decimal Classification.* Albany, N.Y.: Forest Press Division, Lake Placid Education Foundation.
Miksa, F. (1980). "The 19th Dewey: A Review Article." *Library Quarterly* 50 (October): 483-9.
Miksa, F. (1998). *The DDC, the Universe of Knowledge, and the Post-Modern Library.* Albany, N.Y.: Forest Press, A Division of OCLC Online Computer Library Center.

doi:10.1300/J104v42n03_02

Teaching the Dewey Decimal
Classification System

Arlene G. Taylor

SUMMARY. The Dewey Decimal Classification (DDC) system is a
logical approach to a hierarchical categorization of recorded knowledge
that makes sense to many people. It both illustrates classification theory
and provides a practical way to organize information. It is taught in several different settings with content relying upon the purpose of the education or training. With reference to communications from colleagues,
the author identifies some problems in teaching DDC, followed by some
of the content covered and some methodologies used to overcome the
problems. Several examples of teaching tools are included as appendi-
ces. doi:10.1300/J104v42n03_03 *[Article copies available for a fee from The
Haworth Document Delivery Service: 1-800-HAWORTH. E-mail address:
<docdelivery@haworthpress.com> Website: <http://www.HaworthPress.com>
© 2006 by The Haworth Press, Inc. All rights reserved.]*

Arlene G. Taylor, PhD, MSLS, BA, is Professor Emerita, Library and Information
Science Program, University of Pittsburgh (E-mail: ataylor@mail.sis.pitt.edu).

The author wishes to thank A. Wayne Benson for reading and commenting on the
manuscript.

DDC, Dewey, Dewey Decimal Classification, OCLC, WebDewey, and WorldCat
are registered trademarks/service marks of OCLC Online Computer Library Center,
Inc. The Dewey Decimal Classification system is Copyright 2003-2006 OCLC Online
Computer Library Center, Inc. Used with permission.

[Haworth co-indexing entry note]: "Teaching the Dewey Decimal Classification System." Taylor,
Arlene G. Co-published simultaneously in *Cataloging & Classification Quarterly* (The Haworth Informa-
tion Press, an imprint of The Haworth Press, Inc.) Vol. 42, No. 3/4, 2006, pp. 97-117; and: *Moving Beyond
the Presentation Layer: Content and Context in the Dewey Decimal Classification (DDC) System* (ed: Joan
S. Mitchell, and Diane Vizine-Goetz) The Haworth Information Press, an imprint of The Haworth Press,
Inc., 2006, pp. 97-117. Single or multiple copies of this article are available for a fee from The Haworth
Document Delivery Service [1-800-HAWORTH, 9:00 a.m. - 5:00 p.m. (EST). E-mail address: docdelivery@
haworthpress.com].

KEYWORDS. Teaching, education, classification theory, categorization, number building, DDC, Dewey Decimal Classification

INTRODUCTION

People outside the field of library science often believe that the Dewey Decimal Classification (DDC) system surely is no longer taught to anyone beyond elementary school. Especially in academia, where so many libraries in the United States have switched from classification with DDC to classification with the Library of Congress Classification (LCC), people have the idea that DDC, being more than 125 years old, must be too out of date to be relevant today. They are mistaken. Not only is DDC kept up-to-date by continuous revision, it is a hierarchical scheme that makes sense to most people, and it has faceting capabilities (i.e., ability to designate subparts of the whole topic) that have a potential to improve online retrieval of information. It presents challenges for teaching, however, because of its complexity. This article addresses some of the challenges, concentrating especially on standard master's level cataloging education.

SETTINGS IN WHICH DDC IS TAUGHT

DDC can be taught in several different kinds of settings for several kinds of purposes. It is often taught to elementary school students in an overview manner with the purpose of giving them an understanding of how a library is organized, and perhaps secondarily, in order to give them an introduction to a hierarchical way of arranging concepts.

A second setting for the teaching of DDC is in a college technical arts program designed to produce paraprofessional librarians to work in technical services departments. Such a program is likely to emphasize the understanding of DDC notations (along with techniques for shortening very long ones) and the creation of complete call numbers by adding Cutter numbers to the DDC notations.

DDC is also taught in Schools of Library and Information Science to students who are preparing to be professional librarians. In these programs, DDC may be introduced as an example of a hierarchical classification scheme. Theory of classification may be emphasized, and students may or may not be taught DDC number-building techniques in introductory classes; although number building is certainly covered in advanced classes.

DDC is taught in various kinds of continuing education training courses. Such courses may be aimed at working professionals, para-professionals, or clerical level personnel. They may run for a half day or a full day or longer, depending upon the purpose of the training.

Finally, there is on-the-job training. Some places hire subject specialists without prior DDC study or experience and then must teach them to apply DDC to their subject knowledge. In other cases, newly hired personnel are considered to have had inadequate preparation for creating DDC notations and must have their previous training supplemented. And there seems always to be some degree of "how we do it here" to be taught to any newly hired person.

PHILOSOPHY OF TEACHING DDC

In each of the settings just described a teacher always has to determine what approach will be used in presentation. Education vs. training (or theory vs. practice) is almost always an issue, although it is more of an issue in professional education settings than in the others. Much has been written about the virtues of teaching theory vs. practice, and most writers have come to the conclusion that in the area of the organization of information, including cataloging, it is necessary to teach some of each. The proportions of each, of course, cannot be dictated, and depend very much upon the personal philosophy of teaching held by the instructor.

Whether the course is an introductory one or an advanced one also affects the philosophy of the way a course is taught. Introductory courses need to cover the basics of principles and patterns of the system. In professional schools introductory courses often are required for every student, while advanced courses are often elective. In introductory courses that are preparing professional librarians, and some think for the other groups also, an introduction should explain how DDC fits into classification theory. For example, DDC is basically hierarchical in its approach to knowledge, but it inevitably becomes somewhat enumerative as time goes along and it is required to respond to literary warrant (i.e., provide notations for topics that are being written about).

Introductory courses also should impart an understanding that classification systems, including DDC, are organic. While they reflect the culture of the time of their origin, they change with the times, and one can even trace changes in cultural, political, and social mores by studying the changes of locations and arrangements of those entities throughout the existence of a classification scheme, especially one like the

DDC which has an overseeing body that has made sure that the scheme has changed with the times. At the same time there is inevitably bias in any classification, and it is important to admit this while teaching about the attempts to lessen the bias and update the scheme.

It is also important to examine the faceted nature of DDC in courses for professional students. Faceting has tremendous potential for use in online systems. Professional librarians, going out into an increasingly online-dominated information world, will need tools especially adaptable to online environments if they are to continue to organize and provide access to information.

Advanced courses need to review the concepts covered in introductory courses and then go on to the difficult task of teaching the more intricate aspects of the principles and patterns. Such courses must cover actual methods of choosing basic notations, which may seem to some to be non-professional learning; but making sure the "right" discipline has been chosen requires one to think philosophically, not just by rote. And because the schedules themselves show only a small proportion of all potential DDC notations, it is essential to teach future users how to do number-building using several different approaches, including tables external to the basic schedules, tables within the schedules, and numbers or parts of numbers from the schedules themselves.

PROBLEMS OF TEACHING DDC

In preparing to write this article, I enlisted assistance from colleagues who teach in the area of organization of information and who subscribe to a discussion list called EDUCAT.[1] I explained that I was writing an article about teaching Dewey, and that while I have my own experience to draw upon, I would like to be able to add ideas from others also. I asked the following questions: "What things do you find particularly problematic about teaching Dewey? What innovative methods have you tried that worked? What didn't work? How does teaching Dewey compare with teaching other classifications (usually LCC, but also UDC)? How does it mesh with the teaching of classification (or categorization) as a general concept?" I received responses from twelve people.[2] All were thoughtful and helpful. I will be referring to some of the responses in the next few pages.

The first question was about problems of teaching DDC. It seems that a continual problem in teaching DDC is lack of time. There seems never to be enough time to cover even the basic material, and certainly not enough to get into details of special cases. Time seems to be a perennial problem for any topic in the organization of information; even so, the area continues to be given shorter and shorter time periods because of the persistent belief by educators outside the area that organization of information will soon be accomplished by computers, and it is therefore unnecessary for humans to learn how to do it. Marjorie Bloss comments, "I am troubled by the profession's underplaying the importance given to the organization of information/knowledge in general and cataloging and classification in particular. The concepts of consistency, uniformity, and standardization are even more important in today's technological world than before, as we continue to improve upon our methods for handling traditional technical services functions."[3] Speaking specifically of lack of time for DDC, Shawne Miksa writes, "Many students want a 'quick fix'–a nice tidy lesson in how to classify, but that simply isn't possible, especially with DDC."[4]

A problem that has arisen recently is the online teaching of DDC. Many instructors find that students struggle to gain an appropriate conceptual model of the DDC system if they start with WebDewey. Cheryl Boettcher Tarsala states, "The page images and experience with the physical volumes that anchor our understanding of how DDC works are not obvious to students who encounter it as a new database. . . . Additionally, WebDewey is so complex that beginners can get lost in it easily, even if they avoid a number of browser-related quirks that may crop up when students use it at home."[5] Despite such complications, library schools are not purchasing multiple copies of the print volumes because WebDewey is included in OCLC library school accounts. (And even before WebDewey, many schools had long ago quit purchasing enough copies of the print volumes so that every student in a class could be looking at the DDC at the same time.) This has left classroom instructors with the options of making enough copies of enough multiple pages of Dewey to teach from, or making projection copies of pages and hoping students can see from the back of the room, or teaching from WebDewey with its conceptual-model difficulties (and often the same problem with seeing from the back of the room) and hoping to somehow get the model across anyhow. Instructors in distance education mode can give students PDF copies of Dewey pages, but otherwise, must use WebDewey.

Another problem mentioned several times is the difficulty of teaching number building. The instructions are sometimes difficult to follow because they may lead to numbers that then lead to other numbers. This is especially difficult on the Web. With the print volumes, students sit with all four volumes and with fingers holding two or more places in two volumes, trying to remember which place led to another. This is not possible on the Web, and there may not even be a realization on the Web that instructions are available because they are off the screen. The fact that instructions have hierarchical force (i.e., instructions at a higher level of hierarchy apply at lower levels) is often not apparent to students, and is more difficult to teach on the Web than with print where such instructions may be higher on the page where the lower level number is found or on a preceding facing page.

Terminology can also present teaching difficulties. While there is an excellent glossary, and the introduction has become more clearly written with each new edition, there are several concepts in DDC that are not encountered elsewhere, and they are difficult to remember. Such concepts include "approximate the whole," "citation order," "preference order," "hook numbers," and "rule of zero." And, seemingly just to confuse things, the "rule of three" is a concept shared with descriptive cataloging and Library of Congress Subject Headings but is applied differently in DDC. Marjorie Bloss comments, "Perhaps one of the most difficult concepts to get across is the Rule of Zero. I have noticed that often students believe it tells them to eliminate the '0' from the standard subdivision number. . . . For many students, this is the first time they've ever confronted the various concepts of classification, and in many cases, it will probably be their last."[6] Unfortunately, such terminological difficulties can drive away people who would rather believe that computers will soon do all the organizing that is needed–they wonder why they should struggle with such "arcane" concepts.

Keeping workbooks and handouts up-to-date also is difficult. And in any situation where exercises are given that include "answers" at the end, there are going to be differences of interpretation as to what constitutes the "correct" answer, not to mention the typographical errors that inevitably occur when notations consisting of numbers, some lengthy, are typed one after another.

Finally, several people mentioned the difficulty of teaching the 800s in particular. Joanna Fountain observes, "The reason, IMO, is that the user is forced to use both the schedules and the tables just to create even basic numbers. This part of the scheme is unnecessarily unwieldy."[7]

DDC is more difficult to teach than is Library of Congress Classification (LCC). LCC is mostly enumerative. The top few levels of LCC are hierarchical, but not too far into the hierarchy, one encounters lists of concepts, often in alphabetical order, or alternatively, locations where the user is invited to create enumerative notations through the use of an alphabetical cuttering scheme. Students are often able to get to the appropriate place in the scheme simply by doing a keyword search. Although students also try to use WebDewey by doing keyword searching, they must be much more aware of the hierarchy and the potential for number building when using DDC than when using LCC.

CONTENT

Given the problems just outlined, it is useful to share some ideas about content that various educators have found essential in teaching DDC. Several of my correspondents mentioned the necessity of first learning subject analysis. After commenting that she finds it important to determine what an item to be classified is about, Beverley Chartrand adds, "Not to do so would be putting the cart before the horse, or flying madly off in all directions, but you might be surprised at the number of trainers who neglect this step."[8]

The content requirement mentioned by almost everyone who wrote to me is that students must be taught to get to the right place in the hierarchy, because most individual topics can fall into various disciplines. This is a concept that seems obvious to the seasoned DDC user, but new students find it a challenge. An example given by Hur-Li Lee is that when she gives students the concept "women in librarianship," half of them will choose a base number for women's occupations in Economics, regardless of the fact that the concept does not contain any economic aspects.[9] Barbara Albee says that part of the problem is "the fact that Dewey classification separates as it collocates; the system pulls things together but also takes things apart; for example, automobile racing is classed in sports 796.72, but ethics of auto racing is 175–this is difficult to get across to students."[10]

I have used the concept "children" to illustrate a subject that can be treated in almost every discipline, e.g.:

Children's libraries	027.625
Children–psychology	155.4
Children–Christianity–religious education	268.432
Children–legal status	346.0135
Children's diseases–medicine	618.92
Children–cooking for	641.5622
Children's parties	793.21
Children–literature	808.803523
Children's Crusade, 1212	944.023

Another suggestion from several of my correspondents is that the Introduction to DDC must be required reading. There the student will find explanations of the parts of the system (e.g., glossary, Manual, Relative Index, etc.), what classification is, a brief history, the conceptual framework of DDC, and the basic principles. One is also "walked through" the process of classifying with DDC, and key features of the schedules and tables are discussed. The process of number building is explained in some detail. There may be more detail in the introduction than is considered necessary for an introductory library science course, but I cannot imagine teaching an advanced course without requiring its reading.

The necessity to follow instructions is so obvious with DDC, that the teaching of this process may not be seen as an important area of content. However, students are often in a hurry and/or short on time, and they cannot imagine that they have to "read the fine print and follow it," as Kristine Kuhns wrote.[11] They must be reminded that the instruction to "add to the base number . . . the numbers following . . . " is often followed by "then add further as follows. . . ." Or an instruction to add to a base number may be followed by: "however, for [specific topic], see [another number]."

Because classification is often taught after subject headings, students must grapple with the concept that, unless they are entering records into a classified catalog, they can choose only one DDC notation to represent an item; whereas they are able to choose several subject headings for the same item. This requires discussion of the possibilities of more than one location and the implications for different types of library settings. Hope Olson says: "One thing I try to address in all aspects of teaching cataloging and classification, including DDC, is that not every real life example will fit perfectly; so as I progress through examples I add some that will have more than one right answer and some that won't fit perfectly. The latter may fall between topics or may have multi-faceted topics that can be only partially represented."[12]

A positive comparison with subject headings that can be made is that Table 1 in DDC is quite similar to the concept of free-floating subdivisions that can be added to main subject headings. It is important here to distinguish Table 1, which has general applicability, from Tables 2-6, which can be used only where instructed to do so.

METHODS USED IN TEACHING DDC

In a discussion of teaching methods, it is useful to separate introductory methods from those used for more advanced learning. It seems to me that in the teaching of organization of information classes it is essential to teach the broad concept of classification as the way humans categorize the world in order to be able to find things in it. I try to get beginning students to think about and try to answer such questions as:

- How do humans categorize?
- How is subject content expressed symbolically in bibliographic records?
- How is categorization used in the arrangement of physical information packages?
- How can categorization be used in the organization of Web resources?
- How is categorization used in the arrangement of surrogate records?
- What are the pros, cons, issues, etc., involved in the following classification concepts:
  - broad vs. close classification
  - classification of knowledge vs. classification of items on shelves
  - integrity of notations vs. keeping pace with knowledge
  - fixed vs. relative location
  - closed vs. open stacks
  - location device vs. collocation device
  - classification of serials vs. alphabetic order of serials
  - classification of monographic series (classified separately vs. classified as a set)
- What purposes are served by classification schemes?
- How are the major classification schemes organized?
- What are the weaknesses and strengths of the major classification schemes?
- How does faceting in classification systems work?
- What is the potential for faceted classification in searching?
- How are taxonomies being used on the Internet?
- What is the role of the classified catalog for the Internet?
- What is the role of automatic classification in organizing information?
- How can artificial neural networks assist in organization and retrieval of information?

With respect to the faceting question, Olivia Frost agrees, writing, "because of the faceted nature of Dewey, along with its hierarchical structure, one can show how this scheme has the potential to be used for online retrieval, although this potential has not been truly realized."[13]

The questions addressing major classification schemes apply to DDC and LCC, for the most part, although some attention is sometimes given also to Universal Decimal Classification (UDC). For introductory courses covering DDC, I believe there are two essential understandings: the hierarchical nature of DDC, and how to determine the meaning of a particular DDC notation. In order to teach these concepts, I copy a few pages from the schedules and from Tables 1 and 2, and create "handouts" with them. These pages are carefully chosen so that they have examples of most of the different kinds of instructions that one encounters in DDC. After some introductory explanation, I give a few examples of notations whose meaning can be deciphered from the sample pages the students have in hand, and we work through determining the meanings of those numbers. Then I give more notations that can be deciphered using the handouts, and students work together in groups of two or three to determine the meanings. A sample assignment that I then give the introductory class students is given as Appendix A.

Another approach sometimes used in introductory courses to help students understand classification is to have them create a classification scheme of their own. Olivia Frost writes:[14]

> The methods that I have tried that work best are ones where I ask students to design their own classification systems, drawing upon established schemes. The best projects that have resulted from this have been projects that incorporate features of Dewey. Students have let their imaginations soar and have come up with some truly innovative Web-based schemes. Another successful type of project is to have students create a specialized scheme drawing upon the structure of Dewey. This has resulted in schemes ranging from a system to organize historical cookbooks to a system for Islamic religious law. It forces the student to think critically about the scheme and how it can be adapted to specialized needs. A third type of project that I have found successful is to have students examine the history of a political or social movement and see how it has been reflected in Dewey. This engages the students who are more interested in social thought than cataloging per se, and demonstrates how cataloging and classification are part of a living, evolving social system, shaped by cultural values. Of course, this type of exercise can be done with other schemes, but no other

scheme has the historical or iconic import of Dewey, and using Dewey really brings home the ideas, both the broader intellectual and cataloging points.

In advanced courses, in continuing education training, and in on-the-job training, a major goal is to teach participants to create DDC notations. It is necessary to explain how DDC works. Lois Chan introduces "Principles" (which include classification by discipline, hierarchical principles, and faceting) and "Patterns" (including mnemonics and facet indicators).[15] Marjorie Bloss finds the flowcharts found in the Manual in volume 1 to be helpful.[16] Hur-Li Lee has found that students benefit from a basic flowchart for the concept of number building, before getting to the more complex flowcharts in the Manual. A copy of her basic flowchart is given as Appendix B.

Almost all of my correspondents emphasized the necessity to work through many examples. Many start from the top down. Christine Todd comments, "I used an exercise of identifying the number for a topic by working 'Top Down' through the main classes–looking at every likely possibility and only eliminating areas that definitely didn't apply–until we reached a suitable number for a topic."[17] Of course, students prefer to start with the Relative Index and look up the several topics found until one seems to fit. They need to be shown that although this may be an appropriate short-cut for experienced users, it can get beginners in trouble by putting them in the wrong discipline, as discussed earlier.

In order to teach number building I find it useful to give students a prepared handout in which I have cut out appropriate pieces from photocopied Dewey pages and then have taped them onto a page in the order in which they are used. This shows all the pieces from which a number has been built. A sample page from such a handout is given as Appendix C. I also have a handout that walks students through some basics of number building. Each page explains a new concept and then gives several problems for the student to work on to create numbers that will require them to use the concept that was explained on that page. Included are pages on: standard subdivisions, using the geographic area table, adding whole numbers and parts of numbers from schedules, using internal tables in the schedules, citation order, preference order, and the classification of literature using Table 3. Because the difficulty of teaching the 800s was so often mentioned by people who responded to my request for ideas, I am including my literature handout as Appendix D.

In order to teach distance education students on the Web, a module has to be created for each part of the course to give the distance learner all the resources needed for completion of the learning objectives. A discovery I have made is that those modules are also useful for on-campus students, because the material is presented in a logical fashion and can be returned to as many times as needed until understanding has been reached. That is, the face-to-face student does not have to rely completely on hearing and remembering what a teacher has said in class. The module I have created for the teaching of DDC is offered as Appendix E.

CONCLUSION

Not only is the Dewey Decimal Classification system still being taught, it is being taught thoughtfully and creatively, whether it be in a college technical arts program or in a School of Library and Information Science. And well it should be, for the DDC is a logical approach to classification. DDC teaching is as varied as the material to be classified, and various methods are used to lead the students to understand the simplicity and the complexity of the system, whether it be by challenging them to try their own hand at classification or by giving them as many examples as possible to help them understand the DDC number-building capabilities. Teaching and learning about classification in general and Dewey Decimal Classification in particular is an exercise that is well worth the effort, because human beings have a basic need to categorize, and DDC is a satisfying way to categorize recorded knowledge.

REFERENCES

1. Discussion list for issues related to cataloging and metadata education and training <EDUCAT@loc.gov>.

2. Responses were received from: Barbara L. Albee, School of Library and Information Science, Indiana University-Purdue University Indianapolis; Marjorie Bloss, Graduate School of Library & Information Science, Dominican University; Lois Chan, School of Library and Information Science, University of Kentucky; Beverley Chartrand, Subject Cataloger (retired), Library and Archives Canada; Joanna F. Fountain, Library Cataloging Consultant, Austin, TX; Olivia Frost, School of Information, University of Michigan; Kristine A. Kuhns, Cataloger, Ketchikan Public Library; Hur-Li Lee, School of Information Studies, University of Wisconsin-Milwaukee; Shawne Miksa, School of Library and Information Sciences, University of North Texas; Hope A. Olson, School of Information Studies, University of Wisconsin-Milwaukee; Cheryl Boettcher Tarsala, Graduate School of Library and Information Science, University of Illinois at Urbana-Champaign; Christine Todd, Bibliographic Services, National Library of New Zealand.

3. Marjorie Bloss, personal e-mail communication, 4 February 2005.
4. Shawne Miksa, personal e-mail communication, 31 January 2005.
5. Cheryl Boettcher Tarsala, personal e-mail communication, 3 January 2005.
6. Marjorie Bloss, personal e-mail communication, 23 January 2005.
7. Joanna Fountain, personal e-mail communication, 26 January 2005.
8. Beverley Chartrand, personal e-mail communication, 25 January 2005.
9. Hur-Li Lee, personal e-mail communication, 11 January 2005.
10. Barbara L. Albee, personal e-mail communication, 5 January 2005.
11. Kristine A. Kuhns, personal e-mail communication, 25 January 2005.
12. Hope A. Olson, personal e-mail communication, 21 January 2005.
13. Olivia Frost, personal e-mail communication, 22 January 2005.
14. Ibid.
15. Lois Chan, personal e-mail communication, 3 January 2005.
16. Marjorie Bloss, personal e-mail communication, 23 January 2005.
17. Christine Todd, personal e-mail communication, 26 January 2005.

doi:10.1300/J104v42n03_03

APPENDIX A. Example Introductory Course Exercise

I. Decoding classification notations.

A. Dewey Decimal Classification. (Use 22nd edition of DDC or WebDewey.)

Follow this example:

Example: 634.9097282

    600   Technology
      630   Agriculture and related technologies
        633-635 Specific plant crops
          634   Orchards, fruits, forestry
           634.9 Forestry
           [634.90,… Standard subdivisions *]
              09   Historical, geographic, persons treatment
               [093-099 Treatment by specific continents, countries,
                  localities…]
               [T2--4 - T2--9 Modern world, extraterrestrial worlds]
              7   North America
                2   Middle America   Mexico
                  8   Central America
                    2   Belize

This is a work on forestry in Belize.

* This means you have to go to Table 1 for Standard Subdivisions. Click on the "Tables" button in the upper right corner of WebDewey window.

- Give a *hierarchical interpretation* of the following notations. **Do not skip hierarchical levels!**
- Follow this with a *sentence that gives the gist of the topic*, as in the example above.

1. 305.55409415

2. 709.04042074

APPENDIX B. DDC Number Building by Hur-Li Lee

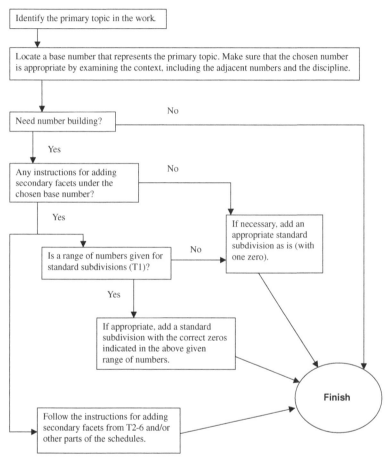

Reprinted with permission.

APPENDIX C. Sample Page from Synthesis of Notation Handout

To create a notation for a work on discrimination against Moravians in North Carolina:

305   **Social groups**

Including interactions, problems, role, social status of social groups

Class here culture and institutions of specific groups; subcultures of specific groups; consciousness-raising groups; group identity, social identity; discrimination; social stratification, equality, inequality

· · ·

SUMMARY

305.2	**Age groups**
.3	**Men and women**
.4	**Women**
.5	**Social classes**
.6	**Religious groups**
.7	**Language groups**
.8	**Ethnic and national groups**
.9	**Occupational and miscellaneous groups**

· · ·

.6   **Religious groups**

Add to base number 305.6 the numbers following 2 in 230–299, e.g., Christians 305.67, Christians in Indonesia 305.67598, Christian Scientists 305.6895, Christian Scientists in France 305.689544, Orthodox Jews 305.696832

Notation 230–299 replaces notation 2 from Table 7 with the result that many numbers have been reused with new meanings

· · ·

---
284   *Denominations and sects of Christian church*   **284**

.6   **Moravian churches**

For Hussite churches, see 284.3

[.609 4–.609 9]   Treatment by specific continents, countries, localities in modern world

Do not use; class in 284.64–284.69

.64–.69   Treatment by continent, country, locality

Add to base number 284.6 notation 4–9 from Table 2, e.g., Moravian churches in Germany 284.643

· · ·

T2   *Table 2. Areas, Periods, Persons*   **T2**

—75   **Southeastern United States (South Atlantic states)**

Class here southern states, *Piedmont, *Atlantic Coastal Plain

For south central United States, see —76

SUMMARY

—751	**Delaware**
—752	**Maryland**
—753	**District of Columbia (Washington)**
—754	**West Virginia**
—755	**Virginia**
—756	**North Carolina**
—757	**South Carolina**
—758	**Georgia**
—759	**Florida**

Full DDC notation for this work: 305.6846756

APPENDIX D. The Classification of Literature in DDC

The order of application of "characteristics of division" in the literature (800) class in Dewey is as follows:

If one author: Literature + Language + Literary form + Time period

If more than one author:

                                        Subdivision
Literature + Language + Literary form +   <u>or</u>
                                     Time period + Subdivision

        <u>or</u>

                                                  Subdivision
Literature + standard subdivision (if no one lang.) + Literary form +   <u>or</u>
                                                       Time period + Subdivision

[Literature that consists of miscellaneous writings has a slightly different order. Consult instructions in Table 3-B.]

Literature is always 8.

Language is spelled out in the schedules and is sometimes represented by a single digit, and sometimes by several, e.g.:

    2 - English
   69 - Portuguese   0 - international
 917 - Russian
 397 - Swedish

Works in English originating in the Western Hemisphere are classed in 810, not in 820 with the rest of English literature.

A standard subdivision comes after literature only when there is no language characteristic of the work to be cataloged. These standard subdivision designations are found under 801-809 and are similar to the standard subdivisions used throughout Dewey.

The notation for literary form is constant: (found in Tables 3-A – 3-B)

   1 - poetry   5 - speeches
   2 - drama   6 - letters
   3 - fiction   7 - satire and humor (found in Table 3-B)
   4 - essays   8 - miscellaneous writings

APPENDIX D (continued)

Examples:

English poetry - 821 (8 + 2 + 1)
Portuguese drama - 869.2 (8 + 69 + 2)
Russian fiction - 891.73 (8 + 917 + 3)
Swedish essays - 839.74 (8 + 397 + 4)
20th century English poetry - 821.91 (8 + 2 + 1 + 91)
20th century Portuguese drama - 869.24 (8 + 69 + 2 + 4)

Subdivisions are obtained from Table 3-B and apply only to works by more than one author:

01-07 are standard subdivisions from Table 1

08 Collections of literary texts in more than one form

09 History, description, critical appraisal of works in more than one form

Time period tables are found under 810-899 in DDC.

Remember that every notation must contain 3 digits but need not contain every characteristic, e.g.:

800 means a work about literature (without one specific language, standard subdivision, form, or subdivision);

820 means a work about English literature (not by form or subdivision)

PRACTICE EXERCISE 7: LITERATURE AND TABLE 3 EXERCISES

1. The Poems of Longfellow
2. The Poems of Great American Poets
3. The Crucible, by Arthur Miller
4. Best Plays of the American Theater, 1982. (Consider that all are by American playwrights.)
5. Charlotte's Web, by E. B. White
6. The Short Stories of Edgar Allen Poe
7. Great American Short Stories
8. An Encyclopedia of American Drama
9. A History of American Humor
10. A Critical Companion to Edgar Allen Poe
11. A Critical Companion to American Novelists
12. Great German Speeches of the Later Nineteenth Century
13. The Complete Plays of William Shakespeare
14. The History of Portuguese Letters
15. A Collection of 18th Century Chinese Poetry

APPENDIX E. Sample Module for Teaching DDC

Module 3:
Dewey Decimal Classification

Required readings:

Langridge, *Classification*, pp. ix-23, 26-38
Hunter, *Classification Made Simple*, pp. 34-59
Taylor, *Wynar's Intro. to Cat. and Class.*, chapter 9, "Classification of Library
Materials"; and chapter 12 [sections entitled "Introduction" (p. 324) and "Cutter numbers
devised by Charles A. Cutter" (p. 324-326)].
Taylor, *Intro. to Cat. and Class.*, 10th ed. mss., chapter 15, "Decimal Classification"
Chan & Mitchell, *Dewey Decimal Classification: Principles and Applications*, chapters
2-3, 5
Saye, *Manheimer's Cataloging...*, chapter 6 (especially exercises with answers)
Dewey 22, v. 1, pp. xxxi-lvi

Recommended readings:

Scott, *Dewey Decimal Classification, 22nd Edition: A Study Manual and Number
Building Guide*
Foskett, *The Subject Approach to Information*, chapter 17
Taylor, *The Organization of Information*, chapter 11
Thomas, "Implementing DDC20"
Olson, *Subject Analysis in Online Catalogs*, pp. 209-238
Comaromi, *Book Numbers* (skim)
Marcella and Newton, *A New Manual of Classification*, chapter 1

Questions to ponder:

Why is the system called "decimal"?

What is the difference between Schedules and Tables?

What are the functions of Tables in DDC?

How are numbers built using auxiliary tables? adding from other parts of the schedules?

How are the Index and the Manual to be used in creating DDC notations?

APPENDIX E (continued)

Activities:

 Review PowerPoint presentation on DDC basics. [Remember to close separate window in which presentation opens in order to come back to this module.]

 Become familiar with the following classification tools:

Abridged Dewey Decimal Classification and Relative Index. 14th ed., edited by Joan S. Mitchell, et al. Dublin Ohio: OCLC, 2004.

BUBL Link Service. Available: http://www.bubl.ac.uk/

CyberDewey - DDC. Available: http://www.anthus.com/CyberDewey/CyberDewey.html

Dewey Decimal Classification and Relative Index. 22nd ed., edited by Joan S. Mitchell, Julianne Beall, Giles Martin, Winton E. Matthews, Jr., Gregory R. New. Dublin, Ohio: OCLC, 2003

WebDewey [requires authorization and password] Available: http://connexion.oclc.org

OCLC. *Dewey Services: Dewey Decimal Classification* [home page]. Available: http://www.oclc.org/dewey/

OCLC. *Dewey Services: Updates*. Available: http://www.oclc.org/dewey/updates/default.htm

Cutter, Charles Ammi. *C.A. Cutter's Three-Figure Author Table*. Swanson-Swift revision, 1969. Distributed by Libraries Unlimited, Littleton, Colo. **SIS REF: f Z698 .C94**

Cutter, Charles Ammi. *C.A. Cutter's Two-Figure Author Table*. Swanson-Swift revision, 1969. Distributed by Libraries Unlimited, Littleton, Colo. **SIS REF: f Z698 .C93 1969**

Cutter-Sanborn Three-Figure Author Table. Swanson-Swift revision, 1969. Distributed by Libraries Unlimited, Littleton, Colo. **SIS REF: f Z698 .C95 1969** Also Available: http://librarian.or.kr/reference/mark/cutter1.htm

Three sites that present the basics of DDC in "cute" and clever ways are:

Funkhouser, Ann, and Virginia Vesper. "Let's Do Dewey" http://www.mtsu.edu/~vvesper/dewey.html

Nettleton Intermediate Center (Jonesboro, AK). " 'Do We' Really Know Dewey? http://www.columbia.k12.mo.us/dre/dewey/

OCLC. "The Dewey Decimal Classification: A Multimedia Tour" http://www.oclc.org/dewey/about/ddctour/index.htm

Study handout on basics of the Dewey Decimal system and handout on Synthesis of Notation in DDC.

Study number-building flowchart (created by Hur-Li Lee)

Learn how Dewey 22 differs from earlier editions: "Dewey 22 offers many updates to Dewey users worldwide" by Joan S. Mitchell, Editor-in-Chief, Dewey Decimal Classification
http://www5.oclc.org/downloads/design/e-newsletter/n261/ddc22.htm

Learn how to use *WebDewey* by taking the tutorial: *Using WebDewey: An OCLC Tutorial*. You may go through the whole tutorial at once, or you may do it in sections by use of the tutorial's main menu. http://www.oclc.org/dewey/versions/webdewey/

Practice applying DDC using exercises from the following:

    Ferguson, *Subject Analysis*, pp. 59-78. (Dewey 21)

    Saye, *Manheimer's Cataloging and Classification*, pp. 177-188. (Dewey 21)

    Mortimer, *Learn Dewey Decimal Classification (Edition 21)*.

Practice creating Cutter numbers that can be used to make complete call numbers using the following exercises:

    Ferguson, *Subject Analysis*, pp. 79-82.

Complete the DDC half of the Classification Assignment, assigning DDC call numbers to the class information packages.

Classifying the Popular Music
of Trinidad and Tobago

Lorraine M. Nero

SUMMARY. The classification of Caribbean popular music poses problems to cataloguers. The paper discusses the problems which have been encountered by cataloguers in Trinidad and Tobago using Dewey Decimal Classification (DDC) and Library of Congress Classification (LCC). Some of the creative solutions adopted to circumvent these issues are discussed. Further, the paper offers recommendations on how

Lorraine M. Nero, MLS, BA, is Cataloguer, The University of the West Indies, St. Augustine Campus, Trinidad and Tobago (E-mail: lnero@library.uwi.tt).

DDC, Dewey, Dewey Decimal Classification, OCLC, WebDewey, and WorldCat are registered trademarks/service marks of OCLC Online Computer Library Center, Inc. The Dewey Decimal Classification system is Copyright 2003-2006 OCLC Online Computer Library Center, Inc. Used with permission.

[Haworth co-indexing entry note]: "Classifying the Popular Music of Trinidad and Tobago." Nero, Lorraine M. Co-published simultaneously in *Cataloging & Classification Quarterly* (The Haworth Information Press, an imprint of The Haworth Press, Inc.) Vol. 42, No. 3/4, 2006, pp. 119-133; and: *Moving Beyond the Presentation Layer: Content and Context in the Dewey Decimal Classification (DDC) System* (ed: Joan S. Mitchell, and Diane Vizine-Goetz) The Haworth Information Press, an imprint of The Haworth Press, Inc., 2006, pp. 119-133. Single or multiple copies of this article are available for a fee from The Haworth Document Delivery Service [1-800-HAWORTH, 9:00 a.m. - 5:00 p.m. (EST). E-mail address: docdelivery@haworthpress.com].

the relevant sections of the classification schemes can be amended to provide for Trinidad and Tobago as well as Caribbean popular music. doi:10.1300/J104v42n03_04 *[Article copies available for a fee from The Haworth Document Delivery Service: 1-800-HAWORTH. E-mail address: <docdelivery@haworthpress.com> Website: <http://www.HaworthPress.com> © 2006 by The Haworth Press, Inc. All rights reserved.]*

KEYWORDS. DDC, Dewey Decimal Classification, music, Trinidad and Tobago, Calypso, chutney music, soca, parang, popular music, Library of Congress Classification

INTRODUCTION

The organization of music in classification schemes has been a problematic area for cataloguers. Among the issues discussed by writers on the subject is the inability of various schemes to capture all types of music.[1] This discourse will continue since the time frame for the review and publication of classification standards cannot match the rapidity with which music is created. Nonetheless, attempts must be made to broaden the scope of current classification tools to facilitate world music. Trinidad and Tobago is an excellent case to consider, since it has several indigenous music traditions including calypso, soca, chutney, parang and their various hybrid forms. This paper focuses on the two main standards used by libraries in Trinidad and Tobago, Dewey Decimal Classification (DDC) and Library of Congress Classification (LCC). It examines the solutions adopted by these libraries and provides practical examples on how to accommodate world music in these schemes.

THE MUSIC OF TRINIDAD AND TOBAGO

Trinidad and Tobago[2] has a multiplicity of ethnic groups which have produced their own music traditions. According to the *Annual Statistical Digest* of Trinidad and Tobago, the racial distribution is as follows:[3]

East Indians	40.3%
Afro Trinidadian	39.9 %
Mixed	18.4%
Chinese and other	1.2%
White	0.6%

These groups interact with each other, consequently, the music has also begun a hybridization process. Table 1 shows the major music types

TABLE 1. Music in Trinidad and Tobago

Group	Traditional	Contemporary	Hybrids
Spanish	Parang		Parang soca
French	Creche	Zouk*	
Africans	Folk songs	Calypso	Soca
		Reggae*	Ragga Soca
East Indians	Tan singing*	Chutney	Chutney soca
Other		Rap	Rapso

*This music type did not originate in Trinidad and Tobago.

in the country, covering traditional to contemporary genres and presents some of the hybrid forms.

Calypso is the musical genre that is most recognized internationally as being the music of Trinidad and Tobago. The growth and popularity of the music are attributed to the fact that it was the medium of expression used by the masses to air views on social and political issues as well as to honor and celebrate many aspects of human achievements. Calypso is the music that is performed in the annual carnival celebrations held in the Caribbean and the festive offsprings in other countries such as Canada and United States. As a result, every year many new calypsos are produced to satisfy this market. Versions of calypsos have been popularized by singers such as The Andrews Sisters, who produced a cover version of "Rum and Coca Cola" that became a number one hit in 1945; Harry Belafonte's recordings in the 1950s; and more recently the Bahia Men's cover version of "Who let the dogs out." There is no estimate of the number of calypsos that have been written and recorded. The collection at the National Library of Trinidad and Tobago is in no way indicative of the total figure. Initiatives are on the way to acquire as complete a collection as possible.

Chutney is a new musical genre which is "emerging as a distinctive adaptation of Indo Caribbean folk traditions into public and pop culture."[4] The genre merges East Indian traditional music with Caribbean influences. Although East Indian music was part of the Trinidadian musical landscape since the inception of Indian immigration in the 19th century, it remained in the bosom of the East Indian community. Chutney music has gained in popularity and transcended these boundaries, primarily because the rhythms are quicker to match the up tempo beats of other popular dance music. The lyrics inculcate both Hindi and English languages.

The Hispanic music of Trinidad and Tobago is called parang. It is unclear whether the music came with the Spaniards during their occupation of Trinidad or with the migration of immigrants from the mainland Venezuela. Parang music is associated with the Christmas celebrations and like chutney, the songs are now sung in English. This has facilitated appreciation by all groups and has laid the foundation for further hybridization.

In the latter half of the 20th century, the musical scene in Trinidad and Tobago exploded with the experimentation of new music through the mixing of different sounds from the various ethnic groups. In a community where the modern day Trinidadian required a more upbeat form of music, new forms emerged. The first of these is Soca, a term which combines the So from soul and the Ca from calypso. Created by the deceased Garfield Blackman (Ras Shorty I), this form is said to combine the rhythms of the African and Indian descendents. The second generation of these hybrid forms includes chutney soca and parang soca. As the 20th century came to a close, other experimentations resulted in the mixing of some international musical forms with Trinidadian music to produce new genres, e.g., ragga soca, rapso. See the hybrid results in Table 1.

The history of the evolution of music in Trinidad and Tobago shows the dynamism of the cultural environment; hence, classification schemes need to be equally dynamic to assist in adequately classifying the resources.

MUSIC IN DDC

The public library network of Trinidad and Tobago is part of the National Library and Information System Authority (NALIS). This public library component of NALIS uses DDC to classify its resources. The branch libraries possess small collections of music and music literature; however, the Heritage Library which functions as the National Library of Trinidad and Tobago has a growing audio visual collection.

The Technical Services Division of the network is a centralized unit responsible for acquiring, cataloguing, and processing all items for the branch libraries. The cataloguers in this division perform a large amount of original cataloguing and contribute records to the OCLC online bibliographic services. Some of these catalogue records are for the musical albums produced in Trinidad and Tobago. This unit dictates the cataloguing policies for all the public libraries; thus, any changes adopted will have a wide reaching effect in the country.

DDC makes provision for the classification of music in the 780s. 'Renowned' western music traditions like jazz are extensively covered in DDC. However, 'new' music and other musical experimentations are difficult to accommodate within the DDC scheme. For example, in spite of calypsos' long history, consistent production and popularity, the music does not have its own notation in DDC. Under DDC contemporary western music traditions are classified as follows:[5]

Example 1	781.63	Popular music
	781.64	Western popular music
	.642	Country music
	.643	Blues
	.644	Soul
	.645	Ragtime
	.646	Reggae
	.649	Rap
	.65	Jazz

(.647 & .648 are currently unused)

In this scheme, numbers are provided primarily for the music that comes from the North American tradition with the exception of reggae which originates from Jamaica.

Calypso is indexed at 781.64 in the DDC. This number also hosts other forms of western popular music without a specific number, e.g., funk music, disco. The published index does not provide individual notations for chutney, soca and contemporary parang; however, some of the music expressions have been mapped from DDC to Library of Congress Subject Headings by OCLC. These include Ragga 781.646, Soca 781.646, and chutney music 782.42164155409729. The number 781.646 places raga and soca with reggae, but the differences in form warrants that each genre be given a separate number.

Local libraries tend to classify these forms at 781.64 in the absence of a specific number and also because the genres are considered western popular music. The notation 781.64 is therefore assigned to a wide cross section of music types. Caribbean libraries have found that this number is inadequate. A look at several Caribbean catalogues has shown that some attempts are being made to offer some specificity. Table 2 includes some of the numbers libraries are currently using for these music

TABLE 2. Class Numbers Used for Music of Trinidad and Tobago

Music Genre	DDC Class number
Calypso	781.640972983
	782.42164
	781.64
Chutney music	780.899140729
	781.6409
	782.42164
	781.64
Chutney soca	781.640972983
	781.64
Soca	781.64
	781.640972983
Soca parang	781.723
	781.64

traditions. In the examples given, the number that is common to all is 781.64.

The cataloguers at the National Library of Trinidad and Tobago have sought to create a solution by adding the geographic country notation to the 781.64 stem. All music of Trinidad and Tobago would therefore be classed at 781.640972983, where 72983 is the country notation. The music of another Caribbean island like Barbados is classified at 781.640972981. This adds some specificity to the number and allows the national library to differentiate the music by each Caribbean territory; however, it does not separate the diverse traditions of music that are available within a country. This has made it difficult to assess collections and for users to browse and locate items.

This problem is not unique to Trinidad and Tobago. Sweeney, in his assessment of DDC, noted the "need to re-examine the treatment of music in non-European traditions."[6] DDC did undergo a radical change with the 20th edition. These changes and implications are documented and discussed by Forrest and Smiraglia[7] as well as Thomas.[8] According to the preface of the 20th edition, the aim of Dewey is "to be accommodating to other cultures." This process was started in the 20th edition, but did not progress much further in the 21st edition since new notations were only added for ragtime, reggae, and rap. The 22nd edition has not added any new traditions.

McKnight notes that one particular problem with DDC is that it has failed "to keep abreast of new developments . . . not sufficiently covering music of non-western cultures or western idioms."[9] This statement aptly describes the problem that continues to plague the classification of the music of Trinidad and Tobago.

Proposal I

Within the DDC scheme, there are options which can be expanded to include Trinidadian music as well as other world music. The ideal solution would be to assign one of the unused numbers in DDC to the more established tradition, calypso. Taking the first unused number as an example, notations can be further developed for hybrids of calypso as follows:

Example 2	781.647	Calypso
	.6472	Soca
	.6473	Ragga Soca
	.6474	Rapso
	.6475	Chutney Soca
	.6476	Parang Soca

This recommendation ensures that the tradition of calypso is separated from the generic number 781.64 and provides room for growth with the hybrid forms. In this example, the hybrid forms of chutney soca and parang soca are accommodated, but the weakness is that the root traditions of chutney and parang would be without a place in the scheme. To complement this recommendation, one would also suggest that the other unused number 781.648 be assigned to the iteration of all other western music traditions, e.g., funk. Thus, chutney can be assigned to 781.6485 and parang 781.6486. The ending digits 5 and 6 were chosen to be consistent with the numbers used for the hybrid forms of chutney soca and parang soca in Example 2.

Proposal II

DDC also provides an option for classifying the traditions of music at 781-788. The scope note states that "781-788 may be used for only one tradition of music; in that case, class all other traditions in 789." This option is feasible for special libraries that may want to emphasize one tradition. By using the example of calypso, the classification scheme may then be arranged and adapted as follows:

Example 3   781.64   Calypso music
           .642   Hybrids of Calypso & Country Music
           .643   unassigned
           .644   Soca (SOul & CAlypso)
           .645   unassigned
           .646   Hybrids of Calypso & Reggae (ragga soca)
           .647   Chutney soca
           .648   Parang soca
           .649   Rapso
           .65   Calypso & jazz

The proposed scheme listed in Example 3 is constructed following the precedence established by the original numbers taken from the DDC schedule in Example 1. In the DDC scheme, 781.642 represents country and western music; in this adaptation the number is used for hybrids of calypso and country and western music. In the cases where the hybrids for a particular form are not yet available, the space has been left unused. The number 781.645 is not assigned because there is no known hybrid of calypso and ragtime music. The original scheme has left two unused numbers; these two numbers can then be assigned to the hybrids of calypso with other local music, e.g., 781.647 for chutney soca and 781.648 for parang soca.

The advantage of this option is that it caters to any projected development in calypso music as it combines with other genres. Yet, in its present state, this scheme is still limited since it can only facilitate the classification of one tradition. Space has only been provided for the hybrids of calypso with other local music but not for chutney and parang.

The DDC scope note to accompany the option described in this proposal also indicates that all other traditions are to be classed under the 789 notation. The 789 scheme in DDC 22 is as follows:

Example 4   789.4   Western popular music
          .42   Country music
          .43   Blues
          .44   Soul
          .45   Ragtime
          .46   Reggae
          .5   Jazz
       (789.47 & 789.48 unassigned)

The unused numbers 789.47 and 789.48 can then be assigned locally to chutney and parang respectively. The success of the implementation of these recommendations is also dependant on the unassigned numbers in DDC remaining free.

Proposal III

The main recommendation for proposal III involves using one of the unassigned numbers and developing faceted notations for all un-iterated western music traditions. This recommendation differs from proposal I because it is not dependant on calypso being assigned its own number in the scheme. Here the main number 781.647 remains unassigned to a specific genre and the first digit after this stem represents one tradition, thus calypso is 781.6471 and chutney 781.6472. New notations can be added under each number as hybrid forms evolve.

Example 5	781.647	unassigned
	.6471	Calypso
	.64712	Soca
	.64713	Ragga soca
	.64714	Rapso
	781.6472	Chutney
	.64721	Chutney soca
	781.6473	Parang
	.64731	Parang soca

The numbers available from the span 781.6474-781.6478 can be used to classify other world music. The number 781.648 remains unassigned and available for future development. The option to add country numbers to these stems should also be available. This adds further depth to the specificity of the numbers. These adaptations of the DDC can eliminate some of the problems, but it should be noted that in a bibliographic record sharing environment these numbers would not be understood by all participants. Cataloguers will also have to reclassify items from shared services to fit into the adaptations.

MUSIC IN LCC

The Library of Congress Classification scheme (LCC) is used primarily by the libraries of two institutions which are at the forefront of tertiary education in Trinidad and Tobago, the College of Science, Technology and Applied Arts of Trinidad and Tobago (COSTAATT) and the St. Augustine campus of The University of the West Indies (UWI). COSTAATT is a collegial network established in 2000 through the amalgamation of several government-assisted tertiary institutions. The COSTAATT libraries focus on providing information relevant to the diploma and associate degrees being taught. Consequently, the music collection at COSTAATT is now in developmental stages.

The nature of the UWI is different because it is part of a wider Caribbean network of campuses. The main campuses are in Jamaica, Trinidad and Tobago and Barbados. Smaller centres are present in other Caribbean territories; thus, the focus of the collection development has to be regional. The programmes lead to the award of first and graduate degrees. The current humanities curriculum has been expanded to include degrees in cultural studies as well as certificate programmes in steelpan and carnival arts. The libraries have to fulfill the mandate to support teaching by collecting popular culture resources inclusive of musical material. Prior to the existence of a national library, the main library of the UWI also functioned as one of the principal collectors of the heritage of Trinidad and Tobago. This ensured the start of a music collection. The music collection is not limited to items from Trinidad and Tobago, but also includes selections from various Caribbean islands and as the collection grows, the cataloguers have had to find solutions to organize the material within LCC.

LCC is first and foremost created to serve the needs of the United States national community. New numbers are added to the scheme based on the holdings of the Library of Congress and recommendations from institutions participating in the SACO programmes. Class M is used to sort music into recorded music, music literature, and music study. As with DDC, music cataloguers have debated the strengths and weaknesses of LCC and have found the functional separation of music from music literature to be an advantage.[10] Also, the comprehensive treatment of subject matter by country has been lauded. This preference for citation according to country is not always expedient for the organization of the collection. The problem which the cataloguers have found with LCC is not with the coverage by country but in the genres listed under popular music and the limitations of M1681.

LCC has offered several numbers to classify the music of Trinidad and Tobago, but the problem is that these numbers are too general. More specificity is needed. Some of the options available are:

Example 6

<u>Section M Music</u>[11]
M1681.T7   Secular vocal music

<u>Section ML Literature on music</u>
ML207.T7   History and criticism
ML1038.S74   Steel drum

ML1414   Vocal music
ML1714   Secular vocal music
ML2614   Secular vocal music, songs
ML2814   Solo songs
ML3414   Dance music
ML3486.T7   Popular music
ML3565   National music of the Caribbean (not country specific)

<u>Instruction</u>
MT725.S7   Steel drum

The number M1681.T7 is set aside for recorded vocal music of Trinidad and Tobago. Like the DDC number 781.64, this LCC number is used as the generic number for all types of secular music. The cataloguers at the main library of the UWI, St. Augustine Campus have implemented a dual classification system to put further order to the items classified at this number. This dual system includes an LCC number with a triple cutter and an in-house index number.

For example, there are several albums by the soca artiste Austin Lyons whose sobriquet is Superblue. Two of these are "Joy" and "Matrix" These albums were assigned LC numbers as follows:

M1681.T7 S8 J6   Joy
M1681.T7 S8 M2   Matrix

In M1681.T7 S8 J6, the first cutter represents the country, the second is derived from the album's main entry (in this case Superblue) and the third is the title of the album. The pattern was derived from the principle used to classify literature in the PR schedule where a cutter for the author and title of work is used. This classification policy allows all albums by a particular artiste to be held together on the shelves.

The third alphanumeric cutter, e.g., J6, was adopted to avoid the clumsiness which was occurring as a result of using only two cutters and extending the second cutter. One such case is that of Slinger Francisco (Sparrow), a calypsonian, who has no less than thirty albums in the collection. Some of these albums have been published in the same year and the initial title words are often similar. Table 3 has a sample of Sparrow's album titles.

It was found that creating unique class numbers for the growing body of his work using the year of publication and extending the second cutter proved to be unwieldy. In addition, the cataloguers had to consider albums from other artistes that were being given cutters within the same area as Sparrow's work. Although the second and third cutters are being used, calypso, soca, chutney and other music styles are still interfiled. The in-house classification scheme was introduced to provide genre separations.

The in-house scheme was created to serve two purposes: to facilitate keyword searching and to organize the collection according to genre. This scheme is used only on the recorded music items. At the time of the development of the scheme, the terms chutney, soca and rapso were not available in the Library of Congress Subject Headings and the department needed to generate numerical lists by genre. Thus, it was necessary for the scheme to serve these two purposes. The number from this scheme consists of the genre, an incremental number and the artiste's name, e.g., Soca : 40 . Superblue. These measures in time will produce other challenges as the collection grows. The solution will be to address the changes within the current LCC scheme.

The two schemes work in tandem with each other. The recorded music collection is housed separately according to the in-house scheme. These in-house numbers are not displayed in the OPAC. The LCC num-

TABLE 3. Sample of Sparrow's Albums

Album Title	Year Produced
Casanova	2000
Cokie eye rooster	1999
Comi-kal cat fight	2000
Corruption	2000

bers provide one point of access for the users who liaise with library staff to use the material. Discussions are continuously taking place in the organization about the merits and demerits of each scheme. The librarians recognize that one of the best ways to address this is to influence the future developments of LCC.

Proposal

The popular music category in ML3505.8-3541 provides a list of types and styles. Among those covered are reggae, jazz, disco and funk. The list is more comprehensive than DDC; however, none of the styles associated with Trinidad and Tobago are included. In the current class M, considerations could be given to adding calypso, chutney, soca, and parang to the list and assigning numbers as follows:

Example 7

ML3522	Calypso
ML3522.8	Chutney
ML3529.7	Parang
ML3536.8	Soca

Another M table could also be created for use under all types and styles listed in the span of numbers ML3505.8-3541. The table is constructed using the pattern established for jazz found in Example 8.

Example 8

Jazz

ML3505.8	Periodicals
ML3505.9	Congresses
ML3506	General works
ML3507	Addresses, essays, lectures

By region or country

ML3508-3508.8	United States (Subarranged by Table M9)
ML3509.A-Z	Other regions or Countries A-Z

The new table which for convenience is called M11 would therefore use the categories in Example 9.

Example 9

x	Periodicals
x.1	Congresses
x.2	General works
x.3	Addresses, essays, lectures

By region or country

x.4	United States (Subarranged by Table M1)*
x.5A-Z	Other regions or Countries A-Z

*Table M1 is currently in the LCC scheme and offers a list of the states and regions of United States

Therefore using the numbers listed in Example 7, a conference on calypso would be at ML3522.1 and calypso in Trinidad and Tobago would be classed at ML3522.5 T7. This proposal would enhance the collation of music literature not only for Trinidad and Tobago but for all genres.

It is noted that in the section M for recorded music, the following pattern has been established for many countries:

General
    Popular music
    Collections
    Separate works

This pattern should also be incorporated into the M1681 numbers which are used for Caribbean music. The introduction of this pattern will offer more specificity within the area, though not as precise as the triple cutter system.

CONCLUSION

In Trinidad and Tobago, the libraries that have adopted DDC and LCC as the schemes of choice have had problems in classifying the local music. One purports that this is not a deficiency of the cataloguers, but is a result of the inability of the schemes to clearly identify spaces and a number for new forms of music. Yet within the current order of the schedules it is possible to create spaces for local music. The paper has presented models whereby other countries that face the problem of accommodating indigenous music can begin the exploration process of incorporating new genres into the classification schemes.

REFERENCES

1. Many of the arguments are covered by the writers in *In Celebration of Revised 780*. 1990. Canton, MA.: Music Library Association.

2. The creation and evolution of the steelpan (musical instrument) is an integral part of the music history of Trinidad and Tobago. Although the paper does not focus on the classification of this instrument, the music generated by experimentation with this instrument is also difficult to place in conventional musical genres.

3. The figures were calculated from the statistics available in: Trinidad and Tobago Central Statistical Office. 2003. *Annual Statistical Digest.* Port of Spain: CSO.

4. Manuel, Peter. 2000. *East Indian music in the West Indies.* Philadelphia: Temple University Press. p. 11.

5. Dewey, Melvil. 1996. *Dewey decimal classification and relative index.* 21st ed. Albany, NY: Forest Press.

6. Sweeney, Russell. 1990. Grand Messe des 780's: With apologies to Berlioz. In *In Celebration of Revised 780: Music in the Dewey Decimal Classification, Edition 20*, ed. Richard Wursten. Canton, MA: Music Library Association, 1990. p. 28-38.

7. Forrest, Charles and Richard P. Smiraglia. 1990. Radical change with minimal disruption: the effect of revised 780 music on the University of Illinois library shelf arrangement. In *In Celebration of Revised 780.* Canton, MA: Music Library Association.

8. Thomas, Pat. 1990. A music muddle? DDC 20 in the public library. In *In Celebration Revised 780.* Canton, MA: Music Library Association.

9. McKinght, Mark. 2002. *Music classification systems.* Canton, MA: Music Library Association, p. 13.

10. Bradley, Carol. 2003. Classifying and cataloguing music in American Libraries: a historical overview. *Cataloging & Classification Quarterly* 35 (3/4): 467-481.

11. Library of Congress. 2005. Classweb [online]. http://www.classificationweb.net.

BIBLIOGRAPHY

Myers, Helen. 1998. *Music of Hindi Trinidad.* Chicago: University of Chicago.

Redfern, Brian. 1978. *Organising music in libraries. Vol 1. Arrangement and Classification.* London: Clive Bingley.

Rohlehr, Gordon. 1990. *Calypso & society in pre-independence Trinidad.* Trinidad and Tobago: Gordon Rohlehr.

Smiraglia, Richard P. 1989. *Music cataloguing: the bibliographic control of printed and recorded music in libraries.* Englewood, Colorado: Libraries Unlimited.

Taylor, Daphne Pawan. 1977. *Parang of Trinidad.* Trinidad and Tobago: National Cultural Council.

Williams, Eric. 1970. *From Columbus to Castro: the history of the Caribbean 1492-1969.* London: Andre Deutsch.

Williams, Eric. 1944. *History of the people of Trinidad and Tobago.* London: Andre Deutsch.

doi:10.1300/J104v42n03_04

Dewey Decimal Classification (DDC)
at the Swiss National Library

Patrice Landry

SUMMARY. The Swiss National Library adopted the DDC as its classification scheme for its open access stacks collections and the structure of its national bibliography, Das Schweizer Buch, in 1999. The paper explains why the library decided to adopt the DDC and how the decision was made. The factors leading to the decision are explained, namely the use of the DDC in Europe and the decision taken by libraries in Germany to translate and adapt DDC 22 in German. The article also describes the implementation process of the DDC and the results so far attained at the Swiss National Library. doi:10.1300/J104v42n03_05 *[Article copies available for a fee from The Haworth Document Delivery Service: 1-800-HAWORTH. E-mail address: <docdelivery@haworthpress.com> Website: <http://www.HaworthPress.com> © 2006 by The Haworth Press, Inc. All rights reserved.]*

KEYWORDS. DDC, Dewey Decimal Classification, Swiss National Library, classification schemes, DDC Deutsch 22

Patrice Landry, MA, MLS, is Head of Subject Indexing, Swiss National Library, Hallwylstrasse 15, 3003 Bern, Switzerland (E-mail: patrice.landry@slb.admin.ch).

[Haworth co-indexing entry note]: "Dewey Decimal Classification (DDC) at the Swiss National Library." Landry, Patrice. Co-published simultaneously in *Cataloging & Classification Quarterly* (The Haworth Information Press, an imprint of The Haworth Press, Inc.) Vol. 42, No. 3/4, 2006, pp. 135-145; and: *Moving Beyond the Presentation Layer: Content and Context in the Dewey Decimal Classification (DDC) System* (ed: Joan S. Mitchell, and Diane Vizine-Goetz) The Haworth Information Press, an imprint of The Haworth Press, Inc., 2006, pp. 135-145. Single or multiple copies of this article are available for a fee from The Haworth Document Delivery Service [1-800-HAWORTH, 9:00 a.m. - 5:00 p.m. (EST). E-mail address: docdelivery@haworthpress.com].

INTRODUCTION

This paper describes how and why over a period of a hundred years the Dewey Decimal Classification (DDC) was first used as the basis for the library's initial subject catalogue, then replaced by the Universal Decimal Classification (UDC) and reintroduced as a classification and shelving scheme in the late 1990s. Many librarians working in libraries with a long tradition of using a standard classification scheme such as the DDC or the Library of Congress Classification (LCC) may consider this an odd undertaking by a national library. One may wonder, rightly so, why a national institution would still be looking for a standard classification tool so late in the 20th century.

The answer to this question can be found in the heterogeneous development of various classification schemes in Europe during the 20th century. Libraries in most European countries used a variety of classification schemes, among which the Universal Decimal Classification (UDC) played a prominent role. But throughout the century, the development of the UDC as well as other schemes suffered from a lack of sustained and coordinated cooperation across Europe. Linguistic and cultural differences as well as the lack of a strong organisation that might have supported a classification scheme across Europe were partly responsible for this situation.

In the 1990s, the Swiss National Library[1] (SNL) undertook a major reorganisation of its operations and structures in order to improve its delivery of goods and services. Some of these changes involved the improvement of bibliographic access to its collections. Many of the bibliographic practices of the library had not kept up with current international standards and thus needed to be reviewed. This evaluation led to many changes such as the introduction of USMARC (now MARC21) in 1993 as the communication format for its library automation system. It also resulted in the replacement of the indexing system based on the UDC by the Schlagwortnormdatei (SWD) and the Regeln für den Schlagwortkatalog (RSWK) in 1998[2] and more recently in the introduction of the Anglo-American Cataloguing Rules (AACR2) for descriptive cataloguing.

The final stage of the reorganisation process of the library was the physical renovation of the library building. Started in 1999 and completed in 2001, this renovation of the building made it possible to expand and create new public access collections. In order to prepare for these new services, the tasks of collection development and access policies were undertaken as early as 1997. A study was conducted in 1998 to select a classification system that would allow the library to organise and arrange documents in the following public access collections:

- Forschungsbibliothek Schweiz (FBCH): a collection of about 20,000 documents that emphasize major aspects of Swiss culture, politics, history, environmental and technical developments
- Reference collection (Lesesaal): a collection of 10,000 reference documents
- Schweizerisches Literaturarchiv monographs collection: approximately 10,000 literary works by Swiss authors and secondary literature.

The ideal classification scheme that was sought should not only permit the physical arrangement of documents on shelves by call numbers but should also provide a systematic access to these documents by a subject field (classification) in the library's online system. Furthermore, the chosen classification scheme should permit the systematic organisation of the national bibliography, Das Schweizer Buch, according to IFLA and UNESCO recommendations. Changes to the National Bibliography had been planned for its 100th anniversary in 2001 and it seemed logical and more efficient to select a classification scheme that would answer all these specific needs.

THE SELECTION PROCESS

The search for a classification scheme was conducted using criteria that would ensure that the chosen scheme would meet the current as well as the long-term needs of the library. The guiding principle of the study was to find a classification scheme that could be used for a variety of bibliographic and physical access tasks. These requirements, though fairly extensive, are probably similar to those of other national libraries and national bibliographic agencies. Because of its commitment to ensure bibliographic control and access through standard bibliographic tools, the library did not seek to develop its own classification nor choose a local or regional system. To meet this goal, the selection process was undertaken using the following criteria:

- Standards: The classification scheme should be a recognised system, either national or international, that follows established classification theory and principles. Basically, the scheme should contain concepts that are described topic by topic and arranged in a classified or logical order. The standard should be maintained by an organisation that would revise and publish on a regular basis changes in the organisation of disciplines.

- Scope: The classification must be comprehensive in scope as well as flexible and expansive (notion of hospitality).
- Use: The classification scheme should be used widely in Europe and North America and its data available in bibliographic records though major bibliographic agencies. The use of classification schemes in Switzerland following these criteria should also be considered.
- Language: Ideally, the scheme should be published in German, as most indexers/classifiers at the Swiss National Library are German speaking. If not in German, it should at least be published in English or in French.

DECISION

For most libraries, the selection of a classification scheme would be a fairly easy process. For North American libraries and English speaking countries, the choice is between the Library of Congress Classification (LCC) and the Dewey Decimal Classification (DDC). In Switzerland, there are four national languages, three of which are widely used, namely German, French and Italian. The Swiss National Library had to take in account this multilingual reality and the use of various language based standards. The goal was finding a scheme that would reflect the needs of these three languages as well as English.

A starting point for our evaluation was to look at the use of classification schemes by other national libraries, in particular European national libraries. Two reasons motivated this process: the use of a classification scheme in a national library usually has an impact on the use of that scheme in other libraries in that country. This increases the quantity of bibliographic records with the specific notations. Secondly, the Swiss National Library preferred to use a classification scheme that is common to many European libraries in order to foster cooperation. The publication, *An Annotated Guide to Current National Bibliographies* by Barbara Bell,[3] was a first step in getting an overview of the use of classification schemes in national libraries. Dewey Decimal Classification was one of the most widely used schemes. In Europe, it is used by Italy, the United Kingdom, and Norway. Since 1998, it is the classification standard for the Bibliothèque nationale de France.

Another important source for our considerations was the work of the "Expertengruppe Klassifikation" of the Deutsches Bibliotheksinstitut. The mandate of this group was to propose one or several classification schemes that could be used in Germany. The group also looked at how the schemes could be used in the OPACs of individual libraries and networks. Lastly, the group was asked to propose ways to establish concordances between various classification schemes. In the report *Klassifikationen für wissenschaftliche Bibliotheken*,[4] the Expertengruppe recommended that the Dewey Decimal Classification be used by the Die Deutsche Bibliothek for its national bibliography and that the Regensburger Verbundklassifikation (RVK) and Basisklassifikation (BK) be retained as the classification scheme for the library networks currently using these schemes. The report recommended that concordances be established between these and the Dewey Decimal Classification (DDC). Published in 1998, the report was a timely source for our evaluation. It provided us with a clear view of the classification situation in Germany and the commitment by the DDB to proceed in implementing a German version of the DDC.

Also in 1998, the French edition of DDC 21[5] was published. The translation and publication of the DDC 21 undertaken by three national libraries, namely the Bibliothèque nationale du Canada, the Bibliothèque nationale de France, and the Bibliothèque nationale du Québec, was the first full French Dewey edition since the 18th edition published in Québec in 1974. This marked an important step in the collaboration between three francophone national libraries and more importantly, the commitment of the Bibliothèque nationale de France to adopt and to promote the Dewey Decimal Classification in France.[6]

As we proceeded to evaluate the various classification schemes and their applications, it became obvious that the Dewey Decimal Classification represented the most used and prominent classification scheme at the present time. Used in 138 countries by over 200,000 libraries (and 62 national bibliographies) and translated in more than 30 languages, it is the most widely used classification scheme in the world. The fact that the DDC is supported by OCLC and that development and revisions of the schedules are maintained by the Decimal Classification Division of the Library of Congress was for us an important aspect of stability.

We concluded that the Dewey Decimal Classification was a very reliable classification system that met our requirements (standard, scope, use and language criteria). It could be used for our national bibliography, for stacks arrangement, and for an improved online access. It was well maintained and, in the last few years, has been translated in many languages. We were particularly impressed by the fact that Italy and France were using the DDC 21 in their own language and that Germany had undertaken the commitment to publish a German edition. We thought the DDC was now a classification scheme that could be used and developed for European collections.

One practical question still remained without a clear answer: could the DDC be applied easily at the SNL? Our internal tests had shown that generally the DDC could be used without too many difficulties and there was no need to create too many local modifications. There was still the concern that the so-called American bias of the DDC, notably in its terminology and structure, would be a constraint. In tests conducted, certain terms and instructions were misunderstood and the guiding principle of classifying by discipline was sometimes difficult to follow. Nevertheless, the overall value of the DDC and its potential outweighed these concerns.

Our decision proved to be an interesting twist in the library's use of classification schemes. In fact, it marked the return of the DDC at the library. When the Swiss National Library was created in 1895, one of the goals of the first director, Jean Bernoulli was to "[create both an alphabetical and subject catalogue that would be based according to the American method]."[7] By this, he was referring to the cataloguing and classification practices used in American libraries. The wide acceptance of the DDC in American libraries[8] had been noticed by Bernoulli and it was through his initiative that the Decimal Classification and relative index (5th edition) was purchased by the library. In 1899, immediately after having received a copy of this index, the task of creating a classified catalogue was undertaken, initially using the DDC notations and gradually integrating the UDC notations as they became available through the work of the Institut international de bibliographie in Brussels (IIB). By 1906, when the Swiss National Library published a systematic and alphabetical index to the subject catalogue *Systematische und alphabetische Übersicht zum Realkatalog der Schweizerischen Landesbibliothek*,[9] the DDC application at the library had followed the same path as the Italian one at that time by being more of the "Brussels brand."[10] By 1919, the library had adopted the UDC as the basis for the development of its subject catalogue.

IMPLEMENTATION

Eighty years later, the Dewey Decimal Classification returned to the Swiss National Library. The decision to adopt the DDC was officially taken in September 1999 and the SNL proceeded right away to implement this decision. The primary objective was to start work on classifying the documents for the open access collections in the early part of 2000. This allowed for about six months to organise the work procedures and training programme for the classification of the public access collections and the use of the DDC for the organisation of the national bibliography, Das Schweizer Buch.

The first question to resolve was to decide which Dewey language edition to use. Even though all of the members of the Subject Indexing Service are fluent in many languages (either French, English or Italian), the intricacies of the DDC were sometimes difficult to interpret correctly. Without a German DDC edition, it was decided to use the English and French DDC 21. Some solutions were nevertheless needed to assist the indexers to use the schedules correctly and apply the DDC in a coherent and consistent manner. Our solution was to set up an Access database as a working DDC database and online shelf list. An alphabetical index using SWD terms linked to a DDC number was also established. It also acted as an authority file, where the different steps in the number building of a DDC notation would be presented. This function had the advantage of controlling the number building process. The database was used for about two years until the data was loaded in the library online system, VIRTUA, when the library public access collections were opened to the public.

A training programme was thus established with the goal of achieving a fairly good knowledge and application of the DDC in six months. In the first three months, teams of 2 or 3 persons were set up in particular fields or disciplines (social sciences, sciences and technology, history, etc.) and, using a study manual and exercises, learned to apply the DDC. Weekly meetings were organised to analyse and solve problems. At the end of this first phase (3 months), a weeklong course on the DDC was given by a Dewey instructor from the National Library of Canada. A combination of theory and practical applications was given, often using as examples problems discussed in the first phase of the programme. This course resulted in achieving a better understanding of the application's rules and a means to measure the progress made in the previous months. The second phase that lasted three months consisted in applying the DDC to the collections under supervision and review. Contacts with the Canadian instructor were kept in order to resolve particular problems and help in setting up guidelines on how to use particular notations.

A further consideration concerned the work procedures, which involved the creation of class numbers and call numbers and the eventual loading of data in the library automation system according to MARC21. Our purpose in using the DDC was to offer not only notations that refer to the physical location of the items (call number) but also offer a bibliographic subject access (class notation) that consists of full Dewey notation. Instructions were written to specify that documents should be classified using the full potential of number building offered by the DDC. From that notation, the call number would be created using a maximum of 10 digits, roughly based on the DDC segmentation principles.

Special call numbers were designed for the monographic collection of the Schweizerisches Literararchiv (SLA) to allow for the works (various literary forms) by one author to be classed together. As the DDC organises literary works by form, the standard DDC call number had to be modified. The chosen approach taken was inspired by the method used by the Bibliothèque nationale de France for its organisation of literary works in its public access collections.[11]

The decision to modify the classification arrangement of the national bibliography, Das Schweizer Buch (SB), from 24 subject groups to using the proposed Dewey's Hundred Divisions meant that the overall redesign of the publication had to be accomplished in time for the 2001 edition. In 2000, this task was undertaken to prepare the display of the 100 categories in 5 languages (German, French, Italian, Rhaeto-Romanic, and English). Cataloguing work processes were modified so that descriptive cataloguers could assign these broad categories to the bibliographic records of the SB. Instructions were drawn up by the subject indexers to facilitate this work and tests were conducted in the later part of 2000 to validate the work procedures.

RESULTS

Having started in early 2000, the staff of the Subject Indexing Service had, by the end of 2004, classified approximately 27,000 documents including 4,500 bibliographies and reference works, 12,000 in the Forschungsbibliothek Schweiz (FBCH), and about 10,000 monographs in the collection of the literary archives. This classification work was accomplished mostly without additional resources as the DDC task was gradually integrated into the regular tasks of the staff of the Subject Indexing Service.

The practice of assigning Dewey numbers gradually improved as indexers became more familiar with the various DDC principles and rules. Many of the early difficulties lay in determining the discipline of a work. For many multi-subject documents, the challenge resided in applying in a constant and coherent manner the DDC rules to choose the appropriate subjects within a particular discipline. For example, documents in interdisciplinary domains such as ecology and environmental studies proved to be difficult to classify in a coherent manner in order to bring similar documents together. It was only through trial and error and with many discussions that a clear understanding of the principles was attained.

For guidance, the indexers could rely on bibliographic sources for records that contained DDC numbers. Records from national libraries using the DDC, from the Library of Congress catalogue, and from OCLC's WorldCat were the most often used sources and accounted for about 30% of derived classification. Most of these sources had a valid DDC number while others had a LCC number that could be converted (for difficult cases) to a DDC number using the conversion tables established by Mona L. Scott.[12] These sources were especially important to indexers at the beginning to help them gain the necessary confidence in assigning DDC numbers to the documents.

The new version of Das Schweizer Buch (SB), organised according to the Dewey's Hundred Divisions, was received favourably by SNL's subscribers. Book dealers indicated that they had an easier time locating books by discipline and, in particular, filling standing orders for North American libraries requesting Swiss books in selected subject areas. From all of the comments received, it appeared that no one missed the former organisation based on the 24 subject groups.

PROSPECTS

The work of the DDC Deutsch Konsortium has been well documented and promoted in the German speaking countries. Since 2002, the Swiss National Library has received many requests for information from Swiss libraries looking for a shelving system for their public access collections and requesting our help in using the future DDC German edition. The library has so far assisted a few libraries in establishing a work plan to migrate to the DDC as well as giving in depth information about the use of the DDC. This level of interest is quite remarkable considering the library has made very little effort so far in promoting the DDC in Switzerland, pending the publication in German.

With the advent of the publication of the German edition of DDC 22 in 2005, the Swiss National Library will be drafting a work plan that should define the level of support the library will be prepared to give to Swiss libraries interested in using the DDC. As there are currently very few Swiss libraries using the DDC, the primary goal will be to define how training should be organised and coordinated. With its limited resources, the library will surely be looking at partnerships with other institutions in order to offer maximum support for the development of the DDC in Switzerland.

CONCLUSION

Introducing the DDC at the Swiss National Library was a calculated risk. While the objective factors (use, scope, standard) indicated that the DDC was a solid choice, the fact that it was not a German classification standard increased the difficulties in using it in a German language environment. To overcome this risk, much work and energy had to be invested in training and maintenance of skills.

Today, the DDC is used without difficulties, at least no more than in other libraries. Indexers are generally at ease with the DDC structure and with the application principles and rules. They have learned to cope and have adjusted to the quirks of a North American classification scheme.

The final validation of our decision will come this year with the publication of the German edition of DDC 22. The Swiss National Library will benefit from having a standard work in German that will complement the French and Italian editions. The availability of DDC notations in German bibliographic records will be a definite asset to the SNL and Swiss libraries using the DDC. The SNL will closely monitor the impact of that publication on Swiss libraries and try to assist those who will adopt it as their classification scheme. On a European level, the German DDC 22 edition will certainly be another opportunity that will increase cooperation between the SNL and German library networks and increase existing collaboration between the SNL and the Die Deutsche Bibliothek. New possibilities of cooperation between other European national libraries will probably occur within projects of the Conference of European National Librarians (CENL) and in particular within The European Library Service where plans are underway to use the DDC for collection descriptions.

REFERENCES

1. The official names of the Swiss National Library are: Schweizerische Landes-bibliothek (German), Bibliothèque nationale suisse (French), Biblioteca nazionale svizzera (Italian), Biblioteca naziunala svizra (Rhaeto-Romanic).

2. Patrice Landry, "SWD/RSWK at the Swiss National Library: Celebrating 5 years of Indexing and Cooperation," *International Cataloguing and Bibliographic Control* 33, no 4 (2004): 82-85.

3. Barbara Bell, *An Annotated Guide To Current National Bibliographies*, 2nd completely revised edition (München: K.G. Saur, 1998).

4. *Klassifikationen für wissenschafliche Bibliotheken: Analysen, Empfehlungen, Modelle* (Berlin: Deutsches Bibliotheksinstitut, 1998).

5. *Classification décimale Dewey et index*, 21e édition, éditée par Joan S. Mitchell, Julianne Beall, Winton E. Matthews et Gregory R. New, version française sous la coordination de Raymonde Couture-Lafleur et Louis Cabral (Montréal: Editions ASTED, 1998).

6. *Dewey Decimal Classification: Francophone Perspectives, Papers from a Workshop presented at the General Conference of the International Federation of Library Associations and Institutions (IFLA), Amsterdam, Netherlands, 1998*, edited by Julianne Beall and Raymonde Couture-Lafleur (Albany, NY: Forest Press, 1999).

7. Bibliothèque nationale Suisse, "Premier rapport annuel, 1895 présenté par la Commission de la bibliothèque," (Berne: C.-J. Wyss, 1896): 7. The text in French is: Le catalogue principal servira, selon la méthode américaine, simultanément de catalogue alphabétique et de catalogue des matières.

8. Francis L. Miksa, *The DDC, the Universe of Knowledge, and the Post-Modern Library* (Albany, New York: Forest Press, 1998).

9. Schweizerischen Landesbibliothek, *"Systematische und alphabetische Übersicht zum Realkatalog der Schweizerischen Landesbibliothek"* (Bern: Rösch & Schatzmann, 1906).

10. Daniele Danesi, "Translating Dewey into Italian," in *Dewey: An International Perspective. Papers from a Workshop on the Dewey Decimal Classification and DDC 20; Presented at the General Conference of the International Federation of Library Associations and Institutions (IFLA), August 24, 1989, Paris, France*, Robert P. Holley, ed. (München: K.G. Saur, 1991): 54-63.

11. Bruno Béguet et Catherine Hadjopoulou, "Les collections en libre accès de la Bibliothèque nationale de France: Organisation par départements et usage de la Dewey," *Bulletin des bibliothèques de France* 41, no 4 (1996): 40-45.

12. Mona L. Scott, *Conversion Tables*, 2nd edition (Englewood: Libraries Unlimited, 1999).

doi:10.1300/J104v42n03_05

DDC German–
The Project, the Aims, the Methods:
New Ideas for a Well-Established
Traditional Classification System

Magda Heiner-Freiling

SUMMARY. The paper will give a short outline of the project DDC German. The project is not limited to a mere translation of DDC 22, but aims at the implementation of Dewey in the library networks of the Ger-

---

Magda Heiner-Freiling is Senior Reference Librarian, Deputy Head of Department of Classification and Indexing in Die Deutsche Bibliothek, and Director of the Project DDC German, Die Deutsche Bibliothek Adickesallee 1 D-60322 Frankfurt a.M., Germany (E-mail: heiner@dbf.ddb.de).

The author wishes to thank Joan Mitchell (OCLC) and Julianne Beall (LC) for their help and encouragement in the project DDC German and for their advice concerning the English version of this paper. Further thanks go to Heidrun Alex and Lars G. Svensson of the project team DDC German for their contributions and helpful criticism and to Nobuko Ohashi (LC) for her excellent examples concerning World War II and persecution of witches.

The project DDC German is a common effort of librarians in three countries. Very often when German or Germany is mentioned in the following paper, the project partners in Austria and Switzerland are included as well.

[Haworth co-indexing entry note]: "DDC German–The Project, the Aims, the Methods: New Ideas for a Well-Established Traditional Classification System." Heiner-Freiling, Magda. Co-published simultaneously in *Cataloging & Classification Quarterly* (The Haworth Information Press, an imprint of The Haworth Press, Inc.) Vol. 42, No. 3/4, 2006, pp. 147-162; and: *Moving Beyond the Presentation Layer: Content and Context in the Dewey Decimal Classification (DDC) System* (ed: Joan S. Mitchell, and Diane Vizine-Goetz) The Haworth Information Press, an imprint of The Haworth Press, Inc., 2006, pp. 147-162. Single or multiple copies of this article are available for a fee from The Haworth Document Delivery Service [1-800-HAWORTH, 9:00 a.m. - 5:00 p.m. (EST). E-mail address: docdelivery@haworthpress.com].

man-language countries. Use of DDC mainly for retrieval purposes, not for shelving, leads to certain new approaches in classifying with Dewey which are described in detail and presented together with the German web service Melvil. Based on the German experience of cooperation and data exchange in the field of verbal indexing, the paper develops some ideas on future Dewey cooperation between European and American libraries. doi:10.1300/J104v42n03_06 *[Article copies available for a fee from The Haworth Document Delivery Service: 1-800-HAWORTH. E-mail address: <docdelivery@haworthpress.com> Website: <http://www.HaworthPress.com> © 2006 by The Haworth Press, Inc. All rights reserved.]*

KEYWORDS. DDC German translation project, Die Deutsche Bibliothek (DDB), DDC Deutsch 22, DDC German web service, Melvil, MelvilClass, MelvilSearch

1. DDC GERMAN–
OUTLINE OF THE TRANSLATION PROJECT

The translation of DDC 22 and the identification of adaptations necessary for use of DDC in German libraries together with a German Dewey web service with a component for retrieval as well as a tool for the classifier were the central aims of a feasibility study on DDC German which was published in 2000.[1] The authors, an expert group with classification and indexing specialists from Germany, Austria and Switzerland, were nominated by the "Standardisierungsausschuss"–a committee including representatives of the library networks and the national libraries in the three German-speaking countries, the ministries of education and culture and the Deutsche Forschungsgemeinschaft (DFG). The translation work was funded by the DFG and based at the University of Applied Sciences in Cologne with faculties for translation, and information and library sciences. Die Deutsche Bibliothek (DDB), the German national library, organised and coordinated the input of more than 60 specialists for the different subjects, and developed a concept for the future German DDC web service Melvil and for the integration of DDC numbers in the national bibliography and other bibliographic services.[2]

The translation work began in November 2002 and started with the establishment of German equivalents for the specific Dewey terminology. The DDC had never before been translated into German, and generally accepted German terms for items such as centered entry, decimal point, dual heading or Relative Index did not exist before. At the same time an editorial system for the translation, mainly using open-source products, was developed by Pansoft, a software company from Karlsruhe. It handles the XML data of DDC 22 delivered by OCLC and produces an XML file for the German web version, and pdf files of schedules, tables and Relative Index for the German print edition. The editorial system allows the parallel view of the English text of a class and the translated German class together with all connected index terms. It supports the storage of standard phrases, the integration of extra index entries and the creation of new classes. It also includes features for the handling of the DDC Summaries.

The translation of DDC 22 started in April 2003 when the data of the complete DDC 22 were integrated into the editorial system. Corrections and changes distributed by OCLC until the end of 2004 were integrated in the German version of DDC 22. DDC 22 is now completely translated, and was published in October 2005 by K. G. Saur. The publication by K. G. Saur of a German translation of *Dewey Decimal Classification, Principles and Application* by Lois Mai Chan and Joan Mitchell, translated by the project team, is scheduled for March 2006, when DDC German will be presented at the annual congress of the German librarians in Dresden. *Die Dewey-Dezimalklassifikation, Theorie und Praxis* will be the first DDC textbook for students and classifiers available in German.

Due to the needs of academic and national libraries, the German translation is based on the full edition, contrary to the general practice to start with an abridged version when DDC is translated into a certain language for the first time. The editorial policy statement for DDC German includes considerations for national or language options: no such options will be developed because international data exchange and easy access to Anglo-American bibliographic records carrying Dewey numbers with them are the main reasons for implementing Dewey in Germany. It is, however, one of the main concerns to integrate additional terminology for specific German, Austrian and Swiss institutions, practices or points of view, for instance in law, education, administration or religion. Difficulties for German and central European DDC users may also be caused by different traditions and different placement of certain subjects within an academic discipline. Though proposals such as the classification of Slavic languages and literatures with the other European languages, revision of outdated positions in engineering science and placement of certain topics in parts of the social sciences were made, the expert group DDC German decided to accept the present arrangement of subjects in Dewey. Difficulties for the German or central European arrangement of subjects were also caused by the splitting of archaeology between the different geographically bound classes for history; by the split between public education (in 370) and family education (in 640); and by the scattering of environmental studies.[3]

Additional index entries, additional notes and explanations in the Manual, and, in very few cases, integration of extra classes by expansions were planned to make classifying and retrieval with Dewey in a German-language environment easier. With the help of the Dewey editors, expansions for new classes in religion and politics (German translations of the Bible and German political parties) were developed. Built numbers for the German parties had already been integrated in the standard edition of DDC 22. The Editorial Policy Committee also accepted proposals for revisions and expansions in the history of Germany and Austria and in the area notation 43 in Table 2. The acceptance of these proposals was an important positive signal for the German librarians interested in the integration of Dewey in their services; for the first time, future cooperation in fields of genuine German interest and with German need for improvements was tested between American and German specialists in classification.

Further steps in the project DDC German are presentation and testing of the tools which form the future Dewey web service of Die Deutsche Bibliothek. They are described in detail in section 5 of this paper. The practice of classifying with Dewey by the bibliographic agencies of Germany (DDB) and Switzerland (the Swiss National Library in Berne) was discussed in detail by the expert group DDC German and in working groups with different institutions and libraries which either use Dewey already for cataloguing or for web presentations, or are interested in doing so in the near future. These considerations took into account the pros and cons of traditional DDC application and led to some ideas about improved integration of Dewey in OPACs or web-based services which might be a challenge for the present Dewey community in the United States and Anglophone countries in general. They are presented in the following parts of the paper.[4]

2. BUILT NUMBERS–
A CHALLENGE FOR RETRIEVAL

Built numbers are one of the features playing a major part in criticism of Dewey in general. The length of many numbers with two or three added notational elements is one of the crucial points. The other point lies in the difficulty in determining the meaning of parts of built numbers, which makes access to these elements in retrieval so complicated. Whereas UDC uses certain symbols to indicate the process of synthesis, the nature and function of the added elements DDC does not offer these possibilities. It must be admitted, however, that the simpler and shorter structure of DDC numbers (compared to UDC) was one of the positive characteristics mentioned in the German discussion about international classifications which led to the recommendation of Dewey for the national bibliography.[5]

In the case of built numbers, retrieval currently is limited to access to the base number, and to notation that can be taken directly from the base number's associated add note. So far, no possibilities exist for direct access besides pure truncation. Even if some algorithms could be quickly developed for simple and often used cases (T1—09 followed by notation from Table 2), there are so many exceptions and special cases that decomposition remains a difficult process. Many numbers in Table 2, Table 5 and Table 6 would be desirable as access points for retrieval; the same can be said for add table notation or parts of numbers from the schedules. Songqiao Liu's thesis[6] has demonstrated that decomposition of built numbers is possible, but what he did for the 700 classes (DDC 20) has not been proven to work for all classes of DDC 22, and to our knowledge there is no complete DDC number decomposition tool for all possible built numbers.

The Gemeinsame Bibliotheksverbund (GBV), in cooperation with the State and University Library of Goettingen, has started a project to build on Liu's work, because about 3 million foreign bibliographic records in the GBV's union catalogue consist mainly of Anglo-American data and carry DDC numbers with them as their one and only subject information element. Retrieval for all relevant information hidden in a built number will be made possible by using a tool under development by Ulrike Reiner.[7]

The partners in the project DDC German, however, want to offer access to all elements in built numbers from the beginning. The data model developed for the German national bibliography and for others classifying with Dewey such as the virtual libraries in the vascoda group will offer separate fields for the different elements in Dewey numbers.

The first field is reserved for the complete (often a built) number, connected with information about the Dewey edition used such as

[DDC22eng] for all titles classified before the publication of DDC German, or [DDC22ger] for titles classified since October 2005. This "official" Dewey number is generated during the classification process.

The classification process starts with

A. the field for the base number, followed by
B. the field for an added number (or parts of an added number) from other schedules,
C. the field for numbers from the tables, always marked by the name of the table, e.g., T1—03 or T2—43155, and
D. the field for numbers from add tables.

Fields A-D are repeatable, mainly for notation from Table 1 or from Table 2.

It has not yet been decided whether all notation from internal add tables will also be stored for retrieval. The information carried by add table notation makes sense only in connection with the number or span of numbers to which it applies and does not carry much relevance for retrieval by itself. For example, in the period tables for specific literatures in 800, notation 4 stands for the years 1625-1702 in English literature (820.1-828), the years 1517-1625 in German literature (830.1-838), and the years 1917-1991 in Russian literature (891.701-.78). In medicine, for instance, in the internal add table associated with class 616, notation 042 represents genetic diseases; in the arts in class 746 (textile arts) the same notation is used for stitches. So programming these features for classification and retrieval is more complex and will be postponed to a later stage of the implementation process.

Yet the separate storage of notation from add tables will be possible, and a field for this purpose has been reserved in the German DDC data model for bibliographic records so far. Further considerations have to take into account that the MARC format for classification data offers a possibility for the storage of this kind of information in the context of an authority file. Experience with separate fields for all elements of built numbers has to be collected during the first year of classification with Dewey in the national bibliography. The establishment of an authority file for all built numbers (additional to MelvilClass or as a part of it) is under discussion. It will be a crucial question whether built numbers with all notational elements from schedules or tables will be stored, or whether Table 2 (and also perhaps Table 5 and 6) with a huge number of possible combinations will be handled differently. It could, for instance, be a solution to store only built numbers with the more general elements from Table 2 (e.g., combinations with—43), but not with all the more specific numbers for parts of Germany beginning with—43. Of course an authority file would be an excellent way to save time in the process of notational synthesis and reduce the number of mistakes.

3. APPROXIMATELY THE WHOLE AND STANDING ROOM

The introduction of separate fields for parts of built numbers also offers an opportunity to avoid another disadvantage of Dewey for retrieval purposes. In Dewey, number-building techniques are not permitted for topics that do not "approximate the whole" of a class. Such topics are said to be in "standing room." For beginners in classifying with DDC, it is difficult to understand which topics are in standing room, especially in those cases in which the topics are not mentioned explicitly in including notes. This leads to serious losses for retrieval, especially in the case of items with geographic aspects not represented in the notation. Separate fields for added notation will allow the classifier to preserve important information, even in cases where built numbers are not allowed because the subject does not cover approximately the whole of the base number. For example, black widow spiders do not approximate the whole of the class of poisonous spiders (595.44165). Therefore a work on black widow spiders in California would be classified in 595.44165, not in 595.4416509794. In spite of the fact that geographic notation cannot be added to 595.44165 for specific poisonous spiders such as black widow spiders, T2—794 can be stored separately, and everybody looking for specific poisonous spiders and other arachnida in California would find this title when using the truncated number 595.4? and T2—794 for retrieval.

Whenever a topic of a document does not approximate the whole of a particular class, classifiers can of course stop by assigning the basic number, and neglect any additional aspects and thereby save some time. Yet, from the German point of view, it seems helpful, or even necessary for a satisfying retrieval, to take the time for storing information accessible through notation in Tables 2-6 in cases where number building is forbidden. The bibliographic data of the German national bibliography will store these additional elements, even if the base number is presented as the one and only "official" Dewey number in the printed issues of the bibliography.

4. UNCONVENTIONAL WAYS OF USING DEWEY NUMBERS WITHOUT NOTATIONAL SYNTHESIS

Discussions among different institutions interested in using Dewey in Germany have gone even so far as to query the necessity of built numbers in general and to propose the filing of isolated notation which, as a whole, would represent all relevant information in the classified document. This desire of avoiding the time-consuming and error-prone process of number building is due to the fact that some of these parties are working for retrieval purposes alone in connection with the project vascoda, an initiative of virtual libraries. Here masses of web documents, often with quickly changing names and contents, will be classified with a very limited staff and under pressure of time. No printed bibliographies, no shelving and no other conventional library services are connected with these activities, just electronic presentation of information in pathfinders, portals, etc. The topics in which these virtual libraries are specialized often have strong geographic components such as Middle East or North America Studies, history and cultural anthropology. Here number building will be necessary for most documents classified, but also considerations connected with the "standing room" principle have to be respected in many cases. A complete splitting of the Dewey number into several elements might be quicker and more effective, but may appear very unorthodox and even alarming for the Dewey community in general.

Therefore, this practice is not acceptable for the national bibliography and for all national and university libraries with a strong interest in national and international data exchange. With a rising interest in Dewey in Germany, one could even imagine use of the system for shelving in some libraries. The development of a component for number building within the Melvil service will probably make it easier to synthesize numbers in the regular way without paying too much time and attention to the rule of zero and other difficulties for beginners. Together with an increasing number of ready-made built numbers in the classification tool, this unconventional use of Dewey may be only a preliminary stage in the implementation process in Germany.

A similar perspective has another application of Dewey under discussion: the use of Dewey on a "medium level." The limited number of classes in the abridged version does not offer the necessary degree of specificity, but numbers from the DDC Abridged 14 are used as a basis and enriched by a couple of additional classes from DDC 22. This topic was raised in connection with the enormous number of theses in medicine where no regular indexing with subject headings had been possible so far in Germany. Neither the German national library of medicine (Zentralbibliothek fuer Medizin) in Cologne nor Die Deutsche Bibliothek have staff resources for such a service, and the same has to be considered for detailed classification with Dewey at full length. Based on DDC Abridged 14 and DDC 22, a hundred classes have been identified in medicine which can be applied quickly. These classes offer possibilities for an improved retrieval of medical theses without detailed content analysis and time-consuming number building.

Problems, however, are caused by interdisciplinary aspects and the scattering of medical theses, which often cover topics in the social services (360) or life sciences (570-590). Another difficulty is the significance of the add tables in medicine, which hold a lot of relevant information and have to be considered also for retrieval. All classifiers involved in this process are aware of the fact that a formal solution based, for instance, on the Third Summary (as used by the British Library for reports and theses until 2003) or the abridged edition would be preferable, but is not sufficient for the needs of retrieval in medicine. Therefore, alternatives with a limited number of relevant Dewey numbers varying between 3 and 6 digits are being tested and should be used for the future services of the national bibliography, but not for the organisation of the bibliography itself (where all titles are listed under 610 Medicine). Similar ideas are under consideration in the neighbouring disciplines of life sciences, veterinary medicine and agriculture by some of the virtual library projects.

5. ONE, TWO, THREE DEWEY NUMBERS PER TITLE?

A great deal of time, effort and controversial discussion is necessary to understand and accept the handling of complex interdisciplinary topics in Dewey, especially in fields where common central European traditions would lead to different solutions. This is also an issue when the first-of-two rule and the rule of three have to be applied in cases where a document comprises two or more topics. Experienced Dewey classifiers seem to internalize these rules and place titles usually without hesitation. However, whenever identical or similar documents are compared in the bibliographic data delivered by the Library of Congress, WorldCat or the British Library, it becomes obvious that even here discrepancies in the placement of certain topics can be observed. These rules and practices of Dewey will cause problems and inconsistencies when beginners have to learn and respect them.

As a first step for the implementation of Dewey in German library services, Die Deutsche Bibliothek (DDB) introduced a Dewey-based organisation of the German national bibliography. This development includes 100 subject categories corresponding to the Second Summary, but with some minor changes due to literary warrant and the expectations and wishes of German clients. For example, it includes separate categories for 791 Public entertainment, film, broadcast; 792 Theatre, dance; and 796 Sports. On the other hand, the development has only one subject category for 100 Philosophy, which also comprises documents belonging to other fields of philosophy in the classes 110, 120, 140, and 160-190.[8] This was an opportunity to learn a lot about placement of topics in Dewey even before classification with full Dewey numbers and synthesizing of built numbers starts in 2006. The Swiss national library introduced a similar arrangement with 100 subject categories based strictly on the Second Summary in 2001.[9] In 2004, DDB, in cooperation with the Swiss national library, published a manual for the placement of topics in the subject categories of the Deutsche Nationalbibliografie (DNB) to assist classifiers in the two branches of DDB in Frankfurt and Leipzig as well as their clients (the users of the national bibliography in libraries, book trade and publishing). The manual defines certain cases in which application of a second or even a third subject category (Sachgruppe in German) is possible for interdisciplinary topics or for more than one topic treated in a document or in cases where American and German views differ on the placement of certain topics within a discipline. In some cases the necessity of more than one subject category can also be a hint that more than one Dewey number would be sensible for retrieval purposes as soon as documents are classified with complete numbers in 2006. For now, the main (first) subject category of a document in the national bibliography (and in the future the first number of a completely classified title) will be equivalent to the "official" Dewey number.

Decisions for the placement of topics and titles in Dewey are, in most cases, clear and non-controversial, as are the application of the rules for two or more topics. Nevertheless, the assignment of Dewey numbers to documents with slightly changing emphases on one or the other topic, and differences in the personal views of classifiers offer possibilities for variant numbers and may lead to inconsistencies. What is even more frustrating is the loss of information if numbers are not permitted according to strict use of the first-of-two rule or the rule of three. If Dewey is mainly used for retrieval purposes and not for shelving, the requirement for one and only one number cannot be regarded as a dogma. Dewey will not be primarily used for shelving purposes in most German libraries, because strong local and regional traditions have led to other solutions and the well-known classification systems will not be abandoned, but rather connected with DDC by concordances.

The German decision for repeatable fields for complete numbers facilitates the representation of complex topics in a document by two or even three Dewey numbers; in many cases, such numbers are built numbers. Each additional number means extra work for the classifier; this could lead to the consequence that in most cases the one and only generally accepted Dewey number will be regarded as sufficient. For the purposes of the national bibliography, the "official" number will always be the first indicated and carry with it the information about the edition and language used for classifying such as [DDC22ger], or, in the years before publication of DDC German, [DDC22eng].

Typical situations where a second and sometimes even a third number seems to be desirable are exemplified by the following three cases.

1. The rule of three leads to a rather general position of the topic in the DDC scheme (in the 400s or 800s), and important specific information in the document has to be neglected, for example, in a comparative linguistic or literary study where one or two interesting and unusual languages are included.

In this case, an additional number for the specific subject, e.g., one language or literature in the 490 or 890 classes, can be constructed. For example, it would be useful to assign additional numbers in the case of an academic thesis that includes a general comparison between different languages or literatures in connection with a certain linguistic or literary phenomenon, followed by a detailed study of one specific language or literature, such as Russian, Arabic, Chinese, or Japanese.

2. A document covers two different topics with nearly equivalent importance and space in the text. It is perhaps influenced by the interest of the classifier which topic he or she finds more interesting and prefers for number building, but users may find the other aspect interesting for retrieval, too.

The following example illustrates this situation:

Bosch Roig, Gloria: Sprachenpolitik und Deutschunterricht in Spanien, ein Beitrag zu einem begründeten sprachenpolitischen Konzept. Bielefeld, Univ., Diss., 1999 http://deposit.ddb.de/cgi-bin/dokserv?idn=959846948&dok_var=d1&dok_ext=pdf&filename=959846948.pdf.

SWW: Spanien; Kulturpolitik ; Deutschunterricht ; Online-Publik-
ation (subject headings)

1. complete "official" Dewey number: [DDC22eng] 306.44946
2. base number of the "official" number: 306.449
3. notation from tables (here Table 2): T2—46
4. second "additional" complete Dewey number: 430.710946
5. base number of the "additional" number: 430
6. notation from tables (here Table 1 and Table 2): T1—071,
   T1—09, T2—46

The classifier decided that the primary topic of this thesis is "language policy in Spain" and assigned the "official" Dewey number accordingly. Anyone interested in teaching German in Spain might also
find this document extremely helpful and would be able to retrieve it using the second "unofficial" Dewey number. The practice of assigning
more than one number leads, in our view, to more equivalency and less
bias in the classification process, because personal views and interests
are better balanced, and the sometimes time-consuming decision between two possible numbers is replaced by taking the time for building
two numbers and improving retrieval.

3. Dewey rules and practice classify a topic in a class where European tradition would not place it or European (in this case German) users would not expect it. The document is important and interesting for
users with the international (Dewey) point of view as well as for those
with a German point of view.

A typical example is literature about air raids on German towns during World War II, a field of publishing which is rather popular at the
moment because of the sixtieth anniversary of these air raids. Dewey
classifies these titles with World War II in 940.5421 when emphasizing
the air operation or in 940.53 with respect to the direct aftermath on life
on the ground. In the case of Dresden, these numbers would be either
940.542132142 or 940.53432142.

Many books also include a description of civilian life in the destroyed
town and the regional political events during the last months of the war.
A German reader will be interested in these documents from the point of
view (and retrieval) of the regional history of Saxonia and Dresden during World War II and will start the search in class 943 History of Germany. There seems to be good reason to offer the access from a built
Dewey number for history of Dresden in 1939-1945, too, and to use this
as a second "unofficial" Dewey-based way to relevant information.

The practice of assigning multiple Dewey numbers is probably a controversial point in the German considerations for the future DDC application and has to be observed carefully. It could lead, as national or language options did before, to inconsistencies for the handling of certain matters and thereby make international cooperation and exchange of DDC-classified bibliographic data more difficult or less reliable. Experience of some years of Dewey practice in a German-language library landscape, the permanent need to save money and staff resources and perhaps an increasing number of libraries interested in using Dewey for shelving, too, may convince classifiers to accept the principle of the one-and-only DDC number. Yet the increasing importance of Dewey for retrieval has to be taken into account as an argument for more flexibility of Dewey with respect to assigning multiple Dewey numbers to one document.

6. THE GERMAN DDC WEB SERVICE:
MelvilClass AND MelvilSearch

From the beginning there was a common understanding within the DDC German project team and the Consortium DDC German that a German-language based classification tool similar to WebDewey had to be constructed and should be offered by DDB parallel to the print edition. A second component, a retrieval tool, also seemed desirable and was part of the proposal for the DFG funds. Pilot versions of both tools are now available for the project partners and will be tested until the end of the year 2005. Together they form the future DDC German web service named Melvil with two tools MelvilClass (for classifying) and MelvilSearch (for retrieval). From January 2006 on, Melvil will be a regular online service offered by Die Deutsche Bibliothek under similar license conditions as WebDewey.

The user interface of MelvilClass looks very much the same as WebDewey–this was an important feature as many future clients will have some prior experience with WebDewey and perhaps will even continue to subscribe to it additionally because they prefer to work in an English Dewey environment parallel to the German. So they appreciate similar structures and surfaces. Minor changes are made for the representations of the notes connected with a Dewey class. In MelvilClass they are placed in a bar on the right side of the screen, not below the class as WebDewey does it. There is also opportunity to store personal and institutional comments as well as built numbers.[10]

Lars G. Svensson, the IT specialist in the DDB project team, is responsible for the development of MelvilSearch. The retrieval functions of MelvilSearch are not limited to Dewey numbers, but include the complete vocabulary of the German DDC for verbal access, enriched by translated terms for built numbers in WebDewey and–in the future–by the German language elements in new built numbers integrated in MelvilClass with respect to classifying and retrieval purposes of German users. A second way to access Dewey-classified documents via MelvilSearch is an integrated browsing tool which allows browsing through the complete Dewey hierarchy. As soon as it is implemented within an OPAC of a single library or a regional library network, the number of hits connected with each class is visible, separated between hits for documents connected directly with the class and hits connected with the class and all more specific classes deeper in the hierarchy; the titles of documents in the chosen class can be checked directly.

DDB plans to offer this retrieval tool together with MelvilClass and under the same licensing conditions. Melvil as a whole will be a service based very much on the model OCLC has developed for WebDewey with single-user, limited, and unlimited campus licenses. In accordance with the translation agreement between OCLC and DDB, prices correspond to OCLC's guidelines and offer a slight reduction for OCLC members and members of the Consortium DDC German.

Further plans for MelvilClass include a number building tool which will be developed together with the GBV specialist working on the decomposition tool. For all future items within the Melvil service, the same conditions for cooperation with OCLC and mutual exchange of software are planned as for the editorial system for the translation.

7. COMMON PRACTICE IN CLASSIFICATION WITH DEWEY– A PERSPECTIVE FOR AMERICAN-EUROPEAN LIBRARY COOPERATION

There are several fields of activities where cooperation in DDC has already led to positive effects for the classification itself, for the participating institutions and for classification-based library services in general. The development of neglected, under-valued or outdated Dewey classes will always be an important matter for libraries interested in these topics. This can be a subject where academic or special libraries can contribute new terminology or sound proposals for the new arrangement of certain subjects. It can also be found in geography (in Table 2), history, language, literature, or religion of a country where a foreign national library or translators can correct faults or give advice for more precise numbers and new specific classes. Norway's input concerning Scandinavian languages and literatures is an example in DDC 22 as well as Germany's and Austria's contribution to additional or revised numbers for their countries in history and in Table 2.

Another area of cooperation could be the reconsideration of the placement of certain topics or fields of research in Dewey. One example is the recent discussion between Die Deutsche Bibliothek and the Library of Congress about the placement of literature on witch hunting in LC's bibliographic records. The persecution of witches in Europe is usually classified under witchcraft in 133.43094 (the number for witchcraft plus notation for geographic treatment in Europe). From a European point of view, social history is usually in the focus of studies about witch hunting in late medieval Europe as well as in colonial Massachussetts; however, persecutions were usually executed by the state government and courts in cooperation with the church or the inquisition. Therefore, the law as well as church and general history are other possible aspects for the selection of the right Dewey number. The development of a general guideline for a topic which has implications from criminal law and the penal system, but is also often treated as a matter of female discrimination and the destruction of female power in certain fields such as gynecology, seems to be a useful field of cooperation and brings together LC's rich experience in classifying with Dewey and the fresh European perspective on established practices.

A larger project for common endeavours is a review of the treatment of the law of different European countries and of the European Union in Dewey. The Dewey editorial team has already sponsored several meetings of Dewey classifiers and law specialists in order to improve the treatment of legal topics in Dewey. In the last three years, Dewey translators' meetings have also taken place during IFLA conferences. These meetings have led to improved communication about technical support for translations (including a presentation on the German editorial system) and have fostered cooperation between the editors and translators of Dewey in different languages. For example, it would be useful to have access to geographic expansions made for a translation in a neighbouring country with similar needs and interests. The Italian DDC 21 inlcudes expansions for Italy in Table 2 and extra classes or notes for certain features important for Italian classifiers and users. These additions can also offer some interesting input for Germany, Austria, and Switzerland, countries with close relations to Italy and high literary warrant for titles about Italian history, art or music, travelling in Italy or common concerns such as Roman law or Catholic religion.

Die Deutsche Bibliothek and the partners of the project in Germany, Austria and Switzerland have already established valuable and effective cooperative structures in the expert group DDC German and by the foundation of the Consortium DDC Deutsch. Contacts with the British Library and the Bibliothèque nationale de France in other fields of subject approach to information, such as the project MACS, will probably be intensified when the German national bibliography uses DDC not only for the subject arrangement, but for complete classification of documents. For Die Deutsche Bibliothek the year 2006 will be a crucial year in the process of implementing DDC in the bibliographic services. The necessity for close cooperation with the Dewey editorial team will certainly increase as the need arises for the accommodation of new topics, expansions, and additional notes. Designing firm structures for information exchange among all these interested parties will be one of the challenges for the Dewey community in the near future.

REFERENCES

1. Einführung und Nutzung der Dewey Decimal Classification (DDC) im deutschen Sprachraum (Frankfurt a.M.: Die Deutsche Bibliothek, 2000).

2. Goedert, Winfried, "Die Welt ist groß, wir bringen Ordnung in diese Welt: das DFG-Projekt DDC Deutsch," *Information, Wissenschaft & Praxis* 53, (2002): 395-400.

3. Heiner-Freiling, Magda, "DDC Deutsch–formale, terminologische und inhaltliche Aspekte einer deutschen DDC-Ausgabe," *Zeitschrift für Bibliothekswesen und Bibliographie* 48 (2002): 333-339.

4. See also: Einführung und Nutzung der Dewey Decimal Classification (DDC) im deutschen Sprachraum (Frankfurt a.M.: Die Deutsche Bibliothek, 2000).

5. *Klassifikationen für wissenschaftliche Bibliotheken: Analysen, Empfehlungen, Modelle* (Berlin: Deutsches Bibliotheksinstitut, 1998).

6. Liu, Songqiao, "Decomposing DDC Synthesized Numbers," *International Cataloguing and Bibliographic Control* 26, 1997, p. 58-62.

7. Reiner, Ulrike, "DDC-Notationsanalyse und–synthese," *VGZ-Colibri-Bericht 2, 2004.* (VGZ, 2005) and http://134.28.50/mambo/download/colibri_fagei-04-09-03.pdf.

8. Heiner-Freiling, Magda, "Dewey in der Deutschen Nationalbibliographie?" *Bibliotheksdienst* 36, (2002): 709-715.

9. *DDC-Sachgruppen der Deutschen Nationalbibliografie: Leitfaden zu ihrer Vergabe* / edited by Heidrun Alex and Magda Heiner-Freiling (Frankfurt a.M.: Die Deutsche Bibliothek, 2004).

10. More information available under www.ddc-deutsch.de (in German only).

doi:10.1300/J104v42n03_06

CONTENT AND CONTEXT:
A WEB PERSPECTIVE

Users Browsing Behaviour
in a DDC-Based Web Service:
A Log Analysis

Traugott Koch
Koraljka Golub
Anders Ardö

Traugott Koch is Research Officer, Research and Development Team, UKOLN, University of Bath, BA2 7AY, Bath, United Kingdom (E-mail: T.Koch@ukoln.ac.uk). Koraljka Golub is a PhD student (E-mail: koraljka.golub@it.lth.se); and Anders Ardö is Associate Professor (E-mail: anders.ardo@it.lth.se), both at the Department of Information Technology, Lund University, P.O. Box 118, SE-221 00 Lund, Sweden. All the authors are members of the Knowledge Discovery and Digital Library Research Group (KnowLib), Lund University, Sweden.

The Swedish Agency for Innovation Systems provided the main funding for this research. This work was partially funded by European Union (EU) under project ALVIS–Superpeer Semantic Search Engine (EU 6. FP, IST-1-002068-STP). This work also was partially funded by DELOS–Network of Excellence on Digital Libraries (EU 6. FP IST, G038-507618).

[Haworth co-indexing entry note]: "Users Browsing Behaviour in a DDC-Based Web Service: A Log Analysis." Koch, Traugott, Koraljka Golub, and Anders Ardö. Co-published simultaneously in *Cataloging & Classification Quarterly* (The Haworth Information Press, an imprint of The Haworth Press, Inc.) Vol. 42, No. 3/4, 2006, pp. 163-186; and: *Moving Beyond the Presentation Layer: Content and Context in the Dewey Decimal Classification (DDC) System* (ed: Joan S. Mitchell, and Diane Vizine-Goetz) The Haworth Information Press, an imprint of The Haworth Press, Inc., 2006, pp. 163-186. Single or multiple copies of this article are available for a fee from The Haworth Document Delivery Service [1-800-HAWORTH, 9:00 a.m. - 5:00 p.m. (EST). E-mail address: docdelivery@haworthpress.com].

SUMMARY. This study explores the navigation behaviour of all users of a large web service, Renardus, using web log analysis. Renardus provides integrated searching and browsing access to quality-controlled web resources from major individual subject gateway services. The main navigation feature is subject browsing through the Dewey Decimal Classification (DDC) based on mapping of classes of resources from the distributed gateways to the DDC structure.

Among the more surprising results are the hugely dominant share of browsing activities, the good use of browsing support features like the graphical fish-eye overviews, rather long and varied navigation sequences, as well as extensive hierarchical directory-style browsing through the large DDC system. doi:10.1300/J104v42n03_07 *[Article copies available for a fee from The Haworth Document Delivery Service: 1-800-HAWORTH. E-mail address: <docdelivery@haworthpress.com> Website: <http://www.HaworthPress.com> © 2006 by The Haworth Press, Inc. All rights reserved.]*

KEYWORDS. Browsing behaviour, log analysis, user studies, DDC, Dewey Decimal Classification, subject gateways, user interfaces

INTRODUCTION

As many research communities are increasingly concerned with issues of interaction design, one of the current foci in information science is on user behaviour in seeking information on the World Wide Web. A frequently applied methodology for studying this behaviour is log analysis. This approach has several advantages: users do not need to be directly involved in the study, a picture of user behaviour is captured in non-invasive conditions, and every activity inside the system can be tracked.

User log studies mainly use the average analytical approaches of existing software packages for statistical reporting. Such software provides limited knowledge of user behaviour,[1] since it only produces comparatively general insights into aspects of information services, such as number of users per month or the mostly followed hyperlink, and thus tells little about specific navigation behaviour.

A variety of aspects of user information-seeking behaviour using log analysis have been studied previously, in digital libraries,[2] web search engines,[3,4,5] and other web-based information services. Browsing behaviour has not been studied that much.

The common belief seems to be that users prefer searching to browsing: Lazonder[6] claims "... students strongly prefer searching to browsing." Jacob Nielsen[7] states the following: "Our usability studies show that more than half of all users are search-dominant, about a fifth of the users are link-dominant, and the rest exhibit mixed behaviour. The search-dominant users will usually go straight for the search button when they enter a website: they are not interested in looking around the site; they are task-focused and want to find specific information as fast as possible. In contrast, the link-dominant users prefer to follow the links around a site: even when they want to find specific information, they will initially try to get to it by following promising links from the home page. Only when they get hopelessly lost will link-dominant users admit defeat and use a search command. Mixed-behaviour users switch between search and link-following, depending on what seems most promising to them at any given time but do not have an inherent preference."

These observations have implications for building searching-oriented user interfaces. However, those results could be dependent on a number of issues that might have not yet been recognized. One such issue is, for example, the role of the web page layout in "favouring" either of the two strategies. Hong[8] conducted a study on browsing strategies and implications for design of web search engines. The study reports that existing browsing features of search engines are insufficient to users. Even within the Renardus project, an initial belief about potential user requirements was that end-users preferred searching to browsing.[9] After the browsing interface had been built, it showed that browsing was much favoured.

The overall purpose of our project was to gain insights into real users' navigation and especially browsing behaviour in a large service on the Web. This knowledge could be used to improve such services, in our case the Renardus service[10] which offers a large DDC browsing structure. Renardus is a distributed web-based service which provides integrated searching and browsing access to quality controlled web resources from major individual subject gateway services across Europe. (The Renardus project was funded by the European Union's Information Society Technologies 5th Framework Programme until 2002.)

The research aimed at studying the following topics: the unsupervised usage behaviour of all Renardus users, complementing the initial Renardus user enquiry; detailed usage patterns (quantitative/qualitative, paths through the system); the balance between browsing, searching and mixed activities; typical sequences of user activities and transition probabilities in a session, especially in traversing the hierarchical DDC browsing structure; the degree of usage of the browsing support features; and typical entry points, referring sites, points of failure and exit points. Because of the high cost of full usability lab studies, we also wanted to explore whether a thorough log analysis could provide valuable insights and working hypotheses as the basis for good usage and usability studies at a reasonable cost.

The paper provides short background information about Renardus (I. Background); the methodology applied in this study is described in section two (II. Methodology); the analysis, hypotheses and results regarding the general usage of Renardus, the browsing behaviour and the usage of the DDC are presented in the third section (III. Results). A summary of the results and some ideas for further investigation conclude the paper (IV. Conclusion).

I. BACKGROUND

Renardus Service

Renardus[10] exploits the success of subject gateways, where subject experts select quality resources for their users, usually within the academic and research communities. This approach has been shown to provide a high quality and valued service, but encounters problems with the ever increasing number of resources available on the Internet. Renardus is based on a distributed model where major subject gateway services across Europe can be searched and browsed together through a single interface provided by the Renardus broker. The Renardus partner gateways cover over 80,000 predominantly digital, web-based resources from within most areas of academic interest, mainly written in English.

The Renardus service allows searching several subject gateways simultaneously. What is searched are "catalogue records" (metadata) of quality controlled web resources, not the actual resources. There are two ways to search the service, either through a simple search box that is available on the Renardus "Home" page or through the "Advanced search" page allowing a combination of terms and search fields and providing options to limit searches in a number of different ways. A pop-up window of a list of words alphabetically close to the entered word (for title, DDC, subject and document type) supports the search term selection.

Apart from searching, Renardus offers subject browsing in a hierarchical directory-style (cf. Technology | Agriculture | Animal husbandry[14]).

It is based on intellectual mapping of classification systems used by the distributed gateway services to the DDC. There are also several browsing-support features. The graphical fish-eye display presents the classification hierarchy as an overview of all available categories that surround the category one started from, normally one level above and two levels below in the hierarchy. This allows users to speed up the browsing and get an immediate overview of the relevant Renardus browsing pages for a subject. The feature "Search entry into the browsing pages" offers a shortcut to categories in the browsing tree where the search term occurs. The lower half of the browsing pages, as a result of the classification mapping, offers the links to the "Related Collections" of the chosen subject. In case users do not want to jump to the parts of the gateways offering related collections, an option of Merging the resource-descriptions from all related collections is available.

For a more detailed description of Renardus, see, for example, Koch, Neuroth, and Day.[11] All related publications are given at the web page "Project Archive and Associated Research and Development."[12]

II. METHODOLOGY

Before Renardus was finally released and the EU project concluded in 2002, an end user evaluation of the Renardus pilot subject gateway[13] was carried out during Fall 2001 which led to some service improvements. The results and shortcomings of this initial user study stimulated us to try the full study of Renardus user logs which is presented in this paper.

Log analysis was chosen because it costs considerably less than full usability lab studies and has the advantage that it is an unobtrusive means of capturing unsupervised usage. This thorough log analysis required several steps which are described below: cleaning of the log files, defining of user sessions, categorization into activity types and the creation of datasets and structures to allow the creation of statistics and the testing of hypotheses.

Cleaning the Log Files

The log files used spanned 16 months between summer 2002 and late fall 2003. They first had to be cleaned from entries created by search engine robots, crackers (users performing unauthorized activities), local administration, images, etc. The largest group of removed entries, almost half of all log entries, was that containing images and style sheets

(1,107,378). Further, 516,269 entries were removed because they originated from more than 650 identified robots, and an additional 12,647 entries because they were from crackers. Various other entries not relating to real usage of Renardus for information seeking, e.g., 17,586 redirections, about 9,000 local administrative activities, error codes and HTTP head entries, had to be removed.

Thus, in the first step, the total number of 2,299,642 log entries was reduced to 631,711 entries. From this dataset, only some general Renardus usage statistics was derived. For the analysis of real user behaviour in Renardus, several further steps and separate datasets were required.

Defining Sessions

After cleaning, the log all entries were grouped into user sessions. A session was heuristically defined as containing all entries coming from the same IP-address and a time gap of less than one hour from the prior entry from the same IP-address.

Defining Activity Types

Each log entry was classified into one of eleven different main activities offered by Renardus. These activities were then used to characterize user behaviour, via a typology of usages and sequences of activities.

Browsing activities:

- "Gen. Browse"–hierarchical directory-style browsing of the DDC;[14]
- "Graph. Browse"–graphical fisheye presentation of the classification hierarchy;[15]
- "Text Browse"–text version of the graphical fisheye presentation;
- Search Browse"–search entry into the browsing structure;
- "Merge Browse"–merging of results from individual subject gateways;
- "Browse"–DDC top level browsing page on the home page.

Searching activities:

- "Simple Search" with "showsimpsearch" for result display;
- "Adv. Search"–advanced search with "showadvsearch" for result display and "scan" for scanning certain data indices.

Other activities:

- "Home Page"; "Help"; "Other" other informational pages, including project documentation.

Creating Datasets for Studying Information-Seeking Behaviour

To try to make sure that we studied only human behaviour in Renardus, we removed, in a further step, another 82,490 entries judged as probable machine activities. This determination was based on heuristic criteria, for example, all sessions containing only one entry; sessions shorter than two seconds.

Most of the analysis in this paper regarding human activities in Renardus is based on a dataset containing 464,757 entries grouped into 73,434 user sessions. Only in a few calculations (especially in the section "Browsing sessions") did we use a further subset of this dataset. The different datasets were stored in a relational database and SQL was used to query them to create statistical tables and to test various hypotheses against the log file data.

III. RESULTS

Global Usage

Renardus was accessed from 99,605 unique machines (IP-numbers) during the 16 month period studied. With 351 unique top-level domains or countries identified (a considerable part of the IP-numbers could not be identified), it is apparent that Renardus has a truly global audience. IP-numbers from the USA topped the list with about 30%, other .net and .com domains followed with 8-10%. Renardus Project partner countries were led by Finland with 5%. Canada, Australia, the Philippines, Italy, and India were other countries exceeding 1% of the IP-numbers.

The user sessions are of considerable length: 33% are longer than 2 minutes and 10% are longer than 10 minutes. The time users might have been exploring participating gateways after leaving Renardus is not included.

The figures indicate that more than 851 different hosts referred users to Renardus. As much as 56% of all referred sessions came from various Google servers and 24% from Yahoo!

Renardus seemed to be able to attract and keep many "faithful" users during the first 16 months after release. Thirteen percent of all unique user machines were returning to the service, which is a comparatively good value.

A. *Information-Seeking Activities*

Main Activities, Transitions

Figure 1 illustrates the share of each activity and transition in the following ways: the share of each of the main activities is indicated by the circle size; and the share of the major transitions between different activities is indicated by arrow size. Only values above 1% are displayed. It shows that 60% of all Renardus activities are directory-style browsing using the DDC structure (Gen. Browse; for the abbreviations used here and throughout the paper, cf. the description under II Methodology: Defining activity types). Forty-eight percent of all transitions in Renardus are steps from one such topical page/DDC class to another.

FIGURE 1. Main Renardus Features, Indicating Their Share in All Activities, and Major Transitions Between the Activities

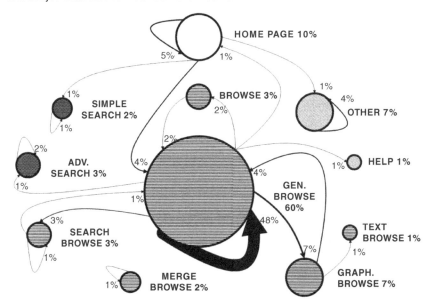

The four special browsing support features are comparatively well used. As many as 45% of the sessions dominated by browsing use two or more different types of browsing activities. As many as 14% use three to five different types (see Browsing sessions below).

Use of the graphical DDC browsing overview (Graph. Browse) is the second most frequent activity in Renardus (7%), after the directory-style browsing. The transition from the dominant directory browsing in the DDC structure to a graphical display is clearly the largest single transition in Renardus, after subsequent directory browsing steps.

Related to Gen. Browse, in 11% of the cases, directory-style browsing has been followed by the usage of the graphical overview (see Figure 2). For further reasoning about these findings see below.

Figure 2 illustrates another important finding. Users tend to stay in the same feature and group of activities, whether it is a single activity like Gen. Browse or a group like browsing, searching or looking for background information, despite the provision of a full navigation bar

FIGURE 2. Transition Probabilities (More Than 5%-Transitions Only)

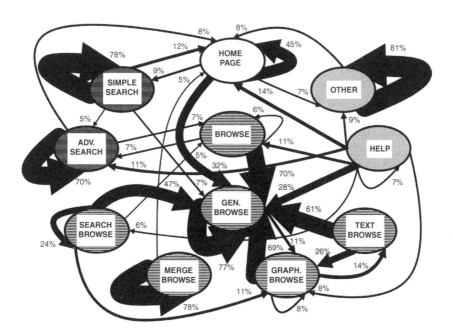

on each page of the Renardus service. In particular, the transitions between browsing and searching activities are less frequent than expected and hoped for. Figure 2 demonstrates this by displaying the main transitions from each feature to other features of the service (the percentages displayed close to the arrows relate to the feature they originate from). For example, 77% of all transitions from one Gen. Browse activity are directed to another Gen. Browse activity and 11% to Graph. Browse.

As the early user study in 2001 showed (in table 18 in the study),[13] the Renardus pilot service was mostly considered very easy or easy to navigate already, although a fifth of the respondents found navigating through the different parts of the service difficult or very difficult. We conclude that advanced online services need to provide some kind of search strategy support. They need to be designed for receiving the user where he/she first enters the system and to assist with user navigation through the whole system with more than a ubiquitous navigation bar (which is offered by Renardus on all pages).

General Navigation Sequences

Many users engage in several different activities during their session: about 46% in one activity, 20% in two, 16% in three different activities. About 18% of the user sessions have between 4 and 11 different activities.

Many users employ a surprisingly rich variety of navigation and browsing sequences and often alternate between many different features. For example, one session has the following sequence (the first number indicates the number of immediate repetitions of the same feature, the second gives the length of this activity in seconds).

home 3 3; genbrowse 4 31; graphbrowse 1 1; genbrowse 3 17; home 1 1 ; browse 1 1; genbrowse 2 3; searchbrowse 1 1; genbrowse 7 152; searchbrowse 1 1; genbrowse 4 24; help 1 1; home 1 1; genbrowse 4 29; graphbrowse 1 1; searchbrowse 1 1; genbrowse 1 1; searchbrowse 1 1; genbrowse 1 1; browse 1 1; genbrowse 3 2; graphbrowse 1 1; genbrowse 2 2; home 2 2

When we look at the most frequent sequences of activity types (immediate repetition of the same type is not counted), we find 4,810 different sequences. The top ten sequences are presented in Table 1. The most frequent sequences, apart from mergebrowse and showsimpsearch, are (in and) between browsing activities.

TABLE 1. Most Frequent Sequences of Activity Types

Type of activity	Sessions	%
(repetitions of) genbrowse	30,606	41.7%
other	7,403	10.1%
genbrowse-graphbrowse-genbrowse	3,860	5.3%
genbrowse-graphbrowse	3,590	4.9%
genbrowse-searchbrowse	2,812	3.3%
(repetitions of) mergebrowse	2,391	3.3%
(repetitions of) showsimpsearch	1,705	2.3%
genbrowse-browse-genbrowse	1,635	2.2%
genbrowse-searchbrowse-genbrowse	1,236	1.7%
genbrowse-browse	1,035	1.4%
all less frequent sequences		23.8%

When we look at a more detailed table of sequences including immediate repetitions of the same activity (not reproduced here), the dominance of browsing and the very high number of variations in navigation is well illustrated. In 73,434 user sessions we find as many as 16,377 different sequences; however, the top 10 most frequent sequences (with more than 1,000 instances each) cover 41.7% of all sessions. In the top 6, and numbers 9-11 among the 11 most frequent sequences, the user exclusively repeats the same activity. Only numbers 7 and 8 involve a switch between different activities (from genbrowse to graphbrowse and from genbrowse to searchbrowse). In the five most frequent cases genbrowse is the repeated activity. The sequences where only the same activity type is repeated cover about 50% of all sessions. This further underlines our earlier finding that a surprisingly large part of the users stay in the same (group of) activities.

Browsing vs. Searching

The levels of usage of the main Renardus features are highly uneven (cf. Figure 1). The most surprising finding is the clear dominance of browsing activities, about 80%. Depending how "dominance of browsing" is defined: 76% of all activities are browsing; 80.5% of all sessions are dominated by browsing. Searching has a much lower share, between 3 and 6%.

This is a highly unusual ratio compared to other published evaluations and common beliefs (cf. Introduction). A possible reason is that most of the browsing pages are indexed by search engines. Seventy-one percent of the users reached browsing pages directly via search engines and start their Renardus navigation at a browsing page. Taken together with the clear tendency to stay in the same (group of) features, these facts "favour" browsing. Additionally, the layout of the home page invites browsing by putting the browsing structure on top of the search box. Still, among users starting at the home page, 57% browse and only 12.5% search (only 22% of all users enter Renardus at the home page/the "front door" of the service, however).

In spite of the dominance of browsing and the tendency to stay in the same group of activities, we see a certain amount of switching between browsing and searching during the same session. In as few as 7.3% of all sessions, users switch between a browse and a search activity, out of which 4.5% of sessions have one switch, 1.9% have two, 0.4% have three, and 0.5% have more than three switches.

The largest number of switches per session is 20. Out of 27 different kinds of switches between browsing and searching, 7 start with a search. Switching from browsing to searching is much more frequent than the opposite. Users at the search pages need to be pointed to the benefits of browsing.

Browsing Sessions

For the calculations in this section we use a subset of our usual dataset, containing 378,267 entries in 58,954 user sessions, defined by a share of more than 50% browsing activities: sessions where "browsing is dominant."

The shares of sessions with a certain number of different activities are almost the same as for all Renardus sessions (cf. the beginning of General navigation sequences). So, even sessions with dominant browsing show as much variety in activities as most other sessions.

Many browsing sessions use more than one type of browsing activity, including the browsing support features: Graph. Browse, Text Browse and Merge Browse. As many as 45% of the sessions dominated by browsing show two or more browsing activities and 14% three to five different types of browsing. We find up to 95 individual browse activities per session, with gracefully degrading numbers from two activities and down.

Two Different Groups of Users

Because of the big influence of referrers like search engines, 71% of the human user sessions start at browsing pages pointed to by referrers, whereas 22% start at the home page (16,300 out of 73,434 sessions). This quantitatively surprising result stimulated us to check if these two "groups" of users show significantly different navigation behaviour. Sessions starting at home have almost twice as many entries per session than sessions starting elsewhere (10 vs. 5.8 entries per session; 35.8% of all entries). Thus, home starters carry out many more activities per session than the other user group.

Users jumping into the middle of the Renardus service are carrying out browsing activities in 87% of all cases and only 2.7% searching activities (Table 2).

Users starting at the Renardus home page/"frontdoor" show a level of browsing of almost 57%, and 12.5% searching. Three times as often they visit other pages and five times as often search pages compared to the other group. These are probably the users who go deliberately to Renardus, whereas a large part of users starting elsewhere, most often in the browsing pages, end up there "ignorantly" after a search in a search engine. The latter overwhelmingly stay in the browsing activities.

People starting elsewhere have a much higher percentage of browsing among their activities. Home starters, however, do considerably more browsing activities compared to their share of all sessions: 53.2% of the sessions show more than 11 browsing activities and 36.8% more than 30 browsing activities.

Figure 3 shows that the home starters clearly dominate the sessions with many browsing activities. A more detailed analysis shows that they are active in browsing activities to a higher and increasing degree starting with 8 browsing activities, compared with their share in all sessions (21%). Quite the opposite is true for users starting elsewhere. They are overrepresented up to the level of nine browsing activities with an ever-decreasing tendency.

TABLE 2. Types of Activities for the Two Different Groups of Users

Type of activity	Starting at home		Starting elsewhere	
	Entries	%	Entries	%
Browsing	94,215	56.6	259,471	87.0
Searching	20,831	12.5	8,099	2.7
Other	51,139	30.9	30,684	10.3
Total	166,503		298,254	

FIGURE 3. Browsing Activities of the Two Groups of Users

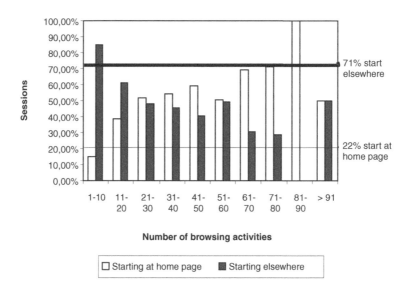

Home starters also exceed their share when it comes to the number of different activity types, all types are counted (in browsing sessions) except when there are three different activities. From five different activities and higher, they have more than twice their share and dominate clearly.

When it comes to the number of different browsing types (in browsing sessions), home starters exceed their share when it comes to carrying out between three and five different browsing types.

B. DDC Usage

DDC Analysis

Analysis of the popularity of DDC sections and classes and the navigation behaviour of users in the DDC structure allow good insights into the distribution of topical interests and the suitability of the DDC system and vocabulary. The findings from the log analysis can, however, only help create hypotheses and need to be complemented by investigative sessions with the users. The most frequently used parts of the DDC hierarchy at the top hierarchical level are given in Table 3.

TABLE 3. Most Frequently Used Parts of the DDC Hierarchy at the Top Heirarchical Level

Entries	DDC	Class
50,784	3	Social sciences
46,209	5	Science
30,955	6	Technology
26,015	2	Religion
22,081	7	Arts & recreation
17,994	8	Literature
16,828	9	History & geography
16,527	0	Computers, information & general reference
13,839	4	Language
13,428	1	Philosophy & psychology

All DDC classes show generally good usage levels (users jumping to one class and not continuing browsing are not counted). Compared to what one would expect in a global Internet setting, Religion ranks surprisingly high and Computers etc. unexpectedly low (see Table 3). Here the vocabulary used in the DDC captions could play a role, e.g., many computing-related terms used in Internet searching do not directly occur in the captions.

On the second hierarchical level, surprisingly large topical areas are Christian denominations (DDC 28), German & related literatures (83), Social problems (36) and Earth Sciences (55; cf. Figure 4).

Unexpectedly frequent visits to individual topics like 552.1 Igneous rocks (the sixth most visited individual page with 2,436 directory browsing activities) could be due to the fact that little information might be found about such a concept in the search engines or to the fact that other sites made prominent links to this topic page in Renardus.

Directory-Style Browsing in the DDC Hierarchy

The directory-style browsing in the DDC-based browsing structure is clearly the dominant activity in Renardus (about 60%). Sixty-seven percent of all browsing activities are DDC directory browsing (254,660 out of 378,264 entries in browsing sessions). Two-thirds of the latter (167,628) appear in unbroken sequences. In these cases, not even browse support features are used between directory browsing steps. While the clear majority of users limit themselves to 10 or fewer steps

FIGURE 4. Most Frequently Used Parts of the DDC Hierarchy at the Second
Hierarchical Level

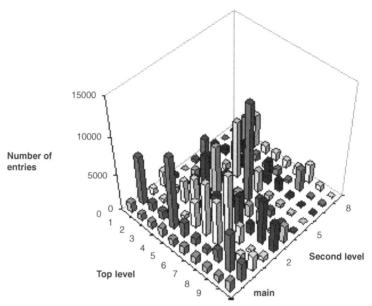

(for distribution see Figure 5), we found surprisingly long unbroken
browsing sequences of up to 86 steps in the DDC directory trees.

These are very unexpected results. People looking for information on
the web are often said to use as few clicks as necessary, switching frequently to other services and activities, having very short attention
spans. Browsing the DDC hierarchies in a directory style of steps at
such quantity and lengths is one of the most significant results of this
log study.

Jumping in the DDC Hierarchy

Since the DDC browsing area in the Renardus user interface displays
the higher levels in the hierarchy, in addition to the "parent" and the
"child" classes, we can find out to what degree users jump levels in the
DDC hierarchy during unbroken directory browsing sequences.

Two of the support features, the graphical overviews and the "search
entry to browsing pages," were designed to relieve users from the "pain"

FIGURE 5. Number of Genbrowse Activities in Sessions (Up to 15)

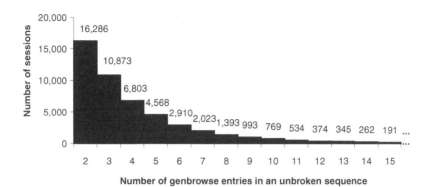

of having to jump around in the hierarchy. Jumping one step up and another step down in the directory-style display is probably faster and easier than using the support features; moving farther away would possibly have been easier using the support features.

The following sequence is an example of a session featuring jumps within unbroken directory browsing:

> start 62-; go to 624; go to 624.1; jump to 62-; go to 625; go to 625.1; go to 625; go to 62-; go to 627; jump to 628; go to 628.1

In sessions featuring unbroken directory browsing, 20.2% of all steps are jumps. Jumps occur in 40.8% of these sessions. In the sessions with jumps, on average 1.7 jumps are carried out. This is a decent number of cases but not excessively high. Many users make use of the support features, especially the graphical overviews, instead of jumping in the directory. This finding indicates, at least, that the necessity to jump in the hierarchy is not putting off users.

As seen from Figure 6, the probability for a user in one session to browse in several main DDC classes increases with the length of the session. This might seem natural but it also implies that the longer the session, the shorter time spent within one main DDC class before moving to another. Each point in the figure is based on several sessions that together contain more than 2,000 browsing entries. Due to the heavy dominance of shorter sessions, the overall mean probability of moving between DDC main classes in a session is 3%.

FIGURE 6. Probability of Moving Between DDC Main Classes

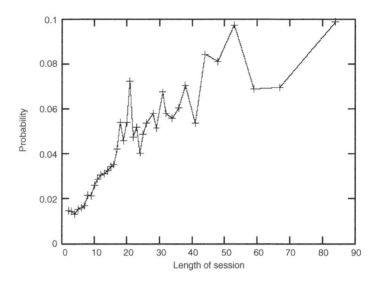

Figure 7 shows a few individual sessions plotted with the number of browsing steps versus the visited DDC classes. For example, all classes within the "1—" branch of DDC are displayed between 100 and 200 on the vertical axis in such a way that the hierarchy is preserved, e.g., the closer two classes are in the hierarchy the closer they are plotted in the figure. Thus a horizontal line indicates that the user stays within a narrow area of DDC while vertical parts indicate jumps between different areas of DDC. The letter "G" indicates that the graphical overview was used while an "S" indicates that the search entry to the browsing structure was used at the indicated points in the sequence.

Keywords and Browsing

We wanted to find out whether the user managed to come close to his/her topic of interest when browsing DDC pages in Renardus. In order to get an indication of that, we compared the keywords entered by a given user into the search engine (Google) respectively entered into Renardus Search with the browsing pages visited subsequently by the same user.

FIGURE 7. DDC Browsing Behaviour Per Session

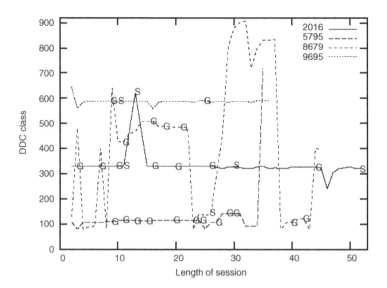

The following list of examples shows keywords entered into Google and the => Renardus DDC class the user selected from the search result:

    ancient continents => History of ancient world; of specific continents, countries, localities; of extraterrestrial worlds

    perspective drawing => Drawing & decorative arts

    "statistics of south america" => General statistics of specific continents, countries, localities in modern world

    writing systems and etymology => Standard language--description and analysis

    kinds of sedimentary rocks => Specific kinds of rocks

The sample studied showed very good hits in the Renardus DDC pages. Most queries matched terms in the DDC caption (which is also used as the title of the page), about 13% of the cases had partial hits there and partial matches in other class and directory "titles" mentioned on the same page (parent, child DDC classes; names of mapped directories from cooperating subject gateways). Most successful questions used 2-3 query terms; only 3% used one term.

It seems that a good initial hit is required to invite users to continue browsing in Renardus (the data here is derived from sessions containing more than one browsing activity).

The result says more about the search engine's ranking algorithm (Google in the case of our sample) than about the Renardus pages and the suitability of the DDC captions. Part of the reason for the share of the good hits we see is the fact that only DDC pages from Renardus where the user's search terms hit several words in the title or top half of the DDC page in Renardus have a chance to appear in the top of Google search results. Only such pages have a chance to be selected and visited by the user.

When checking queries and hits in Other Renardus pages (background and project information), we found great results, too: most hits seemed relevant and we couldn't find many wrong hits on topical questions.

The following examples show search terms entered into Renardus Search (Q:) and DDC classes/pages used during browsing. Each case was gathered from the entire session and was limited to sessions starting with Search and continuing with Browse activities. In the examples, queries and DDC captions are separated by a semicolon.

> Q=chopin; vieuxtemps;
> DDC=Arts & recreation; Music; Composers and traditions of music;

> Q=paperin+valmistus; paperin+valmistus; papermaking; paper+ technology;
> DDC=Technology; Engineering; Engineering of railroads and roads; Engineering of railroads and roads; Engineering of railroads and roads; Railroads; Railroads; Astronautical engineering; Technology; Engineering; Engineering and allied operations; Engineering mechanics and materials; Science; Chemistry; Chemistry; Organic chemistry; Technology; Chemical engineering; Chemical engineering and related technologies; Biotechnology; Biotechnology; Pulp and paper technology; Genetic engineering; Electrical engineering; lighting; superconductivity; magnetic engineering; applied optics; paraphotic technology; electronics; communications

engineering; computers; Electrical engineering; lighting; super-conductivity; magnetic engineering; applied optics; paraphotic technology; electronics; communications engineering; computers; Electronics; Special topics; Optoelectronics; Pulp and paper technology; Conversion of pulp into paper, and specific types of paper and paper products; General topics; Properties, tests, quality controls;

The results of the evaluations of our sample remind us that users frequently follow more than one topic of interest during one session in an information system. In our sample, 70% of all users seemed to pursue one topic in a session, 23% two topics, 2% three topics and 5% seemed to browse around without a specific question. In some cases, topics looked for in Renardus Search are not pursued when browsing, in other cases, a new topic (most often one) is investigated after the switch to browsing.

IV. CONCLUSION

The main purpose of this study was to explore the navigation behaviour of all users of a large web service, Renardus, using web log analysis, in order to improve the user interface and, especially, the browsing features of the system. In addition, we aimed at gaining some more general insights into users browsing and navigation in large subject classification structures, the benefits from system support and the problems and failures that occurred.

Our study indicates that a thorough log analysis can indeed provide a deeper understanding of user behaviour and service performance. Being an unobtrusive means of capturing unsupervised usage and offering a complete and detailed picture of user activities, log analysis can reveal quantitatively comprehensive, sometimes unexpected results, far beyond plain statistics.

In contrast to common beliefs, our study clearly indicates that browsing as an information-seeking activity is highly used, given proper conditions. About 80% of all activities in Renardus are browsing activities. A contributing reason to that dominance is the fact that a very high percentage (71%) of the users are referred from search engines or other linking sites directly to a browsing page in Renardus. The layout of the home page "invites" browsing, which certainly contributes to the fact that even users starting at the home page predominantly use the browsing part of the service.

Our study leads to a hypothesis which deserves further research: browsing is perceived as useful and dominates navigation in services similar to Renardus and under proper conditions.

The good use of the browsing support features, especially graphical overview and search entry to browsing pages, suggests that it would be worthwhile to further develop such support.

Since most visitors jump into the middle of the service, there might be a need to redesign the browsing pages so they would better serve as full-fledged starting points for comprehensive Renardus exploration. The ubiquitous navigation bar seems not sufficiently inviting. In making such changes, it would also be important to better understand the details of site indexing and ranking algorithms in search engines.

The study of navigation sequences shows that users employ a rich variety of navigation and browsing sequences, including rather long and highly elaborate paths through the system. Nevertheless, quantitatively dominating is, to a quite surprising degree, the tendency to stay in the same group of activities or individual activity, whether browsing, searching, or background information. This finding points us to the importance of providing "search strategy" support to the users at the page where their actions take place.

From the behaviour as documented in the log files we could identify two clearly different groups of users: people starting at the home page/ frontdoor of the service (22%), and the majority of the users starting elsewhere. There are dramatic differences in their activity in the service. People starting at the home page show almost twice as many activities per session, and use the non-browsing features three to five times as often. Their share of the browsing activities is smaller, but they primarily engage in the long sequences of browsing activities (8 and longer) and employ more types of browsing activities and more types of other activities in a session. The home page starters are seemingly a minority but represent high quality of usage of the service in a way the system designers have imagined and intended.

The DDC directory browsing is the single clearly dominating activity in Renardus (60%). Two-thirds of it is done in unbroken directory browsing sequences. We see a surprising average and total length of such browsing sequences, opposing the common belief of the short attention span of users of online services.

Thus, we get the surprising hypothesis that sequential, directory style of hierarchical (classification) browsing is found to be popular and useful in large services like Renardus, especially when there is graphical support.

Comparisons between search terms used and topics browsed indicated a very good chance to get relevant results from Renardus browsing when more than one search term was used. People using Renardus Search were capable of finding browsing pages corresponding to their queries. The system invited users to pursue more than one topic during a session.

Future Work

Our findings indicate that log analysis has a clear potential as a method for studying information behaviour and the proper design of information systems. A lot could be gained from future work to investigate questions such as:

- To what degree does the actual design of the system influence user behaviour, especially with regard to the difference in usage levels of browsing versus searching activities?
- Can we identify additional specific usage and browsing patterns and different behaviours of specific user groups?
- What is the influence of the use of end-user adapted and multilingual DDC captions on browsing behaviour?
- How can we provide search strategy support and further improve the support for systematic browsing of large subject structures?
- What is the importance of the details of site indexing in search engines for the discovery of and navigation in large browsing systems?
- How can pages be redesigned so that they better serve as full-fledged starting points?

For more important results and improvements one would need to go beyond the log analysis and:

- Evaluate user behaviour in supervised sessions/usability lab
- Evaluate the accuracy and success of Renardus to help answering user questions
- Use local URLs to identify what pages outside Renardus users explore as a result of Renardus navigation (links to participating subject gateways).

REFERENCES

1. Harry Hochheiser and Ben Shneiderman. "Using interactive visualizations of WWW log data to characterize access patterns and inform site design." *Journal of the American Society for Information Science and Technology* 52, no. 4 (2001): 331-343.

2. S. Jones, S. J. Cunningham, R. McNab, and S. Boddie. "A transaction log analysis of a digital library." *International Journal on Digital Libraries* 3, no. 2 (2000): 152-169.

3. C. Silverstein, H. Marais, M. Henzinger, and M. Moricz. "Analysis of a very large web search engine query log." In: *SIGIR Forum,* 33, no. 1(1999): 6-12. http://doi.acm.org/10.1145/331403.331405.

4. Seda Ozmutlu, Amanda Spink, and Huseyin C. Ozmutlu. 2004. "A day in the life of web searching: an exploratory study." *Journal of Information Processing and Management* 40, no. 2 (2004): 319-345. http://dx.doi.org/10.1016/S0306-4573(03)00044-X.

5. S. M. Beitzel, E. C. Jensen, A. Chowdhury, D. Grossman, and O. Frieder. "Hourly analysis of a very large topically categorized web query log." In: *Proceedings of the 27th annual international conference on Research and development in information retrieval, Sheffield, United Kingdom,* 2004, 321-328. http://doi.acm.org/10.1145/1008992.1009048.

6. Ard W. Lazonder. "Principles for Designing Web Searching Instruction." *Education and Information Technologies* 8 (June 2003): 179-193. pp. 181.

7. Jacob Nielsen. "Search and You May Find." Jakob Nielsen's Alertbox for July 15, 1997. http://www.useit.com/alertbox/9707b.html.

8. Xie Hong. "Web browsing: current and desired capabilities." In: *20th Annual National Online Meeting, 18-20 May 1999, New York, NY, US,* 523-37.

9. User requirements for the broker system: Renardus Project Deliverable D1.2. 2000. P. 23. http://www.renardus.org/about_us/deliverables/d1_2/D1_2_final.pdf.

10. Renardus Home Page. http://www.renardus.org/. [Since the project finished in 2002, this is only a demonstrator.]

11. Traugott Koch, Heike Neuroth and Michael Day. "Renardus: Cross-browsing European subject gateways via a common classification system (DDC). In: "Subject Retrieval in a Networked Environment," *Proceedings of the IFLA Satellite Meeting sponsored by the IFLA Section on Classification and Indexing and the IFLA Section on Information Technology, 14-16 August 2001, Dublin, OH, USA,* 25-33. München: UBCIM Publications New Series Vol. 25, 2003. Manuscript at: http://www.lub.lu.se/~traugott/drafts/preifla-final.html.

12. Renardus Project Archive and Associated Research and Development. 2002. http://www.renardus.org/about_us/project_archive.html.

13. User evaluation report: Renardus Project Deliverable D5.2. 2002. http://www.renardus.org/about_us/deliverables/d5_2/D5_2_final.pdf.

14. For example, see Technology:Agriculture: page. http://www.renardus.org/cgi-bin/genDDCbrowseSQL.pl?ID=10191&node=AAZNG.

15. For example, see Graphical browsing page for Technology . . . : Mining for specific materials. http://www.renardus.org/cgi-bin/imageDDCbrowseSQL.pl?node=ABDPH&ID=10193&pmat=N&pnavnode=Y&pgraph=matcirc.

All electronic resources have been accessed 20 January 2005.

doi:10.1300/J104v42n03_07

HILT:
A Pilot Terminology Mapping Service
with a DDC Spine

Dennis M. Nicholson
Alan Dawson
Ali Shiri

SUMMARY. The role of DDC in the ongoing HILT (High-level Thesaurus) project is discussed. A phased initiative, funded by JISC in the UK, HILT addresses an issue of likely interest to anyone serving users wishing to cross-search or cross-browse groups of networked information services, whether at regional, national, or international level–the problem of subject-based retrieval from multiple sources using different subject

Dennis M. Nicholson is Director (E-mail: d.m.nicholson@strath.ac.uk); and Alan Dawson is Senior Researcher (E-mail: alan.dawson@strath.ac.uk), both at the Centre for Digital Library Research, Department of Computer and Information Sciences, Livingstone Tower, 26 Richmond Street, Glasgow, G1 1XH. Ali Shiri is Assistant Professor, School of Library and Information Studies, University of Alberta, 3-20 Rutherford South, Edmonton, AB, T6G 2J4 (E-mail: ashiri@ualberta.ca). He was formerly Senior Researcher, Centre for Digital Library Research, University of Strathclyde, Glasgow, Scotland, UK.

[Haworth co-indexing entry note]: "HILT: A Pilot Terminology Mapping Service with a DDC Spine." Nicholson, Dennis M., Alan Dawson, and Ali Shiri. Co-published simultaneously in *Cataloging & Classification Quarterly* (The Haworth Information Press, an imprint of The Haworth Press, Inc.) Vol. 42, No. 3/4, 2006, pp. 187-200; and: *Moving Beyond the Presentation Layer: Content and Context in the Dewey Decimal Classification (DDC) System* (ed: Joan S. Mitchell, and Diane Vizine-Goetz) The Haworth Information Press, an imprint of The Haworth Press, Inc., 2006, pp. 187-200. Single or multiple copies of this article are available for a fee from The Haworth Document Delivery Service [1-800-HAWORTH, 9:00 a.m. - 5:00 p.m. (EST). E-mail address: docdelivery@haworthpress.com].

Available online at http://ccq.haworthpress.com
© 2006 by The Haworth Press, Inc. All rights reserved.
doi:10.1300/J104v42n03_08

187

schemes for resource description. Although all three phases of HILT to date are covered, the primary concern is with the subject interoperability solution piloted in phase II, and with the use of DDC as a spine in that approach. doi:10.1300/J104v42n03_08 *[Article copies available for a fee from The Haworth Document Delivery Service: 1-800-HAWORTH. E-mail address: <docdelivery@haworthpress.com> Website: <http://www.HaworthPress.com> © 2006 by The Haworth Press, Inc. All rights reserved.]*

KEYWORDS. HILT Project, interoperability, subject searching, DDC, Dewey Decimal Classification, mapping terminologies

INTRODUCTION: HILT AND DDC

The HILT project[1] began in September 2000 with HILT Phase I and ran for approximately 15 months.[2] HILT Phase I was an investigation into the problems of cross-searching and browsing by subject in a distributed, multi-scheme environment and was charged with determining whether a consensus on the best solution to these problems could be reached in archives, libraries, museums, and electronic services in the UK. It was followed by HILT Phase II, which ran for a similar period between 2002 and late 2003[3] and built an illustrative pilot terminologies server based on the consensus solution arrived at in the Phase I work.[4] At the time of writing (January 2005), a short feasibility study is underway to determine whether the user facilities provided in the Phase II pilot can also be provided via a machine-to-machine (M2M) interface and to determine the likely cost of building such an interface. This is preliminary to possible Phase III work and is expected to lead to an attempt to build these M2M facilities into the pilot service in a full-scale HILT Phase III. The Dewey Decimal Classification (DDC) system has featured in all three parts of the project to date–as a possible solution in its own right and then as a proposed spine for a mapping-based solution in Phase I, and as a spine for pilot terminology services in Phase II and in the Phase III feasibility study.

HILT PHASE I: OVERVIEW

HILT Phase I was a collaborative investigation into the problems associated with cross-searching and browsing by subject in a cross-sectoral and cross-domain environment encompassing libraries, archives, museums, and electronic resource collections in the UK. Its principal aims were:

- To thoroughly research the problem, analyse and document its exact nature in detail, focusing on UK requirements across the various communities, services and initiatives, but setting the study firmly in the context of international requirements and standards.
- To analyse the data obtained, and discuss the results with the various communities, with an aim to reaching a consensus within the project on how best to apply the findings in relation to existing or new subject schemes and thesauri.
- To attempt to reach a similar consensus within the group of stakeholders generally, both at a stakeholder workshop and through other methods.
- Reporting in early 2002,[2] the project determined that:

    - Many different subject schemes and practices are in use in UK services.
    - Subject searching across services is believed to be of value to users.
    - There was a strong consensus across the archives, electronic services, library, and museums' communities in favour of a more practically-focused follow-up project that would develop a pilot service providing mappings between subject schemes, probably using a DDC spine.
    - Further research was required into the effectiveness, level and nature of user need, practicality, design requirements, costs and benefits of such an approach before a long-term commitment to a (possibly expensive) service could be justified.

Further details of the project have been reported in detail elsewhere.[5,6,4]

HILT Phase I and DDC

The key event in HILT Phase I was the stakeholder workshop. Here, well-informed stakeholders were presented with various options:

- Do nothing–on the basis that it was an unimportant problem, that users could cope, that solutions would be found by the artificial intelligence community or by commercial initiatives, or that the problem could not be solved.
- Set up a human process–such as a 'terminologies agency'–intended to lead to a solution in time.
- Adopt a base-level, gradual approach, with an eye on future developments–for example, apply a single scheme to collection-level

descriptions of services, focus only on electronic services, or gradually create inter-community terminology 'cross-walks.'

- Adopt a single scheme under various circumstances–an existing scheme or an entirely new scheme, used in addition to a service's existing scheme or instead of it, with or without retro-conversion of legacy metadata.
- Set up a service that would provide mappings between subject schemes, or set up a pilot service of this kind so that further investigations could be conducted.

DDC was proposed as a strong candidate should a single scheme be the preferred outcome, as it offered the following advantages over other alternatives:

- It is owned by a major worldwide not-for-profit organisation with a clear commitment to continuing to maintain and develop it and a record of consulting key players.
- It is in use in over 200,000 libraries worldwide and in 135 countries.
- It is available in over 30 different languages, including languages with major world coverage such as English, French, German, and Spanish.

Despite being presented as the HILT team's second preference, the option of a single subject scheme (based on DDC or anything else) was almost unanimously rejected by the workshop breakout groups.

However, DDC was identified as having a potential role in the option ultimately chosen by workshop stakeholders as the preferred route to consensus–the pilot mapping service option. One possible design for such a service entailed the use of a central spine and DDC was identified as a possible candidate for this role, primarily in view of the advantages presented above.

HILT PHASE II: OVERVIEW

HILT Phase II was funded to set up a pilot terminologies server based on the mapping approach identified in HILT Phase I, an approach to interoperability used in a range of other projects.[7,8,9,10] The primary aim in this second stage of HILT was to provide a practical experimental focus within which to investigate and establish subject terminology service requirements for the JISC Information Environment[11] and make recommendations as regards a possible future service. There was also a requirement to consider issues such as user needs, collection-level requirements, international compatibility, and costs against benefits. The question of whether or not the pilot service should have a central spine (as opposed to, say, mapping directly between user terms and individual schemes or between the schemes themselves) was left open at the outset, although DDC was identified as a strong candidate as a spine should that approach be adopted.

A spine-based approach was selected, with DDC as the preferred spine, in common with other recent initiatives.[7,12,13,14] The most important reasons for choosing a DDC spine were:

- A spine-based approach was likely to involve less labour-intensive (and, hence, less expensive) manual mapping than mapping between user terms and individual schemes or between the schemes themselves.
- DDC is already extensively mapped to LCSH and has been a favoured option by a wide range of other projects.
- Since multi-lingual mapping was a likely future requirement, a scheme available in more than 30 languages was seen as a leading candidate for the spine.
- The use of DDC was the only evident way of providing the proposed collections finding facility described below.

With this general approach agreed, the project then moved to deal with four primary concerns:

- Designing and building the pilot service.
- Conducting a user evaluation of the resulting service.
- Carrying out a cost-benefit analysis of alternative approaches.
- Making recommendations as to the creation of a possible future operational service.

Much of the remainder of this paper is concerned with a description of the pilot terminology server, with particular reference to the role played by DDC. Further information is available elsewhere on the user evaluation,[15] on early work with users,[16] and on the project outcomes as a whole.[3,17]

THE HILT PILOT: A USER'S VIEW

The HILT pilot is available at http://hiltpilot.cdlr.strath.ac.uk/pilot/top.php. Illustrative examples can be found at http://hiltpilot.cdlr.strath.

ac.uk/pilot/examples/ and in Shiri, Nicholson, and McCulloch.[15] The following is a brief description of the steps involved:

1. The user enters a subject term.
2. The term is matched to the terminology set held by the pilot server (a set that includes terms in the DDC captions, index, and standard subdivisions, and terms from other schemes mapped to DDC).
3. Based on mappings from the terminology set to DDC numbers, the server returns a number of possible subjects from DDC and prompts the user to choose the right one–to disambiguate the options.
4. The DDC number matching the term chosen by the user is submitted to a separate database of collections classified by DDC, to identify collections appropriate to the user's query. If there are no collections matching the DDC number precisely, then the DDC number is truncated until one or more collections are identified that cover a broader subject area than the search term.
5. The collections database sends back recommended collections to search, plus information on the scheme used, the term or terms from the scheme appropriate to the user's search, and, where technically possible, sample retrieval from specific collections.

As is clear from Figure 1, an alternative browse-based route is also available, which takes the user down the DDC hierarchies to a specific subject of interest.

Methodologies

Software and Data Conversion

The pilot server is based on an adaptation of a software package called Wordmap, offered by a company of the same name. The package–described in detail at http://www.wordmap.com/–has three distinct elements:

- A taxonomy database (Oracle) holding terminology mappings.
- A simple user interface that interacts with the database according to staff specifications and user input and feedback.
- A powerful multi-user interface to support sophisticated staff interaction with the database for creation and maintenance of taxonomies and mappings.

FIGURE 1. User Interaction with the HILT Pilot Interface

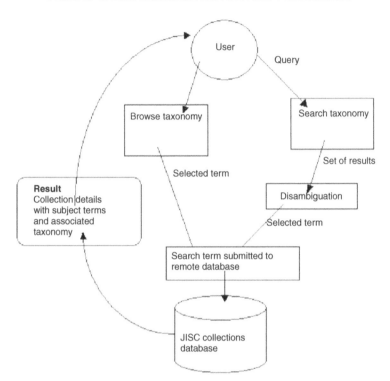

The primary focus of the HILT project was on programming the simple user interface to interact with a database comprising data provided by OCLC supplemented by manual mappings provided by HILT. This offered:

- Access to the whole of the DDC 21 schedules, indexed on the DDC captions, standard subdivisions and Relative Index.
- Mappings of DDC to LCSH as provided by OCLC.
- Illustrative mappings from DDC to UNESCO and MeSH subject schemes, created by HILT.

Further information on the adaptation of the Wordmap database structure for HILT purposes and on processing and importing the files provided by OCLC is available in Appendix I.2 of the HILT Final Report.[3]

Mapping

A literature review was conducted to investigate the problems and issues in integrating and mapping thesauri and classification schemes and the different types of mapping. A list of 19 match types was identified in the review,[18] some mapping exercises were carried out, and example mappings were then selected to build into the server. Examples of common match types are provided in Table 1.

Search Algorithm

The search process is complex and not intuitively obvious. During testing it became clear that no single algorithm could give the best results for all search terms. The resulting process appears to give useful results for most search terms tried, but is not guaranteed to give the best results for all possible search terms. The system goes through the following steps when it receives a query.

1. Look for an exact match against the query term.
2. If there are five or more matches, the results are displayed. If there are between one and five matches, the system will adopt a pattern matching approach, looking for the term with any characters before or after it. For example, a search for 'science' would find 'natural sciences' and 'science and mathematics.' The additional results are appended to the exact matches.
3. If there are no results found for step 2, the system will look for the search term and any characters after it (but not before). For example, if the search term is 'compute' the system will then retrieve 'computer,' 'computerization,' etc.
4. If there are some results, the system offers a 'more results' option. This results in stemming of the search term (removing plurals, 'ing,' 'ed,' etc.), using the Porter stemming algorithm,[19] and pattern-matching search as in step 2.
5. If no results are found following step 3, the system will adopt a pattern matching approach again, as in step 2.
6. If there are still no results, the system will parse the query to identify any individual words, remove stop words such as 'the,' 'in,' 'and,' etc., and then run a search on the individual words using the same steps outlined above. The results will then be merged, de-duplicated, ranked and returned to the user.

TABLE 1. Examples of Common Match Types

Match type	First scheme DDC	Second scheme MeSH
Type 1: Singular plural	Teeth	Tooth

Match type	First scheme DDC	Second scheme LCSH
Type 2: Exact match	Teeth	Teeth

Match type	First scheme DDC	Second scheme UNESCO
Type 3: Exact match	Persons in late adulthood	Elderly

Multi-Word Queries

Before displaying results from multi-word queries, the system removes duplicates and assigns weights to individual items. If the same item has been retrieved as a result of a search with different words, that item gets a higher weighting (ranking) in the display of search results. The merging and ranking of search results gives the same effect as an AND search followed by an OR search. If the user types in Boolean terms such as AND or OR, these will be stripped out as stop words and ignored. Each remaining word is then handled individually.

If a search term is entered as a phrase in quotation marks, it will be treated as a single word and no parsing takes place.

Identifying Collections

A key element in the operation of the pilot server is the identification of network-accessible collections or services appropriate to the user's subject query. The collections database is stored on a separate server and uses different database software to the HILT server. Once the user has selected a term (either by browsing or by search and disambiguation), the system identifies any collections relevant to that term by searching the collections database, then displays the collection name and description along with any subject terms relevant to that collection. Searching the collections database involves the following steps:

1. The system retrieves the DDC number of the user search term from the Wordmap database, along with the corresponding features (subject terms, taxonomy, and match type).
2. Collections relevant to the DDC number are retrieved from the separate collections database. If the DDC number is a range (e.g.,

371.12-.18) rather than a single number, the system retrieves all the collections matching that range.

3. The system also retrieves some broader collections. For example, if the DDC number of the term is 371.2134, the system retrieves collections with DDC number 371.2134, 371.213, 371.21, 371.2, 371, and 370. If there are no results for all these searches, the system adopts pattern searching to retrieve related collections, e.g., all collections starting with DDC number 371.

4. If the selected term is from DDC Table 2 or Table 6 rather than the main DDC schedule, the table number is converted to a DDC number (Table 2 maps to the DDC 900s and Table 6, where possible, maps to the DDC 400s) and then treated as a DDC number when searching the collections database. For example, a search for 'Cairo' will retrieve T2-6216 from Table 2, which will retrieve any collections with DDC number 962.

If the collection allows remote searching by appending a variable search term to a fixed partial URL (as in the OpenURL standard), and if it uses one of the recognized taxonomies, then the system offers the user the option of dynamically searching the remote collection using the appropriate term provided by the terminology server. In order for this function to operate, the collections database has to include the partial URL to which search terms can be appended and remotely submitted. At present, this option is possible with only a small number of collections, a factor beyond the control of the project itself.

OUTSTANDING ISSUES

As the worked examples at http://hiltpilot.cdlr.strath.ac.uk/pilot/examples/ make clear, it is possible to show that the terminology server will work intelligently for the terms chosen, both in terms of the identification of collections appropriate to the subject search in question and in terms of actual item-level retrieval from a specific collection identified by this means. However, the pilot server is only illustrative–it is not, at this stage, possible to claim that the approach will work in practice for the significant number of different schemes used by networked services in the world at large, or for the large number of types of subject query that would have to be handled on a large scale.

The approach adopted in the HILT pilot remains a possible route to a solution, but a good deal of additional research is needed before it will be possible to determine whether its potential can be realised in practice and, if so, how. Particular areas requiring attention are:

- User subject searching needs and associated interface design issues.
- A detailed, large-scale, multi-scheme examination of mapping issues that arise from these user needs.
- Issues associated with the requirement for the terminologies server to interact with users through other services on the network via machine-to-machine (M2M) interfaces.

THE HILT M2M FEASIBILITY STUDY

The HILT Phase II proposal indicated that it would be 'difficult in such a relatively small, relatively low-cost project to fully investigate M2M use of the pilot facility in an operational sense.' It therefore proposed to focus primarily on the use of the pilot server by end users and to cover the M2M needs by 'examining the requirement for this on an ongoing basis at a mainly theoretical level.' An independent examination of the M2M requirement was undertaken by UKOLN, which recommended[20] that an M2M follow-up project should aim to:

- Provide M2M demonstrator services based on controlled vocabularies mapped within Wordmap.
- Develop SOAP-based interfaces[21] between components of the JISC information environment and Wordmap application programming interfaces, and to use these services in the short term as an aid to specify use cases, and in the longer term as a basis for pilot service if still appropriate at that stage.
- Carry out investigative implementation of a Zthes-based solution,[22] with a view to taking advantage of standards-based structured controlled vocabularies (particularly faceted vocabularies) as they become available from third party agencies.
- Track developments within the semantic web and eScience communities, to ensure that decisions made concerning the syntax for structuring vocabularies and the data exchange protocols would take account of forward compatibility.

With this in mind, JISC funded a short study into the feasibility of a project along these lines. This was charged with:

1. Investigating the feasibility of developing a SOAP-based interface between one of the JISC services and the HILT pilot server, whilst also taking into account the possibility of a future Zthes-based solution, relevant implications of work in the eScience and semantic web communities,[23] and developments in vocabulary mapping generally.[24]
2. Determining the scope and cost of the provision of an actual M2M demonstrator based on SOAP.

The study final report is available on the HILT website at the following address: http://hilt.cdlr.strath.ac.uk/hiltm2mfs/0HILTM2MFinalReportRepV3. 1-5.doc. It recommended that a project to create an M2M version of the HILT Phase II pilot be funded, and that it be built around SRW and SKOS-Core. The recommendation was accepted by JISC and HILT Phase III, charged with creating such a pilot, began in November 2005.

CONCLUSION

The DDC and mapping-based HILT pilot described in this paper may provide a basis for resolving subject interoperability issues in a distributed, multi-scheme information environment. However, a good deal of additional research is required before it would be safe either to conclude that it will, or to invest heavily in what is likely to be an expensive (and ongoing) enterprise. A cautious approach to forward development is necessary and appears to be the approach favoured by JISC. At present, the current focus is the creation of an M2M version of the Phase II pilot as indicated above.

HILT has shown that the precision with which DDC can identify concepts gives it the potential to act as a mechanism for mapping between terms in different subject schemes. However, it remains to be seen whether this potential can be realised in a cost-effective production service to assist information retrieval by users of networked information services.

REFERENCES

1. HILT, "High-Level Thesaurus Project" (2005) http://hilt.cdlr.strath.ac.uk/ (March 31, 2005).

2. HILT, "HILT Phase I Final Report" (2002) http://hilt.cdlr.strath.ac.uk/reports/ finalreport.html (March 31, 2005).

3. HILT, "HILT Phase II Final Report" (2003) http://hilt.cdlr.strath.ac.uk/ hilt2web/finalreport.htm (March 31, 2005).

4. D. Nicholson, "Subject-Based Interoperability: Issues from the High Level Thesaurus (HILT) Project," *International Cataloguing and Bibliographic Control* 32 (1) (2003).

5. D. Nicholson and S. Wake. "Interoperability in Subject Terminologies: The HILT Project," *New Review of Information Networking* Volume 7 (2001).

6. D. Nicholson, S. Wake and S. Currier, "High-level Thesaurus Project: Investigating the Problem of Subject Cross-searching and Browsing between Communities," in *Global Digital Library Development in the New Millennium*, edited by Chin-chich Chen. (Beijing: Tsinghua University Press, 2001).

7. CARMEN, Content Analysis, Retrieval and MetaData: Effective Networking, http://www.mathematik.uni-osnabrueck.de/projects/carmen/index.en.shtml (March 31, 2005).

8. LIMBER, Language Independent Metadata Browsing of European Resources, http://www.limber.rl.ac.uk/ (March 31, 2005).

9. MACS, Multilingual access to subjects, http://laborix.kub.nl/prj/macs/ (March 31, 2005).

10. RENARDUS, Evaluation Reports (2002), http://www.renardus.org/about_us/deliverables/d5_2/D5_2summ.html (March 31, 2005).

11. JISC, JISC Information Environment Architecture, http://www.ukoln.ac.uk/distributed-systems/jisc-ie/arch/ (March 31, 2005).

12. R. Heery, L. Carpenter, and M. Day, "Renardus Project Developments and the Wider Digital Library Context," *D-Lib Magazine*, 7 (4) (2001), http://www.dlib.org/dlib/april01/heery/04heery.html (March 31, 2005).

13. T. Koch, H. Neuroth, and M. Day, "Renardus: Cross-browsing European subject gateways via a common classification system (DDC)." Paper presented at IFLA satellite meeting: *Subject Retrieval in a Networked Environment*, OCLC, Dublin, Ohio, 14-16 August 2001 (2001).

14. H. Saeed, and A. S. Chaudhury, "Using Dewey decimal classification scheme (DDC) for building taxonomies for knowledge organisation," *Journal of Documentation* 58 (5) (2002): 575-583.

15. A. Shiri, D. Nicholson, and E. McCulloch, "User evaluation of a pilot terminologies server for a distributed multi-scheme environment," *Online Information Review*. 28 (4) (2004): 273-283.

16. E. McCulloch, A. Shiri, and D. Nicholson, "Subject searching requirements: the HILT II experience," *Library Review* 53 (8) (2004): 408-414.

17. E. McCulloch, A. Shiri, and D. Nicholson, "Challenges and issues in terminology mapping: a digital library perspective. *Electronic Library* (2005). in press.

18. M. A. Chaplan, "Mapping Laborline thesaurus terms to Library of Congress subject headings: Implications for vocabulary switching," *Library Quarterly*, 65(1) (1995): 39-61.

19. Porter, Porter stemming algorithm, http://www.tartarus.org/~martin/PorterStemmer/ (March 31, 2005).

20. UKOLN, "HILT Final Report Appendix J" (2003), http://www.ukoln.ac.uk/metadata/hilt/m2m-report/hilt-final-report.pdf (March 31, 2005).

21. SOAP, "SOAP Version 1.2 Part 1: Messaging Framework," http://www.w3.org/TR/soap12-part1/ (March 31, 2005).

22. "Zthes, a Z39.50 Profile for Thesaurus Navigation," http://www.loc.gov/z3950/agency/profiles/zthes-04.html (March 31, 2005).

23. A. J. Miles, N. Rogers, and D. Beckett, "SKOS-Core 1.0 Guide, An RDF Schema for Thesauri and Related Knowledge Organisation Systems," http://www. w3.org/2001/sw/Europe/reports/thes/1.0/guide (March 31, 2005).

24. D. Vizine-Goetz, C. Hickey, A. Houghton, and R. Thompson, "Vocabulary Mapping for Terminology Services," *Journal of Digital Information* 4 (4) (2004), Article No. 272, 2004-03-11, http://jodi.ecs.soton.ac.uk/Articles/v04/i04/Vizine-Goetz/ (March 31, 2005).

doi:10.1300/J104v42n03_08

Resource Discovery
in the Government of Canada
Using the Dewey Decimal Classification

Deane Zeeman
Glenyss Turner

SUMMARY. Library and Archives Canada (LAC) has capitalized on the Dewey Decimal Classification (DDC) potential for organizing Web resources in two projects. Since 1995, LAC has been providing a service that offers links to authoritative Web resources about Canada categorized according to the DDC via its Web site. More recently, LAC has partnered with the federal government Department of Cana-

---

Deane Zeeman, MLS, is the Lead, Metadata Catalytic Initiative at Library and Archives Canada, 395 Wellington Street, Ottawa, Canada K1A 0N4 (E-mail: deane. zeeman@lac-bac.gc.ca). She is the Canadian member of the DDC Editorial Policy Committee. Glenyss Turner, MLS, is a member of the Metadata Catalytic Initiative Core Team at LAC (E-mail: glenyss.turner@lac-bac.gc.ca).

The authors would like to thank Doug Robinson (Library and Information Science Specialist, Reference and Genealogy Service, LAC) for the literature search foundation of this article and David Murrell-Wright (Chief, Monographs Cataloguing, LAC) and Mark Alexander (Manager, Products & Services, Culture.ca, Department of Canadian Heritage) for the historical perspective.

[Haworth co-indexing entry note]: "Resource Discovery in the Government of Canada Using the Dewey Decimal Classification." Zeeman, Deane, and Glenyss Turner. Co-published simultaneously in *Cataloging & Classification Quarterly* (The Haworth Information Press, an imprint of The Haworth Press, Inc.) Vol. 42, No. 3/4, 2006, pp. 201-211; and: *Moving Beyond the Presentation Layer: Content and Context in the Dewey Decimal Classification (DDC) System* (ed: Joan S. Mitchell, and Diane Vizine-Goetz) The Haworth Information Press, an imprint of The Haworth Press, Inc., 2006, pp. 201-211. Single or multiple copies of this article are available for a fee from The Haworth Document Delivery Service [1-800-HAWORTH, 9:00 a.m. - 5:00 p.m. (EST). E-mail address: docdelivery@haworthpress.com].

Available online at http://ccq.haworthpress.com
© 2006 by The Haworth Press, Inc. All rights reserved.
doi:10.1300/J104v42n03_09

dian Heritage to manage Web content related to Canadian culture in a DDC-based subject tree. Although the DDC works well to organize a broadly-based collection, challenges have been encountered in adapting it for a specific subject domain. *doi:10.1300/J104v42n03_09 [Article copies available for a fee from The Haworth Document Delivery Service: 1-800-HAWORTH. E-mail address: <docdelivery@haworthpress.com> Website: <http://www.HaworthPress.com> © 2006 by The Haworth Press, Inc. All rights reserved.]*

KEYWORDS. World Wide Web, WWW, classification, Web resources, information organization, DDC, Dewey Decimal Classification

INTRODUCTION

The Dewey Decimal Classification (DDC) is a powerful tool for organizing resources, with a proven track record in the world of published information. Researchers have identified possibilities for using traditional bibliographic tools to improve the organization of information resources on the World Wide Web (WWW).[1] Library and Archives Canada, the Canadian national library, has seen in the DDC a potential for playing an authoritative information organization role in other domains and has used the DDC to manage two large collections of links to WWW resources.

LAC EXPERIENCE OF DDC

The National Library of Canada (now Library and Archives Canada, LAC[2]) has been using the DDC since the inception of the institution to help Canadian libraries describe and co-locate similar Canadian publications in both English and French, Canada's official languages. Following IFLA guidelines, *Canadiana*, the printed national bibliography, was organized by broad Dewey numbers since the first issue in 1950, continuing to the demise of the printed publication in 1991. Specific DDC numbers started appearing in the bibliography in 1963; provision of DDC numbers continues at the full and minimal cataloguing level in LAC bibliographic products. The first subject catalogue in the Library was a "classed catalogue" based on the DDC with French and English indexes. This was an excellent adaptation of the DDC that provided a bilingual subject approach to the collection prior to the advent of the *Répertoire de vedettes-matière* (*RVM*), a French language subject headings tool. However, since this classed catalogue was only available to staff, it was not cost-effective and was closed at the end of the 1970s in favour of English[3] and French subject heading catalogues, that is, *LCSH (Library of Congress Subject Headings)* and *RVM*.

THE CHALLENGES

Organizing Information for User Access in the Online World

It is no secret that the growth of information on the WWW has been exponential in the past decade. LAC recognized early on that the ability of users to mine the rich information potential of the Web was being hampered by lack of tools to help them find appropriate content. Too much information with too little relevance has made users feel like they are trying to "take a sip from a fire hose." In addition, users want to find authoritative sites containing reliable information.

LAC saw the DDC as a tool to help users with this dilemma. Providing an organized approach to Web information according to the DDC would supply users with a familiar tool. In addition to organizing Web sites, LAC could assist users with the "authoritativeness factor" by setting selection criteria for sites to be included in a DDC-based structure.

Adapting Tools and Skills for the New Environment

LAC cataloguing staff have extensive experience in applying the DDC to published materials. We realized that we could leverage our knowledge for the new and emerging domain of Web information organization and retrieval by using our skills in Dewey classification in a new way.

THE SOLUTIONS

Canadian Information By Subject (CIBS)

Established in 1995, the objective of the *Canadian Information By Subject* (CIBS)[3] service was to facilitate access to information about Canada, by serving as an "on ramp" to the information highway for Canadians, especially for teachers and students. CIBS provides links to information about Canada from Web resources around the world and arranges them by subject for ease of access.

The subject arrangement is in the form of a hierarchical "subject tree," based on the structure of the DDC (see Figure 1).

The DDC was selected as the organisational underpinning for several reasons: it is the most widely used library classification in the world[4] and is familiar to most public and school library users in North America;[5] it was already proving itself useful for the categorization of Web resources in other contexts such as BUBL Link[6] at the Strathclyde University in Glasgow and the *Renardus*[7] gateway aggregating high quality Internet resources for those teaching, learning and researching in higher education in Europe; and, by using this tool, LAC could leverage its traditional information organization skills for use in a new domain–the Internet. As well, it can play a key role in assuring the development of a balanced collection. Content gaps are easily identified when the content is arranged on the hierarchical tree.

Following the DDC structure, the links to WWW content are attached to nodes or categories on a hierarchical subject tree and listed alphabetically by site name within each category. Geographic qualifiers are added to site names as necessary for clarity. The subject hierarchy is browsable in subject order or alphabetical order. The subject view

FIGURE 1. CIBS Subject Tree

0 Computer science, information and general works
1 Philosophy, parapsychology and occultism, psychology
2 Religion
3 Social sciences
4 Language
5 Natural sciences and mathematics
6 Technology (Applied sciences)
7 Arts. Fine and decorative arts
8 Literature (Belles-lettres) and rhetoric
9 History, geography, and auxiliary disciplines

Source: Library and Archives Canada, Canadian Information by Subject, Subject Tree–Subject. Order: http://www.collectionscanada.ca/caninfo/esub.htm.

shows the top two levels of the subject hierarchy; the alphabetical index lists the subject categories in alphabetical order. The terminology used to label the subjects is taken from standard lists of subject headings: *LCSH* and *CSH* (*Canadian Subject Headings*) for English terminology and *RVM* for French terminology. The terminology of the DDC captions and relative index are rarely used as their purpose is more to explain than to label.

Culture.ca

In June 2001, the Government of Canada announced a new programme, *Tomorrow Starts Today*, with the objective of ensuring a strong and original Canadian presence in new media and digitization "to enable Canadians [. . .] to have broad access to our rich and culturally diverse heritage"[8] using multimedia and the Internet. The programme resulted in substantial Canadian digitization efforts and a corresponding need to provide access to the products to show value for money. As part of this initiative to strengthen the visibility of the arts and culture in Canada, a cultural-based Internet portal was created. The portal, Culture.ca,[9] was to be an online gateway to Canadian culture, to help brand Canada abroad and to reflect the values of Canadian society.[10] The Department of Canadian Heritage was identified as the lead agency for the initiative. Since LAC was already well known for identifying, describing and organizing Canadian Web content in its CIBS service, the Department recognized us as the logical partner to organize the Web resources for this new cultural portal.

The DDC was selected as the organizing tool for the Culture.ca links collection for many of the same reasons it has proved so useful for CIBS: it is scaleable, allowing for organic growth; it is hierarchical, allowing browsing from general to more specific content; and it is language-neutral, a useful characteristic in a bilingual environment. In fact, the cultural content of CIBS was used as the basis for the new portal, enhanced with more metadata, including additional DDC numbers to more fully describe the Web resources selected. Content can be classified with up to three DDC numbers, a policy which allows for a kind of "added subject entry." This was an innovation of traditional classification practice for the electronic world where it is not necessary to find "the" place for a resource; links can be co-located at up to three nodes on the subject tree. Using a standard as the basis for the information organization while potentially using other more fluid means of displaying the content on the portal was identified as an additional benefit.

THE RESULTS

CIBS

The use of the CIBS service on the LAC Web site has been consistently high. Over the years, it has proven to be one of the more popular pages on the LAC site. By 1999, it was receiving an average of 36,000 hits per month.[11] In the first nine months of 2004, almost 2% of total LAC Web site visits were to CIBS, making it among the top 25 areas visited out of over 200 main areas. The DDC works well for this application because the subject content coverage is wide, a good fit with the DDC which is a universal scheme. The top two levels of the DDC are used as categories or "buckets." Content is more narrowly classed, but the goal is to avoid being too specific by aggregating content on very specific subjects at higher levels rather than classifying strictly according to standard practice for published materials. The DDC is a scheme used and well-known to the primary audience of CIBS, teachers, and students.

The domain of a Web taxonomy is defined as the convergence of content, users and business processes. Research undertaken at the Montague Institute has demonstrated that an effective taxonomy is based upon a primary focus (user, content, or process).[12] Organizing and providing access to the CIBS content using the DDC has been successful because the service has a content focus and is designed for a known audience who are comfortable with the organizing principle.

Culture.ca

The DDC works "behind the scenes" in Culture.ca as the organizing structure holding the content. It has not been used as a front-end display taxonomy for two main reasons. DDC was selected as the organizing principle for links to cultural content very early in the development of the project, before the scope of the content and the audiences had been well defined, with the proviso that additional approaches might ultimately be required for browsing. Once a significant pool of links had been classified and relevant terms taken from the DDC captions and relative index were available for display, it became apparent that this terminology set was not user-friendly. DDC terminology explains the concepts to be classed at the specific nodes on the subject tree whereas the need of Culture.ca was for user-friendly categories or "bucket" labels. Moreover, a substantial proportion of the content was classified at nodes deep in the structure because it was about very specific topics. This meant that users would be required to exceed the widely-accepted "three clicks to content" principle to access specific information. Consequently, it was decided to develop a display-layer vocabulary comprised to 6 top level categories (see Figure 2), providing multiple routes to the same content where it seemed useful to do so. A three-layer taxonomy was defined inside each top level category (see extract in Figure 3). After the display taxonomy, known as the Culture.ca Classification (CC Class), was developed by the content team at the Department of Canadian Heritage, the Dewey subject tree was mapped to it (see extract in Figure 4).

The Dewey subject tree was maintained for two reasons. By the time the user-friendly taxonomy was developed, the database of classified links was quite large (the current count is in excess of 14,000 links to Canadian cultural content); it was more cost-effective to map the subject tree to the CC Class categories than to re-do the subject analysis for every link. In addition, there was a concern that the CC Class, which had been developed in a tight timeframe due to project milestone requirements, would be replaced as the portal responded to the identified needs of the its audience. By keeping the DDC as the "backbone" for classifying the database, a new display taxonomy could easily be implemented by re-mapping the Dewey tree.

Problems in reconciling the CC Class, where the same concept may be approached from multiple starting points, with the Dewey subject tree have emerged over three years of experience in building the Culture.ca database. A major concern is that the rigid nature of the underlying organization of the DDC, which makes it such a powerful tool for

FIGURE 2. Culture.ca Top Level Categories

| Arts & Expression |
| History & Heritage |
| Media & Publishing |
| People & Diversity |
| Places & Land |
| Sports & Leisure |

Source: Culture.ca: http://www.culture.ca/.

FIGURE 3. Extract from the 3-Layer Display Taxonomy

Category display name	Code
Places and Land	300
Agriculture	311
Railroads	312
Maps and Geography	320
Atlases and Maps	321
Geographers and Explorers	322
Travel	330
Atlantic Provinces	331
Quebec	332
Ontario	333
Prairie Provinces	334
British Columbia	335
Territories	336
National and Provincial Parks	340
Natural History	350
Heritage and Historic Sites	360
Urban Planning and Architecture	370
Urban Planning	371
Architecture	372
Architects	373
Historic Buildings	374

Source: Library and Archives Canada, Metadata Service.

co-locating and accessing content in the universe of published material, does not lend itself to describing Web content in a narrow domain, nor should it be expected to do so; it was not designed for this purpose. For example, some content on specific Dewey subject tree nodes really maps best to different parts of the CC Class, something we cannot accommodate. The nodes on the Dewey tree are fixed; we are not able to express relationships between subjects in this domain in the flexible ways that we would like in order to deliver content to our users in their terms. Additionally, because of inherent weaknesses in the taxonomy, the mappings from the subject tree are general. Under- or over-popula-

FIGURE 4. Extract from DDC Mapping to Culture.ca Display Taxonomy

English Description	DDC	CC1	CC2	CC3
Mathematical geography, cartography	526.	320		
Surveyors	526.9092	320		
Place names	910.014	320	300	
Atlases, maps	912.	321		
Discovery, exploration	910.9	322	511	
Geographers; Travelers; Explorers	910.92	322		
Sailing ships	387.2043	330	470	570
Automobiles	388.342	330	570	
Bicycles; Bicyclists	388.3472	330	570	
Motorcycles	388.3475	330		
Motorcyclists	388.3475092	330		
Travel–Health aspects	613.68	330		
Hotels	647.94	330		
Restaurants; Bars	647.95	330		
Geography, travel	910.	330		
Geography, travel–Canada	917.1	330	320	

Source: Library and Archives Canada, Metadata Service.
Notes: "CC" refers to the node on the CC Class display taxonomy to which the DDC number has been mapped. Up to 3 mappings are allowed for any DDC number.

tion of CC Class categories is common, and some of the content groupings could be more coherent.

The management of the Culture.ca portal recognises and respects the need for standards, but is concerned by the perceived constraints of the DDC. The strategic direction of Culture.ca is to make it a user-focused service. As users needs become clearer over time, the weaknesses of the present system become more apparent. The basic conundrum is that the organizing infrastructure of the DDC is a content-based classification scheme, whereas the portal is a user-focused service and needs a user-focused taxonomy. Culture.ca is at a crossroads. There is now a sizeable database of classified links and an identifiable audience using the portal. The challenge is to increase the usability of the portal to attract and retain new audiences. Consequently, the continued use of the DDC is in question and the need for overhaul to the CC Class is high on portal management's list of priorities.

Assuming that an improved front-end categorization scheme is developed, a number of ways forward present themselves. The first option would be to follow the original plan and simply re-map the Dewey subject tree to a new user-focused display taxonomy (CC Class 2). Option two would be to gradually phase out the Dewey subject tree and rely solely on the new display taxonomy. As a transitional phase, new content could be linked directly to the user-friendly display taxonomy with a longer-term recon project to re-map the existing content, which could be undertaken as part of regular links maintenance. A third option would be to maintain the Dewey tree and classify new links using both it and the display taxonomy. This approach would obviate the need for a mapping between the two structures, a clear benefit when the structures have such different purposes. This would be an insurance policy, keeping the Dewey backbone in place while a new display taxonomy is validated in practice. No matter which option is selected, the most important consideration is the need for a more responsive display taxonomy regardless of what organising infrastructure acts as the backbone.

CONCLUSION

When LAC started to use the DDC in new ways a decade ago, the WWW was smaller, technologically far less sophisticated and even less prone to the standardization than at present. Now major search engines such as Google and Yahoo play a role in information retrieval undreamed of at that time. We, like many others, were–and still are–grappling with new ways of thinking about information management in the global networked environment.

We have seen that the DDC works well in a service geared to students and educators, possibly because its organizational outline is similar to school subjects. The DDC works well in organizing services, like CIBS, containing a broad spectrum of resources from many disciplines. The benefits of using the DDC strictly to manage and organize Web links in a narrow domain for a specific audience are less clear. Recent research[13] suggests that Web content can be most effectively served up in a user-responsive way using custom multi-faceted taxonomies. Alternatively, the research undertaken by OCLC in presenting the DDC structure in new ways, including work on alternative groupings,[14] may provide a way to improve the display taxonomy while retaining the strength of the Dewey subject tree backbone for Culture.ca.

REFERENCES

1. Saeed, Hamid and Abdus Sattar Chaudry. "Potential of Bibliographic Tools to Organize Knowledge on the Internet: The Use of Dewey Decimal Classification Scheme for Organizing Web-based Information Resources." *Knowledge Organization* 28 (1), 17-26.

2. The National Library of Canada and the National Archives of Canada were merged by legislation in April 2004 to form a new institution, Library and Archives Canada, to serve the information management needs of Canada in the 21st century.

3. Available at: http://www.collectionscanada.ca/caninfo/.

4. OCLC Forest Press. "Dewey Decimal Classification System." Available at: http://www.oclc.org/dewey/about/default.htm.

5. Hickey, Thomas B. and Diane Vizine-Goetz. "The Role of Classification in CORC." *Journal of Library Administration* 34 3/4 (2001), 422.

6. Available at: http://bubl.ac.uk/link/index.html.

7. Available at: http://www.renardus.org/.

8. Department of Canadian Heritage. "Government of Canada Supports Production of New Media Content and International Expositions" (2001). Available at: http://www.pch.gc.ca/special/tomorrowstartstoday/nr-2001-06-19.htm.

9. Available at: http://www.culture.ca/.

10. Department of Canadian Heritage. "Components of Canadian Culture On-Line." (2001). Available at: http://www.pch.gc.ca/special/tomorrowstartstoday/en-back-2001-06-19-fs1.html.

11. "Savoir Faire: Canadian Information By Subject." *National Library News* 32, nos 1-2 (January/February 2000). Available at: http://www.collectionscanada.ca/bulletin/015017-0001-09-e.html.

12. Graef, Jean. *Integrating Taxonomies Course Book*. Montague, Mass.: Montague Institute, 2003, 20.

13. Franklin, Rosemay Aud. "Reinventing Subject Access for the Semantic Web." *Online Information Review* 27, issue 2 (2003), 94-101.

14. Hickey and Vizine-Goetz, 427-428.

doi:10.1300/J104v42n03_09

DeweyBrowser

Diane Vizine-Goetz

SUMMARY. The DeweyBrowser allows users to search and browse collections of library resources organized by the Dewey Decimal Classification (DDC) system. The visual interface provides access to several million records from the OCLC WorldCat database and to a collection of records derived from the abridged edition of DDC. The prototype was developed out of a desire to make the most of Dewey numbers assigned to library materials and to explore new ways of providing access to the DDC. doi:10.1300/J104v42n03_10 *[Article copies available for a fee from The Haworth Document Delivery Service: 1-800-HAWORTH. E-mail address: <docdelivery@haworthpress.com> Website: <http://www.HaworthPress.com> © 2006 by The Haworth Press, Inc. All rights reserved.]*

KEYWORDS. DDC, Dewey Decimal Classification, Abridged Edition 14, DeweyBrowser, Functional Requirements for Bibliographic Records (FRBR), OCLC WorldCat, AJAX (Asynchronous JavaScript and XML)

Diane Vizine-Goetz is Research Scientist, OCLC Online Computer Library Center, 6565 Frantz Road, Dublin, OH 43017 (E-mail: vizine@oclc.org).

The author would like to acknowledge the technical contributions of Harry Wagner, lead developer, and Carol Hickey, research specialist, DeweyBrowser project.

DDC, Dewey, Dewey Decimal Classification, OCLC, WebDewey, and WorldCat are registered trademarks/service marks of OCLC Online Computer Library Center, Inc. The Dewey Decimal Classification system is Copyright 2003-2006 OCLC Online Computer Library Center, Inc. Used with permission.

[Haworth co-indexing entry note]: "DeweyBrowser." Vizine-Goetz, Diane. Co-published simultaneously in *Cataloging & Classification Quarterly* (The Haworth Information Press, an imprint of The Haworth Press, Inc.) Vol. 42, No. 3/4, 2006, pp. 213-220; and: *Moving Beyond the Presentation Layer: Content and Context in the Dewey Decimal Classification (DDC) System* (ed: Joan S. Mitchell, and Diane Vizine-Goetz) The Haworth Information Press, an imprint of The Haworth Press, Inc., 2006, pp. 213-220. Single or multiple copies of this article are available for a fee from The Haworth Document Delivery Service [1-800-HAWORTH, 9:00 a.m. - 5:00 p.m. (EST). E-mail address: docdelivery@haworthpress.com].

INTRODUCTION

In the first paper of this special volume, Karen Markey reflects on the use of classification in online systems over the past forty years. With the exception of classification tools for catalogers, she is disappointed with the library profession's lack of progress in exploiting classification in systems for end users, despite scores of research projects that attempted to do otherwise. She speculates that inadequate technology is partly to blame for the community's failure to fully integrate library classification data into end user tools for subject access, browsing, and display. OCLC's recent experience developing the DeweyBrowser[1] prototype suggest that technology is no longer a significant barrier to delivering classification-based tools for (end) users.

The DeweyBrowser project began in early 2005 as an investigation of OCLC's chief scientist, Thom Hickey, to apply a web development technique called AJAX (Asynchronous JavaScript and XML) to a Dewey browser.[2] Within 6 months of the start of the project, a research team, under the direction of the author, successfully deployed the DeweyBrowser over several million WorldCat records and the abridged edition of the Dewey Decimal Classification (DDC) system. The project team has since introduced several enhancements and is working on a successor interface. This paper provides an overview of three major components of the DeweyBrowser: the collections, the interface, and the technology.[3]

THE COLLECTIONS

The DeweyBrowser allows users to search and browse collections of library resources organized by the DDC. Currently, the DeweyBrowser provides access to two collections of WorldCat records, an electronic books collection (ebooks) and a subset of WorldCat records (wcat). The latter is derived from the set of records that OCLC makes available to web users on search engine sites through the Open WorldCat program. A third collection (a14) is a non-bibliographic database that contains selected data from the abridged edition of Dewey. Table 1 presents the distribution of records by Dewey main class for each of the collections.

The OCLC electronic books collection contains approximately 210,000 ebooks.[4] Over half of these records contain Dewey numbers. Only records with Dewey numbers are accessible through the DeweyBrowser.

TABLE 1. Records by DDC Class for DeweyBrowser Collections

DDC Class	wcat	ebooks	a14
0 Computer science, information & general works	101,888	15,146	216
1 Philosophy & psychology	68,943	4,911	159
2 Religion	115,305	3,434	272
3 Social sciences	545,587	38,114	941
4 Language	39,035	1,530	122
5 Science	184,752	7,705	485
6 Technology	365,047	29,844	618
7 Arts & recreation	241,800	3,915	614
8 Literature	308,613	12,156	146
9 History & geography	248,351	9,732	739
Total	2,219,321	126,487	4,312

The bibliographic records in the ebook collection contain links to electronic versions of the books and many of the records also contain identifiers for the corresponding print books.

Records in the WorldCat collection (wcat) have been grouped based on the Functional Requirements for Bibliographic Records (FRBR) model, group 1 entities (work, expression, manifestation, and item).[5] The OCLC work-set algorithm is used to group the records.[6] For the end user, this means that records for the many expressions (e.g., a translation, an illustrated edition, an abridged edition) of an intellectual work (e.g., Lewis Carroll's *Alice's Adventures in Wonderland*) are brought together. The record from the FRBR work set with the greatest number of library holdings is indexed and accessible through the DeweyBrowser. As a result of FRBR-based grouping of the records, records with and without DDC class numbers (records with Library of Congress Classification numbers and records without any class number) are linked. To increase the coverage of the DeweyBrowser, the project team is exploring using the FRBR groupings to supply DDC numbers for records lacking them.[7]

The a14 collection contains 4,312 classification records derived from DDC Abridged Edition 14.[8] The records consist of the class number, caption, Dewey hierarchy to the third level, Relative Index terms, and mapped terminology. Notes, cross references and other data elements are omitted. The abridged edition is suited for the classification needs of organizations with up to 20,000 resources in their collections.

INTERFACE

The DeweyBrowser is a visual interface that displays search results in successive rows of ten categories based on the three main summaries of the DDC.[9] Users can navigate the Dewey hierarchy by clicking on a category or they can enter a search term. Categories are color-coded to indicate where matching records occur. Categories with the greatest number of records are colored red, orange, and yellow (warm colors) and categories with fewer records are colored green and blue (cool colors). White is used for categories with zero matching records.

The categories in the top row of the display represent the ten main classes of the Dewey system and provide a broad overview of the DDC. The categories in the second row represent the next level of the DDC hierarchy. For example, when a user clicks on 7 Arts & recreation, the ten divisions of that class are displayed. Clicking on a category in the second row, e.g., 79 Sports, games & entertainment, causes the subdivisions of the selected class to be displayed. The third row corresponds to the third summary in the DDC, the thousand sections. When a user clicks on a category in this row, e.g., 798 Equestrian sports & animal racing, a list of records assigned that Dewey number is displayed.

The collections can be searched as well as browsed. For example, a search for "horses" in the WorldCat collection returns results in each of the DDC main classes (see Figure 1). The greatest number of hits is in 6 Technology which contains the subclasses 63 Agriculture and 636 Animal husbandry. Many records are also retrieved in 798 Equestrian sports & animal racing and in the 800s for fiction and literature. Using the color-coded categories of the DDC hierarchy, a user can quickly browse a collection of records to find items of interest.

The interface provides the option of displaying the DDC summaries in several languages, including English, French, German, Spanish or Swedish. Additional languages will be added as they become available. Another option enables users to search and browse for works written in a particular language. This feature is available through the 'More options' link in the interface to the ebooks and wcat collections. When a specific language is selected from the languages menu, e.g., Spanish, the DeweyBrowser displays only records for works written in Spanish; otherwise, matching records in all available languages (more than 200) are displayed. The most frequently occurring languages are English, French, German, Spanish, Italian, Russian, Latin, and Portuguese.

FIGURE 1. Keyword Search for 'Horse' in the WorldCat Collection

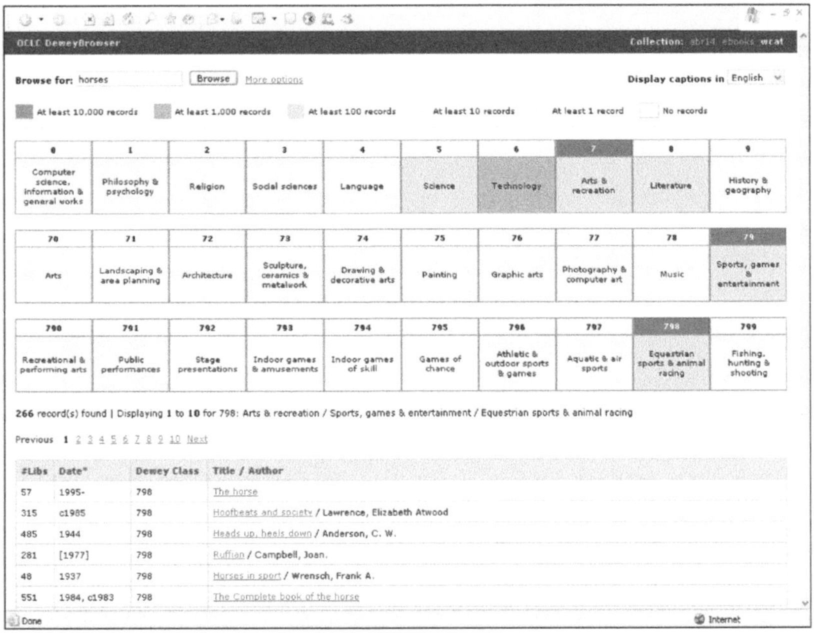

Items in the result lists of the ebooks and wcat collections are linked to the Open WorldCat 'Find in a Library' web service. Items in the ebook collection are also linked to the ebook itself or to the web site hosting the electronic book. An advantage of using collections derived from the WorldCat database is the large number of library holdings symbols (over 1 billion) linked to WorldCat records. Users who select an item from the results list can easily find out which libraries have the item and search for it in the local library catalog or they can identify libraries holding the item in a given city, region or country and search the relevant catalogs.

The interface to the a14 collection presents some features unique to the collection. Items in the results list lead to the display of classification data (class number, caption, and terminology associated with the class) rather than bibliographic data. Figure 2 presents the mapped terms for 798.2 Horsemanship. An experimental feature has been added to the interface to allow authorized users to suggest additional terminology for a class.

FIGURE 2. Sample Classification Record Display in DeweyBrowser for a 14 Collection

TECHNOLOGY

The DeweyBrowser uses AJAX technology.[10] AJAX is a term coined to describe an approach to web interfaces that allows user interaction with a web page without refreshing the whole screen. This technique (often called dynamic HTML) appears on many web pages, but only lately have whole applications, such as the DeweyBrowser, been built using it. Using AJAX speeds up the interface by only requesting parts of a page. This improvement in itself is important, but by maintaining the user's context, such as how far the page is scrolled, it can make the experience more pleasant, since the page is more stable. Refreshing only the part of the screen that changes tends to encourage exploration, a behavior that is central to how the DeweyBrowser was designed to be used.

The DeweyBrowser interacts with the server at OCLC using XML. The XML the server sends is transformed into HTML for display by XML style sheets (XSLT). Within the server the searches are carried out using the SRU protocol (search and retrieve via URL),[11] a web-friendly version of the Z39.50 retrieval protocol that has been used in libraries for some time. The SRU server that searches the DeweyBrowser databases is built in Apache Tomcat using Pears and Gwen, two open source software packages from OCLC Research.[12]

CONCLUSION

OCLC's experience developing the DeweyBrowser prototype suggests that technology is no longer a barrier to delivering classification-based tools for catalogers and end users. The prototype has been well-received by members of the library community who have asked OCLC to explore the feasibility of applying the interface to local library catalogs. They have also asked the project team to investigate new classifier features associated with the a14 collection for application in institutional repositories and learning object metadata creation systems. Despite the uneven progress of the past, the outlook is brighter for integrating classification data into cataloger and end user tools.

REFERENCES

1. The DeweyBrowser is accessible on OCLC ResearchWorks. http://www.oclc. org/research/researchworks/ (accessed 23 March 2006).

2. Hickey, Thom. AJAX and Web interfaces. [Weblog entry.] Outgoing: Library metadata techniques and trends. March 31, 2005. http://outgoing.typepad.com/outgoing/2005/03/web_application.html (accessed 23 March 2006).

3. This section is excerpted from "Getting visual with the DeweyBrowser," NextSpace: the OCLC Newsletter. http://www.oclc.org/nextspace/001/ (accessed 23 March 2006).

4. [OCLC] Electronic Books. http://www.oclc.org/support/documentation/firstsearch/databases/dbdetails/details/Ebooks.htm (accessed 23 March 2006).

5. IFLA Study Group on the Functional Requirements for Bibliographic Records. *Functional Requirements for Bibliographic Records: Final Report.* UBCIM Publications–New Series. Vol. 19, Munchen: K.G. Saur, 1998. http://www.ifla.org/VII/s13/frbr/frbr.htm (accessed 23 March 2006).

6. Hickey, Thomas B., O'Neill, Edward T. and Jenny Toves. 2002. Experiments with the IFLA Functional Requirements for Bibliographic Records (FRBR). *D-Lib Magazine*, 8 (9). http://www.dlib.org/dlib/september02/hickey/09hickey.html (accessed 23 March 2006).

7. Vizine-Goetz, Diane and Thomas Hickey. 2006. Using Dewey Differently. http://www.oclc.org/research/memberscouncil/2006-02/vizine-goetz_rev.ppt (accessed 23 March 2006).

8. Latest versions. http://www.oclc.org/dewey/versions/default.htm (accessed 23 March 2006).

9. Dewey Decimal Classification (DDC) Summaries. http://www.oclc.org/research/researchworks/ddc/desc.htm (accessed 23 March 2006).

10. Singel, Ryan. "You Say You Want a Web Revolution." *Wired News.* 5 Aug. 2005. http://www.wired.com/news/technology/0,1282,68403,00.html (accessed 23 March 2006).

11. Library of Congress. SRU (Search/Retrieve via URL). http://www.loc.gov/standards/sru/index.html (accessed 23 March 2006).

12. Software [OCLC Research]. http://www.oclc.org/research/software/ (accessed 23 March 2006).

doi:10.1300/J104v42n03_10

Index

*For Product Safety Concerns and Information please contact
our EU representative GPSR@taylorandfrancis.com Taylor & Francis
Verlag GmbH, Kaufingerstraße 24, 80331 München, Germany*

T - #0178 - 270225 - C2 - 212/178/14 - PB - 9780789034533 - Gloss Lamination